Soldiers as Citizens

Studies in War, Society, and the Military

Editors

Mark Grimsley
Ohio State University

Peter Maslowski
University of Nebraska

Editorial Board
D'Ann Campbell
Austin Peay State University

Mark A. Clodfelter
National War College

Brooks D. Simpson
Arizona State University

Roger J. Spiller
*Combat Studies Institute
U.S. Army Command
and General Staff College
Fort Leavenworth*

Timothy H. E. Travers
University of Calgary

Arthur Waldron
U.S. Naval War College

Soldiers as Citizens

Former Wehrmacht Officers in the
Federal Republic of Germany, 1945–1955

Jay Lockenour

University of Nebraska Press
Lincoln and London

© 2001 by the
University of Nebraska Press
All rights reserved
Manufactured in the
United States of America
⊗
Library of Congress
Cataloging-in-Publication Data
Lockenour, Jay, 1966–
Soldiers as citizens :
former Wehrmacht officers in the
Federal Republic of Germany, 1945–1955/
Jay Lockenour.
p. cm.—(Studies in war, society,
and the military)
Includes bibliographical
references and index.
ISBN 0-8032-2940-2 (cl.: alk. paper)
1. Veterans—Germany—History
—20th century. 2. Germany—
Armed Forces—Officers—History
—20th century. 3. World War,
1939–1945—Veterans—Germany.
4. Germany—History—1945–1955.
5. Sociology, Military—Germany.
I. Title. II. Series.
UB359.G3 L63 2001
305.9'0697'0943–DC21
2001027145

For Raphael

Contents

Preface	ix
Abbreviations	xi
Introduction	1
1 "Pushed Aside, Persecuted, Prosecuted": Organizational Efforts, 1945–1951	11
2 Creating Soldiers' Opinion: The Verband Deutscher Soldaten	33
3 Service to the Volk: Traditions and the Lessons of Captivity	63
4 Unpolitical Soldiers: Veterans, Politicians, and Military Reform	93
5 A European Fatherland? Anticommunism and European Defense	125
6 The Rift in Our Ranks: 20 July 1944	153
Conclusion	181
Notes	189
Glossary	231
Bibliography	233
Index	247

Preface

Breaking with a time-honored tradition, I will first acknowledge my wife, Andrea, whose support kept me (somewhat) sane. Her editorial work greatly improved what you are about to read.

I incurred many debts during the course of writing this book. For their expert advice, I would like to thank James Diehl, Georg Meyer, and Dennis Showalter. I could not have completed the project without the invaluable assistance of my mentors and colleagues at Temple University and the University of Pennsylvania. I would like to thank Marc Trachtenberg, Lynn Hollen Lees, Werner von der Ohe, and Thomas Safley, all of whom contributed to this book and to my development as an historian. Very special thanks are due to my doctoral adviser, Thomas Childers, for his inestimable aid over the years and his always constructive criticisms of the many drafts of this work. I appreciated the insightful comments and professional advice of my Temple colleagues Richard Immerman and Gregory Urwin. Julia Sneeringer, Dave Kerans, and Jeff Horn are valued colleagues and friends whose help and humor made the task of writing easier.

For the funds to pursue this project, I am indebted to the German Academic Exchange Service, the Mellon Foundation, and the Temple University College of Liberal Arts. The Bundesarchiv-Militärarchiv, the Militärgeschichtliches Forschungsamt, and the Evangelical Academies at Bad Boll and Loccum kindly allowed me to use their materials and facilities. I especially want to acknowledge the assistance of Armin Roether at the academy at Bad Boll and Ernst Bohnenkamp at the academy in Loccum. Maj. Gen. Dr. Jürgen Schreiber (ret.), president of the Verband Deutscher Soldaten, granted me an interview that I found very useful.

I am grateful to Gerald Kleinfeld and the *German Studies Review* for permission to republish "The Rift in Our Ranks: The German Officer Corps, the 20th of July, and the Path to Democracy" from *German Studies Review* 21, no. 3 (October 1998): 469–506, a revised version of which appears as chapter 6 of this book.

Abbreviations

a.D.	*außer Dienst*—retired
BdKK	Bund deutscher Kriegsbeschädigter und Kriegerhinterbliebener—League of German War-Disabled and Survivors
BdO	Bund deutscher Offiziere—League of German Officers
BDS	Schutzbund ehemaliger Deutscher Soldaten—League for the Defense of Former German Soldiers
BGS	Bundesgrenzschutz—Federal Border Guard
BHE	Bund der Heimatvertriebenen und Entrechteten—Block of Dispellees and Disenfranchised
BvW	Bund versorgungsberechtigter ehemaliger Wehrmachtsangehörige und ihrer Hinterbliebene—League of Pension-Entitled Wehrmacht Personnel and Their Next of Kin
CDU	Christlich-Demokratische Union—Christian Democratic Union
CSU	Christlich-Soziale Union—Christian Social Union
DAK	Verband ehemaliger Angehöriger Deutsches Afrika Korps—League of Former Members of the Africa Corps
DDSB	Der Deutsche Soldatenbund
DGB	Deutsche Gewerkschaftsbund— Federation of German Trade Unions
EDC	European Defense Community
FDP	Freie Demokratische Partei—Free Democratic Party
GfW	Gesellschaft für Wehrkunde—Society for Defense Information
GPURKKA	Russian Special Committee on Political Administration of the Red Army
KPD	Kommunistische Partei Deutschlands—Communist Party of Germany
KVP	Kasernierte Volkspolizei—East German People's Police
NATO	North Atlantic Treaty Organization

NKFD	Nationalkomitee Freies Deutschland—National Committee for a Free Germany
NVA	Nationale Volksarmee—National People's Army
PGA	Personalgutachterausschuß—Personnel Screening Committee
SA	Sturmabteilung—National Socialist Storm Troopers
SPD	Sozialdemokratische Partei Deutschlands—German Social Democratic Party
SRP	Sozialistische Reichspartei—Socialist Reich Party
SS	Schutzstaffel—National Socialist Elite Guard
VdH	Verband der Heimkehrer—Association of Former Prisoners of War
VdK	Verband der Kriegsbeschädigten, Kriegshinterbliebenen und Sozialrentner Deutschlands—German Association of War-Disabled, War Survivors, and Social Pensioners
VDS	Verband Deutscher Soldaten—League of German Soldiers
VVN	Vereinigung der Verfolgten des Naziregimes—Union of Those Persecuted by the Nazi Regime

Soldiers as Citizens

Introduction

Explaining the Federal Republic of Germany's success in creating a stable, pluralistic, democratic society is a central mystery of modern German history. Given the disastrous failure of democracy in the Weimar Republic in the 1920s and 1930s, interest in the fate of West Germany's democratic experiment after 1949 has been keen. The economic good fortune that characterized the new republic's first decade, as well as the stabilizing effect of the Allied occupation armies, distinguishes the Federal Republic from its Weimar counterpart. But larger social, political, and cultural forces were also at work that fostered legitimacy and a bond between the Federal Republic and its citizens that never existed in the Weimar era. The effects of World War II, the experience of the Third Reich, and the increasingly threatening Cold War environment combined with decades- and even centuries-old political and historical traditions to help shape a consensus about "democracy," albeit very loosely defined.

One of the most important and least understood of the major social groups that participated in this process were former officers of the Wehrmacht, (the armed forces of Nazi Germany). Because of their high profile, former elite status, and potential for radicalism, the former officers' activities, place in society, and attitudes toward the new state are crucial to understand. Though it has been little acknowledged, the attitudes of former officers are a litmus test for the Federal Republic's success in acquiring stability and legitimacy in the eyes of its citizens. The vast majority of former officers, whose past predilections and postwar predicaments disinclined them to value democracy, ultimately accepted the new democratic regime and gradually assimilated into West Germany's multivalent society.

Significant obstacles impeded the development of a stable democratic society in Germany. When the war in Europe ended on 8 May 1945, all Germans inhabiting the three Western Allied zones of occupation faced numerous and disheartening challenges. Most apparent, the physical conditions in which they lived were miserable. Food supplies were regulated and rationed. In nearly every medium- or large-sized city, the housing stock had been destroyed by Allied bombs or battles in the war's last year. A thriving black market, the physical destruction of industrial facilities, and the lack of a stable currency spelled continuing economic turmoil and unemployment.

Personal relations were also in a state of chaos. Family members, both civilian and military, were dead or missing. Marriages that had survived the strain of long absence and uncertainty now faced the sometimes greater challenge of protracted proximity. Women greeted husbands changed by their experiences as soldiers. Soldiers returned home to find wives changed by the wartime responsibilities they had borne as breadwinners and the targets of Allied bombing raids. The entire society experienced seemingly boundless anxiety about young Germans indoctrinated by the Hitler Youth and utterly lacking a moral anchor owing to the tumultuous conditions of their childhood.

Many people faced the added burden of being refugees. Millions of Germans fled west, both during the war and after, to escape the real and imagined ravages of the onrushing Soviet army. Without homes, without jobs, and without the social networks or personal effects salable on the black market that sustained many West German natives, the refugees were forced to rely on Allied aid programs and the largesse (often grudging) of their new neighbors.

Germans faced political challenges as well. The American, British, and French military authorities exercised dictatorial powers in their zones of occupation. In practice, of course, their generally benign political and economic aims and their reliance on Germans for much of their manpower ameliorated the impact of these dictatorships. Nevertheless, Allied demands regarding denazification, demilitarization, and war crimes trials dominated political life in the Western zones between

1945 and 1948. In short, the West German landscape—physical, political, economic, and personal—still bore the scars of war.

By 1949, however, inspiring signs of change appeared. Though unemployment remained high for a time, the currency reform in the Western zones the previous year had placed the economy on a more stable footing. A state apparatus emerged as the Parliamentary Council began its work, which would result in the creation of the Federal Republic in May. A reliable currency and an increasingly independent West German political system set the stage for the "Economic Miracle" that sent the Federal Republic roaring into prosperity in the 1950s.

Hope extended beyond these practical changes in the social and political environment. The mythological "Zero Hour," which struck on 8 May 1945, despite serving as a means of avoiding confrontations with a horrifying past, also turned many Germans' thoughts to the future. Germans claimed to be fed up with "ideology" (of the National Socialist, democratic, or communist varieties), but many retained a sense of "idealism" that manifested itself in various ways. The country experienced a short-lived religious revival in the aftermath of the war. New political parties and associations formed (and usually faded just as quickly). Activists published countless manifestos, and newspaper editorials expressed a broad band of opinions. Their sense of living in an historical watershed, felt most strongly in the context of the developing Cold War, encouraged many citizens to delve deeply into their consciences and to express themselves, be it privately, in letters to the editor, or at the ballot box.

With more than fifty years of hindsight, one can interpret this period as the beginning of a long, gradual process of political stabilization, social healing, and economic growth that formed the basis for the legitimacy of a democratic state. What can easily be lost in this picture is the sense of contingency and uncertainty that prevailed about the path that Germany should take. The tragic failure of democracy in the Weimar Republic cast a long, deep shadow on the Federal Republic's early years. The more recent, if often suppressed, memories of the crimes and horrors of the Third Reich also profoundly influenced the attitudes and behaviors of Germans in the first postwar decade.

Other anxieties and concerns also shaped the Federal Republic's early political culture. The continuing division of Germany and the temporary character of the Bonn government itself encouraged thoughts of future changes to the governing system. The palpable threat of the Soviet Union emanating from the Eastern zone encouraged efforts at physical and even spiritual defense against communism and its ideology of atheism and world revolution. Though the Korean War would not provide a major spur to rearmament until the following summer, Chancellor Konrad Adenauer had already broached the subject of a new German army in an interview with an American journalist in December 1949.

Former Officers in West Germany

In this tumultuous context, the situation of former Wehrmacht officers is vitally important precisely because the Weimar legacy, the Third Reich, rearmament, reconstruction, and the Cold War environment were so omnipresent. The officer corps had been a key elite for centuries. Since the beginning of the eighteenth century, when Prussian nobility devoted itself to the Hohenzollern monarchy, Prussian, and later German, officers had been the mainstay of those Central European states.[1] German soldiers had fought "With God, for King and Fatherland" against nearly every other European nation and even against their fellow countrymen, if called upon to do so. They sat at the pinnacle of the social order by the end of the nineteenth century, when merely serving in the reserves meant prestige for the status-conscious bourgeoisie. Under Kaiser Wilhelm II, officers played an important role in the formulation of state policy, both formally, as cabinet ministers, and informally, as the emperor's advisers and confidantes. Despite their apparent isolation in the Weimar Republic and the competition from the paramilitary forces under Hitler's command (Sturmabteilung [SA] and Schutzstaffel [SS]), officers remained a privileged elite until 1945, with power, status, and access to wealth denied ordinary citizens.

In the postwar world, however, that situation changed drastically. The Allied occupation regime's first act was to disband the German armed forces. Overnight, officers lost their incomes, careers, and self-identities. Nearly every former officer experienced captivity at least briefly. Hundreds of former officers were defendants in war crimes trials between 1945 and 1947. The socialist-dominated unions initiated an informal boycott that excluded former officers from employment in many fields. Allied efforts aimed at demilitarizing Germany meant that for the first few postwar years, virtually no former career soldiers found jobs in public service, a traditional haven for retired officers. Nearly every major newspaper printed angry letters to the editor denouncing officers as militarists, warmongers, and elitists and blaming them for Germany's current suffering. Officers felt persecuted and believed a defamation campaign was being waged against them. Without addressing the justice of Allied measures, one can nevertheless conclude that by any standard (status, power, wealth), circumstances for the officer corps had taken a turn for the worse.

As former colonel Joachim Wüst summed up, "You know, so many uncomfortable and ugly memories are tied up with the word 'soldier.'"[2] Former officers were unpleasant reminders of continuities with Germany's recent past. They called to mind the failed democratic experiment of the 1920s, when officers passively undermined and actively rebelled against the republic. The army leadership played a crucial role in convincing Reich President Paul von Hindenburg to appoint Adolf Hitler as chancellor on 30 January 1933. The officer corps also had contributed significantly to Hitler's success in achieving control in the years immediately following his seizure of power in 1933.

The officer corps were symbols of Hitler's war as well. The vast majority of officers had done their duty and more in pursuing Hitler's aims and their own career goals, glory, and even wealth.[3] Despite the objections a few officers raised to the Wehrmacht's objectives and methods in World War II, the officer corps embodied many National Socialist values. The officers were patriots, leaders, and warriors. As such, the public naturally identified and excoriated them along with the National Socialists.

Given these continuities, historians as well as contemporaries (including the former officers themselves) made comparisons between veterans after 1945 and soldiers returning home after 1918. While officers in the Weimar era suffered from some stigmatization because of their identification with the imperial regime and wartime sacrifices, they continued to wield influence as a result of their prominent role within the large antirepublican movement. In 1918, officers quickly formed associations, such as the National League of German Officers (Nationalverband Deutscher Offiziere), many of which openly sought to undermine the republican government's authority. Numerous conspiratorial cliques of officers, like National Unification (Nationale Vereinigung), which helped to organize a coup d'etat in 1920 (the infamous Kapp putsch), helped to radicalize Weimar's political atmosphere.[4]

Officers after 1945, by contrast, were initially forbidden to organize by the Allied occupiers. They lacked cohesion because so many of their number remained imprisoned. As noted, many Germans blamed the officer corps for the destruction and the ignominy into which their country had fallen. A significant coexistent train of thought blamed the officer corps less for starting the war than for losing it. Whether they were outright Nazis or merely still under the sway of the "Hitler Myth," many Germans attributed their nation's defeat to a new variation of the "stab in the back" legend that had prevailed after 1918.[5] In their view, the officer corps had squandered the opportunities for conquest that Hitler's military genius had provided by their insufficient initiative, cowardice, or outright treason. Popular resentment of a privileged elite and events such as the attempted assassination of Hitler on 20 July 1944 only strengthened their conviction that Hitler's war had been winnable but for the military leadership's actions. Add to these difficulties the fact that officers had suffered the same losses as other Germans as a result of Germany's defeat in 1945, and one begins to understand the potential for bitterness, isolation, and even radicalism that existed within the former officer corps' ranks.

Defining the Parameters: Who Were Former Officers?

Before we can understand the former officer corps' position in West German society, we must define exactly whom we are talking about. Roughly 260,000 career soldiers (officers and noncommissioned officers) were active in German uniform at war's end.[6] These numbers, while not insignificant, do not reflect the high standing of former officers in society. Officers were important because of their history and prior elite status, as indicated above. The context of the late 1940s and early 1950s also created a situation in which former officers performed an important function as the mouthpieces of "soldiers' opinion" regarding the burning issues of the day, especially rearmament and foreign policy. Because officers led the growing number of veterans' organizations in West Germany at the time, the press and the government frequently turned to them to take the measure of (and to try to influence) the mood of a large and important constituency.[7]

The membership of veterans' organizations, broadly defined, numbered roughly three million men and a small number of widows, next of kin, and female veterans, such as the Wehrmachthelferinnen.[8] There is a marked contrast between the fifteen million or so veterans—that is, the men and women who had served in the Wehrmacht between 1939 and 1945—and those who continued in some way to identify themselves as soldiers by membership in a veterans' organization. Three different sorts of veterans' organizations existed in the Federal Republic after 1949. Each type appealed to a slightly different, though often overlapping, constituency.

One type of veterans' organization was dedicated more to war victims than to veterans as such, and many nonveterans belonged to such groups without considering themselves members of a veterans' organization at all. These groups included the German Association of War-Disabled, War Survivors, and Social Pensioners (Verband der Kriegsbeschädigten, Kriegshinterbliebenen und Sozialrentner Deutschlands—VdK); the League of German War-Disabled and Survivors (Bund Deutscher Kriegsbeschädigter und Kriegerhinterbliebener—BdKK); and the Association of Former Prisoners of War (Verband der Heimkehrer—VdH). The words "soldier" and "veteran" were conspicuously absent from the names of these organizations, though the largest of them, the VdK (with one and one-half million members in 1954), consisted of nearly 50 percent former soldiers.[9] The lack of direct titular connection to military service constituted an important distinction between these "victims' organizations" and their soldierly counterparts. These groups, though concerned with veterans' issues, implicitly and sometimes explicitly denied the uniqueness of the soldierly experience and rather focused on the common sufferings of their membership, which in their eyes justified some sort of compensation from the government.[10] Because of their focus on war victims rather than soldiers per se, these groups played only a small part in defining the officer corps' political attitudes and behavior in the late 1940s.

Larger, more "soldierly," and therefore more significant for our purposes were the tradition societies. Representing units as small as regiments and as large as entire armies, this group included the hundreds of unit-based organizations such as the Comrades of Light Anti-Aircraft Battery 71 (Kameradschaft Leichte Flakabteilung 71) and the Tradition Society of the 65th Infantry Division (Traditionsgemeinschaft 65er Infanteriedivision). These were groups that satisfied the nostalgic urges of many former soldiers. Tradition societies held annual reunions, helped the Red Cross clarify cases of soldiers missing in action, and generally maintained the bonds of comradeship begun in wartime. Much serious historical work remains to be done on the functions and impact of such organizations, which resemble the time-honored German tradition of the *Stammtisch*.[11]

True "soldiers' organizations" constitute the final category of veterans' groups. These associations maintained the uniqueness of the soldierly experience and were the principal proponents in West Germany of a "soldierly ideology." Early restrictions on the former soldiers' right to organize led most groups to bring widows and next of kin into their networks, at least nominally, to avoid the charge of "militarism." Nonmilitary members generally remained in the background, however, as legal window dressing for the organizations' activities which, apart from the recovery of pension benefits, focused on concerns different from those of the other two types of veterans' organizations.

What makes these strictly soldiers' organizations different from the war victims' groups and from many (though not all) of the tradition societies is their more problematic relationship with the past, arising from an insistence on maintaining military traditions and values. To the officers who led these groups, loyalty, honesty, bravery, and discipline—all presumed to have been omnipresent in the Wehrmacht—were absolutely essential for the Federal Republic's survival in a hostile Europe. Communism, motivated by the utopian ideal of a classless society and world revolution, would simply sweep away a Germany devoid of patriotic, responsible, and loyal citizens. Therefore, the soldiers' organizations believed, the military, consisting of the most loyal, responsible, and patriotic Germans, could provide a model citizenry capable of resisting the siren's call of communism. Such a conviction, no doubt augmented by psychological defensiveness, remained widespread in the military subculture of the 1940s and 1950s, especially among the former officers who led the true soldiers' organizations.

Of course, other groups contained far more veterans (certainly more common soldiers and probably more officers too) than any of the above organizations. The Federation of German Trade Unions (Deutsche Gewerkschaftsbund—DGB), for example, had millions of veterans as members, but the DGB never claimed to be a veterans' organization.[12] This reluctance to identify oneself as a soldier elucidates the crucial point that membership in these different types of veterans' organizations implied varying degrees of commitment to a specifically soldierly cause.

Officers as Leaders of the True Soldiers' Organizations

Former officers formed the physical and ideological core of the true soldiers' organizations and were by far their most vocal and active membership. By leading these organizations, officers placed themselves in the political spotlight. Because of press, public, and government interest in "soldiers' opinion" between 1949 and 1955, these leaders played a key political role. The process by which these officers came to espouse democracy and "Western" values in the aftermath of World War II is key to understanding the Federal Republic of Germany. Owing to the occupation and forced division of Germany, the new democratic state in 1949 was destined to face a crisis of legitimacy that rivaled that undergone by the Weimar Republic in 1919. How a social elite like the former officer corps made the transition from a National Socialist dictatorship to a representative democracy helps to explain the success of the Federal Republic. The fact that the Federal Republic has survived longer than any other German state since the Holy Roman Empire's dissolution in 1806 begs an explanation of why this democracy has been so stable. The study of former officers provides remarkable insight into that central question.

We can illuminate this mystery by tracing the former officers' growing acceptance of the Federal Republic to its roots in their training and experiences during the war and postwar era. We can indicate a number of areas, not only in foreign policy, but on domestic and social issues as well, where there is a consonance (if not an identity) among the ideas of former officers, those of large segments of society, and government policies. Officers did not pass easily into the postwar world, but in the larger context of a successful economy, U.S. occupation, and the Soviet threat, their background and experiences sufficed to graft this former elite onto the new society.[13]

One might argue that no other course lay open to the former officers but to accept democracy. The effects of defeat, the revelations of Nazi atrocities, and the Allied denazification campaigns were virtually to exclude authoritarianism and fascism as viable options. The foreign armies of occupation simply would not allow veterans to organize for any more radical purpose than mutual aid. Veterans' ideals are nevertheless important because they represented an alternative to the dominant political discourse. Their proposals retained a militaristic character through an emphasis on the value of hierarchical authority, strictly disciplined education, and the important formative experiences of military service. For officers, comradeship would provide the model for a democratic Germany as it had for their authoritarian solutions of the 1920s.

Despite their misgivings about democracy as defined by those in power, former officers wished to serve Germany in some way and therefore devoted much of their energy to formulating proposals for shaping Germany's future. That these proposals corresponded neither to the desires and plans of the occupation governments nor to the feelings of many other Germans certainly contributed to their obscurity and failure. Unable seriously to alter the course of the Federal Republic's development, former officers never threatened the new state's stability. The study of veteran officers indicates, however, the variety of possible responses to defeat, denazification, and democratization in West Germany. By largely competing to define democracy rather than undermine it, the former officers contributed in their own way to the Federal Republic of Germany's early legitimacy and ultimate survival.

1

"Pushed Aside, Persecuted, Prosecuted": Organizational Efforts, 1945-1951

For six years, the decisive political powers of the Federal Republic—the governing parties as well as the opposition—have conducted a systematic civil war against German soldierdom and have pushed it aside, persecuted it, and prosecuted it.... We have experienced much bitterness at the hands of the victors of the last war and the new German state has not been a good Fatherland. But remember that even today we are still strong if we stick together and work together.[1]

Despite acts of the occupation governments to forbid veterans' organizations, former career soldiers quickly established semiformal contacts among themselves. They wrote to friends and colleagues, former commanders, and even occupying soldiers to enlist their help in the struggle to reestablish the German soldier's "rights" and "honor." They lobbied local and national governing bodies, church officials, and concerned foreign organizations. These early efforts to organize and the contacts that former officers established played a pivotal role in the formation of the veterans' organizations that eventually appeared in the early 1950s and that publicly represented, for better or for worse, the "soldiers' estate" (*Soldatenstand*) within Germany and abroad.

The chaotic conditions of postwar Germany were not conducive to powerful organizations of former soldiers. Indeed, the situation of Germans in the West in general was poor enough: cities were piles of rubble; the economy was a shambles; refugees from the former eastern provinces and the Soviet zone placed extra burdens on already overtaxed housing, food, and transportation resources; and millions of soldiers and civilians were still missing.[2]

Former career soldiers in the Western zones faced all these difficulties and more. Remnants of age-old recruitment policies meant that many refugees were former officers whose residences had been in the Eastern zone of occupation or the lands annexed by the Soviet Union and Poland. They had all lost their means of employment. In fact, the Allies abolished their entire occupation in September 1945. They too lost family members, homes, and their health in the war, and they also faced imprisonment and other legal sanctions. Officers faced difficulties in finding new employment due to the traditional enmity between the armed forces and the socialist-dominated unions, which instituted an informal boycott against high-ranking military personnel in union shops. Most demoralizing for former officers was the hostility of the German people, who were looking for a scapegoat for the horrible experiences since the early 1930s. Former career soldiers were often seen as the embodiment of militarism and, as such, strongly identified with the collapsed Nazi order. From a practical standpoint, as Georg Meyer indicates, "It was much easier to recognize someone as a militarist—that was clear based on the last rank attained with the suffix a.D. (außer Dienst [retired])—than to identify at first glance a former party member or exploiter of the National Socialist system among the general public."[3]

While no systematic, centrally led campaign against former officers existed, they certainly felt victimized by the postwar system and were subjected to enormous pressure from all sides. Defamed by the press, the Allied governments, and an embittered populace; faced with legal restrictions and a union boycott; and subjected to the generally poor economic and living conditions confronting all Germans, former Wehrmacht officers organized in order to address the legal and economic issues facing them as well as to restore their lost honor.

Legal Status

The harsh Allied policy toward former soldiers was part of a larger effort to stamp out "Nazism and Militarism" in German society. Like the denazification procedures instituted in the Western zones, the abolition of the veterans' organizations as "militaristic" created much uncertainty. Laws on the subject were often vague, allowing for broad variations in interpretation, and differences among the occupation zones meant that agencies rarely established clear guidelines. An organization banned in Wiesbaden might be allowed in Kiel. An officer denied his pension in the British zone might be eligible to receive it at prewar levels in an area under French administration. This confusing situation represented both a danger and a promise to organized veterans, who were at the same time the objects of a repressive campaign to wipe out militarism and actors on a playing field with few rules.

Proclamation 2 of the Allied Control Council, issued on 20 September 1945, explicitly forbade organizations of former soldiers as carriers of "military tradition": "War veterans' organizations and all other military and quasi-military organizations shall be completely and finally abolished."[4] Control Council Law 8 (30 November 1945) reiterated that ban, and the proclamation's terms were later reinforced and expanded by Control Council Law 34 (20 August 1946), which dissolved and declared illegal all veterans' organizations along with the Wehrmacht, the General Staff, the officer corps, and any other organization even remotely military in nature. This law, which veterans later criticized as the root of their problems, went even further in invalidating all "laws, orders, instructions, decrees, regulations . . . concerning military service," as well as any legislation pertaining to "disciplinary rights, property, uniforms, decorations, the legal status and privileges of military and ex-military personnel and members of quasi-military organizations and their families." Violation of the provisions of Control Council Law 34 could be punished by the death penalty, though this extreme measure seems to have been rarely, if ever, invoked.[5] Two elements of the law most distressed former officers: the ban on organizations and the revocation of all military pensions, including those owed to widows, crippled soldiers, and veterans discharged before 1933.

Former officers combated the legal strictures placed on them by attacking their common root: the charge that career soldiers were by definition militarists. "Militarism," the officers insisted, was a problem reserved for civilians and especially politicians. "The soldier is merely the executive organ of the power-political will; the carrier of this will is the militarist. Soldierdom is a concept of duty. Militarism is a political doctrine."[6] "Militarism is a political lesson," former admiral Gottfried Hansen wrote in 1947. "Soldierdom, on the other hand, is a conception of duty, of absolute human virtues like love of country and loyalty, obedience, and bravery."[7]

The group of men around Hansen hoped to lend power to their argument by repeated citations of the "Law for Liberation from National Socialism and Militarism," enacted on 5 March 1946, which defined "militarists" as "(1) Persons who attempted to bring life in line with a policy of militaristic force; (2) Persons who advocated or are [sic] responsible for the domination of foreign peoples, their exploitation or displacement; (3) Persons who, for this purpose, promoted armament."[8] By the strict definitions outlined in the law, Hansen hoped that the suspicion that all officers were militarists would disappear, and with it the defamation of the German soldier and the economic sanctions embodied in Control Council Law 34.[9] One group of former officers based in Frankfurt am Main wrote to the minister president of Hesse in 1946 to suggest that a council be formed, with at least one "older" officer as a member, in order to judge former officers based on the provisions of the Law for Liberation. This military counterpart to the denazification procedures would, they hoped, cleanse the officer corps' image by identifying only certain individual officers as "militarists" and thus weakening the notion of the corps' collective guilt.[10] Nothing came of such ideas, however, and the passage of the law had no impact on the payment of pensions or the officers' negative public image. If anything, the Law for Liberation only worsened the situation for former officers by sparking a public debate on militarism, providing many Germans with an opportunity to vent their antipathy toward the officer corps.

Former officers also hoped in vain for a clarification of their status as "militarists" from the final judgment in the Nuremberg trials.[11] The indictment at Nuremberg found the Wehrmacht General Staff and High Command guilty of conspiring to initiate World War II and other crimes against humanity as outlined by the tribunal. The judges declared the Wehrmacht's leadership to be "a ruthless military caste . . . . responsible in large measure for the miseries and suffering that have fallen on millions of men, women, and children." The tribunal concluded the officer corps had been a "disgrace to the honorable profession of arms."

The final verdict, however, stopped short of labeling those organizations "criminal," if only because, in the words of Supreme Court Justice Robert H. Jackson, they were "too loose to constitute a coherent 'group' or 'organization,' [and] not because of any doubt of [their] criminality in war plotting."[12] Admiral Hansen and others insisted in the press and in private letters that this finding amounted to an exoneration of the Wehrmacht and should result in an immediate end to public defamation and a restoration of military pensions. Hansen interpreted the Nuremberg tribunal's verdict to mean that service in the Wehrmacht had been completely honorable.[13]

Control Council Law 34 not only forbade organizations of veterans and revoked career soldiers' pensions, but also prohibited the wearing of decorations. Former soldiers were forbidden to wear uniforms, badges, medals, or citations of any kind, no matter when they were issued or under what circumstances. To many veterans, this ban was an intolerable slight to their honor. According to surveys of the Allensbach Institute for Demoscopy taken in August 1951, roughly half the men in Germany possessed medals or citations from the Third Reich, and most Germans (52 percent) believed they should be allowed to wear them. Many veterans insisted that citations for bravery or service should be respected even if the army that issued them was defeated in battle. Gert Spindler, a man involved in veterans' issues and known for his rightwing political tendencies, even ventured the argument that enough time had passed (in 1951!) that the swastika adorning medals awarded during World War II only denoted the period 1939–1945 and nothing more.[14] A remarkable 54 percent of his fellow countrymen agreed with him.[15]

Even after the Federal Republic's founding in 1949, legal restrictions on veterans remained. Allied High Commission Law 16 (16 December 1949), which superseded previous legislation passed by the Control Council and the military governors, reaffirmed the necessity to eradicate "Militarism and Nazism." The ban on veterans' organizations therefore remained but prohibited only organizations that *required* their members to be war veterans.[16] Veterans easily sidestepped this provision by prominently including widows and next of kin in the titles of their organizations, if not necessarily in the organizations themselves.

The veterans' organizers of the late 1940s saw the legal restrictions, especially Control Council Law 34, as cruel and unjust since they robbed thousands of former officers and their widows (whether needy or not) of monetary support. They also viewed them as defamatory since the laws sanctioned a view of the officer corps as worthy of punishment through the loss of pensions and the ban on wearing medals. As a result, the early organizers devoted a great deal of time and effort to establishing the illegality of the pension revocation by illustrating the hardships endured by the old and needy and indicating the hypocrisy of meting out punishment only to ex-soldiers among all those implicated in the National Socialist system.

Significantly, these laws were enacted by Allied occupation governments and not a German one. Allied governments thus acted as a "shield and lightning rod for German leaders," who were not only protected from responsibility for the postwar situation by restrictions on their sovereignty but were also able to gain valuable political capital for the future by denouncing and occasionally reversing unpopular policies.[17] Veterans may have felt discriminated against, but they often felt grateful for the sympathy and understanding that they received from German officials. Nevertheless, the initial reaction of most former officers was extreme bitterness at being singled out for punishment for the horrors of the Third Reich and the lost war.

Economic Situation

The economic situation of Germany added to the plight of former soldiers after 1945. Many officers were refugees or Displaced Persons. Many more had been crippled by war injuries or lost their homes and families to Allied bombs.[18] While millions of Germans shared the same fate, several circumstances made the former officers' situation unique. The Allies denied all former officers—even those who had retired prior to 1933—their pensions. Officers also faced problems in finding employment because of their association with the Third Reich and the lost war. Allied denazification codes and the hostility of the unions meant that former officers found many doors closed to them.

The situation for former soldiers was often dire. Pleas for assistance that circulated among the early informal organizations recounted stories of extreme hardship. These stories prompted Lt- Gen. Hans von Donat to collect them under the heading "Chronicle of Misery" for later use in his letters to concerned organizations.[19] Another officer collected reports on the suicides of his comrades and their widows to include in a 1949 essay on the former officers' pension fight. According to the reports, many victims explicitly cited economic distress as their motive, although the implication was clear that disillusionment, despair, and lack of pensions led to all of the suicides.[20] While the author obviously selected the stories primarily for their pity-inducing value, the tragedy they describe is no less real.

The occupation powers initially forbade the payment of pensions but left the individual state governments considerable freedom to incorporate former pension recipients into other welfare or support systems. The states did so with varying degrees of speed and generosity.[21] At a fairly early date, the French government renewed the payment of pensions to officers in the French occupation zone, but only to those who had retired before 1933 or who were subsequently discharged or forced to retire for political reasons.[22] The distinction made by the French between older and younger officers was one that many officers themselves made. Max Lebius, an elderly lieutenant colonel who did not have the good fortune to live in the French zone, wrote to Hansen to express his dismay at being punished for the Wehrmacht's "sins." Seventy-one years of age in 1939, Lebius insisted that all he did was "serve three Kaisers and therefore committed no sins, on the basis of which my legally accrued pension should be withheld from me."[23]

Lebius's lack of loyalty shocked Hansen, who expected solidarity even from comrades who did not share in the general association of officers with Hitler and Nazism. But Lebius's tone reflects the bitterness felt by many older officers, especially those too old to find suitable employment. Although many received some assistance from state welfare agencies, some were forced to find whatever work was available, sell their possessions for cash, or rely on the generosity of family members or comrades. Men like Hansen and Donat had access to private funds (the actual source of which is often unclear), which they distributed in cases of dire need to help the less fortunate to pay rent, medical bills, or other special expenses. Donat supported a number of colleagues in the south with the resources collected among his circle of friends and contacts. But such aid was always piecemeal, unreliable, and available to only a select few.

The ratification of the Basic Law (the defacto constitution of the new country) and the creation of the Federal Republic between May and September 1949 presented new opportunities but few immediate and concrete benefits to former officers. On the basis of the new constitution's Article 131, career soldiers finally received some pension benefits. The Parliamentary Council that drafted the Basic Law had originally intended Article 131 to regulate only the pensions of former civil servants who had lost their positions as a result of territorial annexations in or expulsion from the Eastern zones. For lack of viable alternatives, however, the government decided to include former career soldiers under the article's provisions as well.[24]

Though former officers continued to lobby for the complete reinstatement of prewar and wartime benefits granted by the National Socialists, they soon acquiesced to their inclusion under Article 131.[25] Such a tactic appealed to career soldiers since the German and Allied governments' policy regarding pensions in general had long been more favorable toward civil servants than toward soldiers. Civil servants, except those convicted as war criminals, received their pensions after 1945, when soldiers' pensions were abolished. The fact that even government workers who had been Nazi Party members were enjoying their pension benefits while officers who had "merely fought to defend their country" received nothing caused considerable dismay among former officers. Nevertheless, casting themselves as "civil servants of another type" allowed officers to sidestep charges of militarism by claiming merely to have served, just as a postman serves, and to associate themselves with the "apolitical" traditions of the civil service.[26] The general sympathy among West Germans for the plight of those expelled from the East (who amounted to some 17 percent of the Federal Republic's population in the late 1940s) probably also prompted some former officers to cast their lot with that disadvantaged group.[27]

The decision to include career soldiers under Article 131 provided little immediate improvement in their situation. Article 131 merely provided the guidelines for regulating pensions and required further legislation in order for benefits actually to be paid. Between 1949 and 1951, the federal government busied itself with similar legislation regarding other groups of war victims such as refugees, late returning prisoners of war, and war-wounded, many of whom were of course soldiers. That legislation did not, however, deal with career soldiers as such. Not until the passage of the Law Relating to Basic Law Article 131 in 1951 did former professional soldiers begin receiving regular and meaningful assistance. While the level of benefits finally provided may not have satisfied everyone, the law provided some relief and established a framework upon which the veterans could build through further lobbying. The law granted pensions to most long-serving officers but left most noncommissioned officers without support. It excluded officers recruited during the arms buildup of the late 1930s and refused to recognize many of the hasty promotions granted during the war.[28] Revisions of the law throughout the 1950s gradually loosened the requirements for receipt of a pension and increased the level of payment, so that continued complaints on the part of veterans about injustice sounded hollow and eventually (virtually) disappeared by the 1960s.

More significant than the complaints about benefits, however, was the experience that former career soldiers gained in working with the new government as they lobbied for their pensions. James Diehl has called the Federal Republic's approach to special interest group legislation a "corporate, consensual decision-making process."[29] The government actively consulted unions, organizations of veterans and war victims, and other groups whenever it drafted legislation of interest to such bodies. Despite being consulted and involved in the legislative process, however, veterans only gradually got what they requested. The restriction of pensions to those serving before 1935, the limitation on the number of wartime promotions recognized, and the low level of payments irked veterans and resulted in many complaints.

The decision to adopt a corporatist approach redounded to the government's benefit and boded well for the future of the republic. Because the government listened to the soldiers and accorded them a measure of respect and recognition, the soldiers' grumbling remained within certain bounds. Career soldiers were in essence competing with other special interest groups for the government's favor (and resources). They therefore took care never completely to sever their ties and risk forgoing the potential benefits such ties might afford in the future.

Bundestag (Federal parliament) delegates, such as the Social Democrat Carlo Schmid, cajoled and flattered former officers, helping to bring them into mainstream political life. "There are a great, great number of responsible men among the old professional soldiers who are loyal to this state and who are prepared and determined to participate in the building of German democracy," Schmid told the Bundestag in 1950. Honor for these men, Schmid argued, was not something earned or lost exclusively in the past. "This honor is also a matter to be realized today by entering into that loyal relationship to the present state, in its time of need, to which [the soldier]—justifiably—directs his claims."[30] Schmid, by cleverly recognizing the officers' "justifiable" claims and appealing to their renowned sense of honor, did much to diminish the soldiers' disappointment about the low level of payment and the rejection of some of their promotions. By recognizing their legal claim to compensation, the state earned the respect and gratitude of former soldiers. The Federal Republic slowly established its desire to be the soldiers' friend, even if soldiers often reciprocated "only grudgingly."[31]

Employment

The vague provisions of Allied regulations in the late 1940s regarding the treatment of former soldiers meant that employment prospects for ex-officers varied considerably, depending on the hiring agency. The traditional haven for retired or unfit officers, the civil service, provided some positions, but finding a job in the civil service was not without difficulties. First, the large numbers of civil servants expelled from or fleeing the Eastern zones had created a surplus of trained administrators and government workers. Nebulous regulations regarding the exclusion of "militarists" often also meant that applications by former officers were unwelcome. In August 1946, Hansen wrote to the head of the Schleswig-Holstein Office for People's Education (Landesamt für Volksbildung), Dr. Teichert, decrying the office's exclusion of former officers from teacher training programs. Teichert apologized for the policy but insisted that no other option existed given the "current relationships"; he expressed his hope that the "psychosis" that led the German people to vilify former military men would one day die out.[32]

Since officers were identified as militarists in the public imagination, many government offices were wary of hiring former officers because of Allied decrees. Control Council Directive 38, enacted in October 1946, included "militarists" under the heading "Offenders" in its five-stage ranking of those to blame for the crimes of the Third Reich or potentially dangerous to the peace of the Allied zones.[33] That same month, Hansen received a letter from the interior minister of North Rhine-Westphalia, Dr. Schmidt, explaining that the training of former Wehrmacht men made them unfit for service in the police force of that state. Military training deprived soldiers of their sense of self-worth, Dr. Schmidt insisted, making it impossible for them to have the sense of fairness and "sportsmanship" necessary for effective police work.[34]

Despite the hostility of Schmidt and others, according to a statistical survey of former career soldiers (including noncommissioned officers) conducted in 1950, an astonishing 31,001 of the roughly 167,000 respondents (over 18 percent) eventually found employment in the civil service. The greatest proportion of jobs was at the state and communal levels (9,421 and 12,867 respectively), although the railroad accounted for a significant number (4,832), followed by the post office as the next single largest employer of career soldiers (1,292). So while positions of national prominence were often denied to former officers (the significant exception being a number of later Bundestag representatives, including former general Hasso von Manteuffel), many of them found comfortable positions in local or state government offices, making them influential members of the local community.

The traditional hostility between the military and socialists meant that former officers had great difficulties finding work in union-dominated industries. The leaderships of both the Social Democratic Party (SPD) and the German Federation of Trade Unions (DGB) were diplomatic in their utterances concerning the military and in their relationships with the soldiers' organizations. Conditions at the local level were not always so cordial. Certain individual unions, such as the publishing and the metal workers' unions, were openly hostile to former officers. Union members were reluctant to welcome former officers into their ranks because of unpleasant experiences during the war, memories of the Weimar period, or simply a fear of increased competition in the labor market.[35] Finally, however, a combination of governmental pressure on unions, the Social Democratic leadership's desire (especially under Kurt Schumacher) to gain the support of former soldiers for the party's nationalist policy, and the simple passage of time meant that the boycott largely subsided by 1952.[36]

One option that appealed to many veterans was continued military service. The French Foreign Legion's recruitment drives were shockingly successful in postwar Germany. Promises made to soldiers imprisoned in French prisoner of war (POW) camps enticed many to join, as did the dismal conditions inside Germany. Homelessness, unemployment, and family problems motivated almost 90 percent of those who joined, according to one report, which cited the number of Germans recruited between 1945 and 1955 at 232,500.[37] French reluctance to publicize data on the Foreign Legion makes accurate estimates difficult, but at least one former Legionnaire spoke of having served under German officers.[38] While the publicity that the Foreign Legion garnered in the 1950s focused on the threat to youth and the subsequent loss of manpower in Germany, some former officers for whom civilian life in the late 1940s and early 1950s held no promise sought their escape in the jungles of Indochina.

In 1949, Konrad Adenauer made his now famous reference to the possibility of a German contribution to European defense in the *Cleveland Plain Dealer*. Once rumors began to circulate that a new armed force would be created in the Federal Republic, many former officers quickly volunteered. Thinking that Hasso von Manteuffel might have some influence on the selection of the new contingent, ex-officer Hans Bruhn wrote to him, volunteering for a position in the administration. Bruhn eked out a living as an insurance agent, and he was "therefore available at any time for the new position." Life behind a civilian desk apparently had not been kind to Herr Bruhn; a military one might suit him better. Hansen's then fledgling League of Pension-Entitled Wehrmacht Personnel and Their Next of Kin (Bund versorgungsberechtigter ehemaliger Wehrmachtsangehörige und ihrer Hinterbliebene—BvW) received numerous similar letters, which it forwarded to the government.

Service in the Federal Border Guard (Bundesgrenzschutz—BGS) became an option in September 1950, though little information exists concerning how many former officers joined.[39] Many who served in the BGS were later disappointed to discover that they were not permitted to transfer to the Bundeswehr (armed forces of the Federal Republic) upon its creation in 1955. They had signed up thinking that they were serving in the West German army in an age when Cold War politics required such euphemisms as "border guard" instead of "army." After all, were they not supposed to defend against attacks by an East German army with the equally euphemistic name of Kasernierte Volkspolizei (roughly "people's police living in barracks")? On the contrary, the committee in charge of selecting officers for the Bundeswehr (the Personalgutachterausschuß— PGA) decided that any man so anxious to get back into uniform after 1945 did not fit the model of the "citizen in uniform" that was to lead the new army.[40]

Most historians consider the reincorporation of millions of returning soldiers and of tens of thousands of career officers into the economy as a great success story. Meyer asserts that the necessity of finding nonmilitary employment and dealing with a thoroughly civilian political and social milieu on a day-to-day basis helped to demilitarize many veterans, decreasing their potential threat to the Federal Republic's stability.[41] Indeed, Wehrmacht officers became insurance agents, traveling salesmen, civil servants, journalists, truck drivers, farmers, and priests by the tens of thousands.[42] This transition was not without its tense moments and failures, however, especially among former officers. While most acclimated well to the civilian world, many were still filled with notions of "occupational honor" that made it essential for them to receive a "pension" and not "welfare" and that prevented them from seeking employment they did not consider worthy. One officer wrote to U.S. Senator Arthur Vandenberg (then Senate Foreign Relations Committee chairman) warning of the dangers of the officers' declining status. In decrying the United States' continued refusal to pay pensions in its occupation zone, an elderly officer wrote (in broken English), "If an old officer cannot longer pay the study of his children on the university and academie and they must learn a simple profession—and this because the father was a German officer—do you mean that these children will become good democrats? Surely not!"[43]

The formerly privileged officers felt the sting of their diminished status. Anita Sievert, the wife of a former officer, felt abandoned after six Christmas seasons of "misery and danger." The sorry state of her household led to fears of proletarianization for herself and her entire class. Worse yet, she charged in one organization's newsletter, "the monstrous number of suicides among our ranks is being discretely ignored. We demand from the government, which constantly speaks of the equal rights of all citizens, finally our rights as well!"[44] Other letters to Hansen and his colleagues expressed similar fears at being collectively "reduced" to the level of the proletariat and warned of the danger of radicalization should such a decline occur.[45]

The fear of proletarianization on the part of a once privileged class might have constituted a real threat to the emerging democracy in the Federal Republic. However, these stories of misery and discrimination were never translated into calls for radical action. As in the case of the laws concerning militarism and the prohibition of veterans' organizations, veterans gained political experience and a stake in the Federal Republic's fledgling democratic institutions through their participation in the creation of the pension laws, no matter how unsatisfactory. In lobbying the government and the various political parties, the veterans understood that conditions were improving and learned that gains were possible through regular political channels as long as one played the political game.

"Defamation"

In nearly all their correspondence, memoirs, and newspaper articles, former officers linked their material suffering with the psychological trauma caused by the defamation of the military. As noted, mountains of vitriol were heaped on former soldiers, especially officers, by private citizens, foreign governments, newspapers, socialist groups, and even right-wing organizations because of the officers' perceived role in either supporting the Third Reich or contributing to the military collapse in 1945. One representative to the Bavarian Landtag (state parliament) stated simply, "Men who have chosen robbery, plunder, and murder as their life's career are not mere criminals, but are insects that should be punished by being trod upon, not just thrown in prison."[46] To these men filled with notions of both professional and personal honor, such public slander was intolerable. The attacks made upon them provoked a crisis of conscience and forced many former officers into a bitter, defensive stance that hindered them in accepting the new postwar system or effectively dealing with their own past.[47]

Some of the most striking examples of antisoldier feeling appeared in the letters to newspaper editors. At an early date, veterans' leaders identified sympathetic newspapers that would print letters or articles outlining the plight of former officers. These articles often provoked angry responses from readers. One such letter appeared in the newspaper *Echo der Woche* in response to an article on the former officers' struggle for their pensions. "[The generals] are supposed to receive pensions," the reader asked incredulously, "because they kept their oath to a criminal and an oath-breaker? . . . We don't want to see any more 'lead-spangled' heroes' chests. Our requirement for those has been satisfied."[48]

Other readers responded to similar articles in *Die Welt* and the American-controlled *Neue Zeitung* in equally negative terms. Herbert Reben in 1947 was shocked to read in *Die Welt* that officers were demanding special privileges (pensions) while things deteriorated for everyone else. Officers had received subsidies and had such high standards of living before the war that they should have been able to save for their old age, he argued.[49] Frau Wlottkowski, a refugee from the eastern provinces, also expressed her dismay that officers were to be rewarded as though they had won the war while other Germans still suffered. Josef Lauinger preferred the following homely analogy: "Arrogance and Impudence! . . . When someone opens a business, he must allow for the fact that he can go bankrupt. And when I start a war, I must understand from the outset that I can lose it and must then suffer the consequences."[50] Germans obviously both resented the special treatment officers had received before the war and expected them to do their fair share of suffering, especially since many believed the officers were to blame for the war in the first place.

Farther left on the political spectrum, the letters were even more vitriolic. A lengthy letter to the editors of *Süddeutsche Zeitung* (and marked significantly "SPD" by Col. Gen. Johannes Frießner, who cut it out and saved it) suggested that having escaped punishment for their crimes, former generals should slink away into the furthest reaches of Germany. "Instead," the writer frothed, "they let themselves be elected the 'Federal President of *Stahlhelm*,' try to bring their influence to bear again, and they dare, as expert witnesses, to gainsay clear Nazi crimes and murders. A scandalous venture for these journeyman warmongers."[51] The idea of taxpayer-funded pensions for former officers particularly galled many Germans. One subscriber to a communist newspaper suggested that officers "ought to be happy that they are left alone and are not forced to work with shovels and picks" instead of seeking "to be rewarded for the suffering, the misery, and the ruins that they brought on."[52]

Another group of resentful citizens were themselves former soldiers who no longer wished to be identified with the "virtues" of soldierdom. One, Carl Wilhelm Clasen, called the efforts of former officers on behalf of rearmament in the early 1950s an "affront [to] those people who had to endure the pointlessness of the military during the entire last war." Former soldiers, he insisted, "refuse to allow themselves to be clubbed by the military police and muzzled by the parade-ground bullies, only in order to preserve the integrity of the Generals' Club and its wine collection." Clasen closed by expressing his contempt for former officers and his regret that they had not all been imprisoned for their crimes.[53]

In addition to private citizens, some institutions participated in the public outcry against veterans and the "generals' clique." Despite the efforts of men like Kurt Schumacher to patch up old wounds created by decades of animosity between the military and the socialist milieu, prejudices against the military still appeared in journals and speeches of socialists and unionists. As mentioned above, certain unions were particularly hostile to soldiers, as a headline from the publishing union's newspaper, the *Grafischen Post*, illustrates: "The *Stand* [class] most worthy of our contempt is that of the soldier!"[54] The SPD newspaper, *Vorwärts*, was also occasionally guilty of an antisoldier stance, exhibited by a poem published in November 1948:

> *They stood in France and in Poland,*
> *They stood on the Volga and Don,*
> *They have robbed and they have stolen,*
> *And now can't recall what went on.*[55]

Antimilitary doctrines were still being taught to socialist youth. An ideologically schooled young socialist commented at a national meeting of youth groups in Stuttgart in 1955 that an army's influence on society was both inevitable and negative: "The military has always been a reactionary factor in our historical development and has always influenced the forms of our society."[56]

One of the most interesting single instances of defamation as perceived by the career soldiers was the novel and later film trilogy *08/15*. The story, which to the great embarrassment and chagrin of the veterans, was perhaps the most successful film of the first postwar decade, displayed in crude form all the prevailing clichés and prejudices relating to the military. Uneducated and brutal noncommissioned officers abuse new recruits until they are sent to the front to serve under pampered and unqualified aristocratic officers. The title became a synonym for the brutality of the barracks and the senselessness of war. To the former officers, however, the film was an immoral and unconscionable representation of what had been an essentially positive experience for nearly everyone.[57] One concerned veteran wrote, "That this film should be shown on Volkstrauertag [Memorial Day] and in our Fatherland's most fateful hour, as a new protective service is being built on the borders, is a deep insult to all soldiers and mothers and wives."[58]

Studies of public opinion, oddly enough, have shown that Germans held the military in relatively high regard throughout the late 1940s and early 1950s. Asked whether or not soldiers could be reproached for their conduct in the war, only 6 percent of those questioned insisted that soldiers could be condemned, while 76 percent believed either that soldiers were blameless or that only certain individuals could be held accountable.[59] This speaks of a high respect for German soldierdom. Some historians theorize that personal connections to former soldiers were simply too close to allow Germans universally to condemn former military personnel.[60] Everyone had either served or had a father, brother, or husband in uniform. To some extent, this sympathy was granted to the officer corps as well. Former officers were respected members of society, and they became town leaders, Bundestag representatives, journalists, and professors (as noted above). But at the same time, the officer corps and generals' clique were targets of public scorn. To many former officers, this scorn outweighed the tacit forgiveness, and this fact, combined with the officers' extremely broad definition of defamation and their juridical sense of honor, embittered them, making them feel like economic, social, and even moral outcasts.

Early organizations

The perception of these "injustices," embodied in Allied legislation, economic discrimination, and public defamation, catalyzed the first efforts at organization among former officers.[61] They banded together to fight for their pensions and their economic rights. They saw themselves as the bearers of the valuable traditions of German soldierdom and therefore fought just as strongly for the reestablishment of the soldier's honor. Officers maintained contacts made within branches of the armed forces, General Staff, or a specific command and sought each other out when they needed assistance. "Shouldn't the bond of old Wehrmacht camaraderie be strong enough," asked Hansen, "in order to hold . . . even without an officially sanctioned organization?"[62] The early volumes of Hansen's papers are filled with letters from needy comrades and widows requesting assistance. Most had heard through other officers and friends merely that Hansen was "doing something" for former soldiers in the British zone, and they heaped upon him appeals for money and help in finding jobs and housing.[63] Lacking the resources to do much financially for his needy comrades, Hansen lobbied zonal officials, both German and British, church organizations, political parties, and newspapers on behalf of first the members of the navy and later the entire Wehrmacht or previous German armies.

Hansen contacted old acquaintances and established links to former officers working along similar lines across the country. Informal networks of former officers formed around men like Donat and Rudolf Veiel in southwestern Germany and Maj. Gen. Georg von Sodenstern in Frankfurt am Main. Initial contacts were often made when news of the others' work reached one man through mutual friends, prompting an exchange of ideas and experiences that lasted decades.[64]

As the network of acquaintances expanded, Hansen and others wondered about the possibility of forming semiofficial "Emergency Groups" (Notgemeinschaften) to champion their cause by establishing a claim to represent a large number of former career soldiers. The legal status of such organizations was unclear, however. Since Hansen lived in the British zone, he inquired of the British Military Government's attitude. A British official replied that while private meetings did not require the Military Government's sanction, Allied Control Council Law 8 prohibited all "war veterans' organizations." Ultimately, the responsibility was Hansen's to place limitations on any meeting so that the authorities would not have to intervene.[65] This nebulous situation persisted even into 1951, when Axel von dem Bussche, working for the Blank Office, the precursor of the Federal Republic's Defense Ministry, made the following entry in his notes: "According to Control Council Law 16 *all* veterans' organizations are illegal. Until now they have been tolerated. . . . After all, we are also 'forbidden.' . . . Who draws the lines for what is to be further tolerated?"⁶⁶ In the end, the Allies tolerated most veterans' associations. Although the authorities banned a few organizations as rightwing threats in Bavaria and Hesse in 1948, associations such as Hansen's more moderate Emergency Groups survived.⁶⁷

Eventually, the various leaders called for a union of all veterans' organizations to strengthen their position vis-à-vis the government. Early in 1950, Hansen's Emergency Groups formed the BvW. The leaders of other small organizations that had appeared in previous years eventually also associated with the BvW to form the core of organized former officers in the Federal Republic.⁶⁸ Throughout 1951 and 1952, other veterans' associations sprang up all over West Germany. The most numerous were the tradition societies, based on individual units or army groups, such as the Tradition Society Großdeutschland (hereafter *Großdeutschland*) or the League of Former Members of the Africa Corps (Verband ehemaliger Angehöriger Deutsches Afrika Korps—DAK).

Eventually, in September 1951, several of these unit-based organizations, along with the BvW and other broad-based veterans' organizations, formed the League of German Soldiers (Verband Deutscher Soldaten—VDS), which, much like the BvW, represented the economic and pension rights of former career soldiers but also had pretensions to being the home for all former soldiers, officers as well as conscripts. Though the VDS's birth was fraught with dissension and schisms and the organizations that it claimed to represent retained a large degree of freedom, the VDS became the mouthpiece for German soldierdom.⁶⁹ It never represented a majority of former soldiers—or even former officers, for that matter—but it became the organizational home for men and women who shared a set of values and belonged to what they called the "soldier's estate."

The similarity of their goals and beliefs contributed to the fusion of these early associations, despite the jealousies and occasional pettiness of their leaders. The organizations uniformly insisted that they represented only the social and material interests of their constituents, not the political. In announcing the creation of his aid society (Hilfsverein für ehemalige berufsmässige Angehörige der Deutschen Wehrmacht und ihrer Hinterbliebenen) in 1948, Engelbert Frank listed the organization's purpose as purely economic: to relieve the distress of former career soldiers, to help them find work, and to improve their economic situation via a reinstatement of pensions. Rear Adm. Günther Schubert, an associate of Hansen's, prioritized the goals for what would eventually become the BvW in July 1948. Significantly, in Schubert's view, the fight against the defamation of the German soldier preceded the fight for pensions. These two goals were followed by practical aid for ex-soldiers and their families in making the transition to the civilian workforce and by actual financial support for those in extreme need.[70] The BvW branch in Frankfurt am Main demanded an immediate end to the Wehrmacht's defamation, the reestablishment of the right to a pension (even before the issue of financing the pensions was addressed), and an end to the boycott on hiring ex-officers.[71] The stated goals of nearly all the groups combined the material (the fight for pensions and jobs) with the ideal (the fight for honor, the release of POWs, and justice for those wrongly sentenced for war crimes).

The early organizers understood that they were up against not only the various Allied regulations, but also the German public's prejudice. They were aware of a need for effective public relations. In a note circulated in early 1950, Lt. Gen. Gerhard Kühne, head of a group of former officers in North Rhine-Westphalia, established "Guidelines for the Participation of the Press at the Founding of an 'Emergency Group' and Thereafter." It was desirable, Kühne wrote, to publish only a short notice of the founding of a group in the local official press or in a friendly newspaper. Longer notices, which would seem like apologies, were unwelcome. The goal of such press relations was to convince the public that the Emergency Group was interested merely in the question of pensions, not in politics. Kühne also hoped to give readers a glimpse into the suffering of former soldiers and to win the press over in the fight against defamation. He reminded his fellow officers to send such notices to the socialist newspapers as well: "It is worth remembering that many veterans, whose membership we value, belong to the SPD and only read newspapers affiliated with that party."[72] The veterans' leaders were aware of the need to avoid the stigma of a generals' clique, an epithet that circulated widely in postwar Germany whenever soldiers' organizations were mentioned. "I would advise," Hansen wrote in April 1950 to a veterans' representative from Württemberg-Hohenzollern, "that from the very beginning noncommissioned officers and women be brought into the state leadership [of the veterans' organizations], so that our fight . . . does not suffer from the odium of being a purely officers' matter."[73]

By 1950, the early veterans' organizations, especially the BvW, had made significant gains. Hansen and his associates in Bonn, headed by former general Kurt Linde, had successfully lobbied for the inclusion of former career soldiers in the social legislation passed by the Bundestag during its first session. Equally important, Hansen and other veteran officers had established themselves with the government as the "voice of the Wehrmacht." The nascent veterans' organizations were by no means the only voice. Men such as Wolf von Baudissin, Johann Adolf von Kielmansegg, and Adolf Heusinger would later become far more influential from their positions in the Chancellor's Office, especially as regards the issue of rearmament. Yet Hansen, Donat, Sodenstern, and the other veterans' leaders represented a large group of former officers and career soldiers who were concerned to carry on the traditions of German soldierdom.

In responding to their dismal material situation, former officers made idealism a significant part of their program. The attacks on soldiers, whether material or verbal, encouraged solidarity. The veterans' leaders were aware of this, and in their newsletters and speeches they often combined tales of defamation with calls to "close the ranks," pay membership dues, and recruit new members. The former officers' emphasis on the ideal was more than a mere tactical ploy, however. They stressed from the outset the value of their specifically soldierly ideology not simply to their fellow soldiers, but to society as a whole. The articles in their newsletters and the contents of their speeches were directed to a larger audience. They firmly believed that former officers were obligated to provide, as they had in the past, "a national, soldierly conscience" that would help Germany weather the crisis of its total defeat and the threats of the Cold War.[74]

The defamation and the economic, social, and political discrimination against former soldiers led many of them to focus on the idealistic elements of their postwar mission. At the beginning of their struggle, former officers had little else. Many were in prison or in POW camps, unable physically to contribute to the recovery of Germany. Once released, officers were marginalized in society by the ban on organizations and their status as pariahs. Unable to follow their accustomed careers in service of the German people, they fell back on elements of their military worldview that compensated for and explained their inability to gain acceptance. The defamation of soldiers clearly showed, they argued, that the materialist postwar German society lacked the virtues of discipline, service, honor, and honesty that had always been the soldierly profession's hallmarks. As the former officers' material goals were gradually met, the idealistic aspect of their struggle became even more predominant.[75] The experience gained by former officers in representing their material interests to the government has been covered elsewhere.[76] The following chapters will explore the way in which the preexisting soldierly ideology interacted with the demands and conditions of the postwar era to deradicalize former career soldiers and to foster among them a lasting, if not wholly enthusiastic, support for the democratic order in West Germany.

2

Creating Soldiers' Opinion: The Verband Deutscher Soldaten

Dr. Jürgen Schreiber, Bundeswehr major general (retired) and current chairman of the League of German Soldiers (VDS), wrote in the conclusion of *Soldat im Volk* that soldiers returning home after the World War II "looked for and found like-minded people, equally wronged people, and above all a comradeship that after proving itself on the front now would also have a positive effect in civilian life."[1] As we have seen, the first veterans' organizations that formed after 1945 were loosely organized groups of officers and other career soldiers who organized for the purpose of reclaiming both their pensions and their lost honor. These groups formed on a local level and slowly expanded through personal contacts and chance into regional and national organizations, such as the BvW.

Though the Allies still expressly prohibited organizations composed exclusively of veterans, the creation of the Federal Republic, the issue of a West German military force, and the precedent established by Hansen and others created an atmosphere in which the once barely tolerated soldiers' groups flourished, expanding in terms of both membership and number of organizations.

The year 1951 was especially heady though ultimately disappointing for the new groups and for former officers concerned with the future of German soldierdom. In that year both the Kyffhäuserbund and Stahlhelm, veterans' organizations from the pre–Third Reich era, were reestablished.[2] Also in 1951, vast numbers of the tradition societies and other unit-based organizations appeared. Most of these smaller organizations lacked the political influence (or political pretensions) of the larger groups like the BvW, but some unit-based organizations, such as DAK or Großdeutschland, attained considerable importance, encompassing members from all over West Germany. It was also a year of great promise for veterans because of the hopes for organizational unity and political influence engendered by the creation of the VDS. This organization, encompassing all veterans, would be a potential force, by some estimates, of two to three million voters.[3] In September, representatives from eight major soldiers' groups met in Bonn and formed the VDS. However, their dreams of unity were short-lived, as we shall see. Nevertheless, the appearance of so many new (or re-formed) veterans' organizations and the creation of the VDS make 1951 fertile ground for the study of former soldiers' attitudes toward the new German state and their own perceived role within it.

Like many other clubs and organizations, the veterans' groups had membership drives and dues, newsletters and meetings, conferences and parties. Most also developed an "organizational ideology" that defined their mission, justified their demands, and (usually) testified to their loyalty toward the Federal Republic. The later organizations, relying on the principles and precedents set down in 1945–1950 by leaders such as Hansen, Donat, and Veiel, played an important role in resocializing former soldiers by representing their interests to the government (as noted) and creating a structure within which many former career soldiers could express criticism of the new West German political order while staying within the bounds of democratic propriety. Moreover, groups such as the VDS satisfied soldiers' desires for comradeship and safeguarded their collective memories of wartime experiences. By emphasizing the identity of comradeship and democracy, reining in radical members, moderating critical viewpoints, and effectively competing for the state's recognition and resources, such groups also attached the loyalty of many officers to the new state.

Organizational Ideologies

The new organizations shared, to a great extent, the same goals and ideals. The statements of purpose issued by the groups as they made their first public (or semipublic) announcements originated in the language of German soldierdom, especially as modified throughout the late 1940s by the pronouncements of both the government and organizations like the BvW.

In general, the groups of the late 1940s pledged to fight for an end to the defamation of the former German soldier, to lobby for the restoration of his rights, and, as the newsletter of one organization put it, "to fill [the] members with the idea of mutual responsibility for the fate of the Volk and the state and to reincorporate them as an element of order, reliability . . . and integrity in the reconstruction of the life of the German people."[4] Most groups declared their loyalty to the new democratic state but simultaneously claimed to be "above parties" and admonished the government that no honorable soldier would serve in a new army until the war criminal issue had been satisfactorily resolved and certain other soldiers' demands met.[5]

The groups that sprang up in the spring and summer of 1951 followed roughly the same model, though the effects of several years of prior work on the part of Hansen and others to eliminate the stigma that had troubled the earlier veterans' organizations were apparent. Because of the initial legal regulations against the formation of purely veterans' organizations, the earlier organizations tended to publish relatively limited, mostly economic goals. But after the government's will to enforce the strict regulations waned and a number of such organizations had already been formed, their statements of purpose became more ambitious. Their goals ranged from the relatively tame phrases of Großdeutschland— which merely promised to support needy comrades; aid the Red Cross in resolving the cases of soldiers missing in action; and "cultivate the tried and true concepts of discipline, responsibility, and moral bonding"[6]— to the lofty aspirations of Stahlhelm. Stahlhelm claimed to be "a group whose endeavor it was and is to see decency, respectability, and cleanliness realized in all areas of life." According to its declaration, issued 1 April 1951, Stahlhelm "embodies the still silent army of sons of its Volk, who do not want party bickering, class war, and class struggle, but who carry the will to unity in their hearts." The Stahlhelm comrade should lead by example, read the manifesto, and pledge himself to "occidental Christian culture and civilization and its resultant ideas of freedom, rights, and political forms." Stahlhelm stood for "social peace and the right to work for its youth." It protested against "the abuse of Germans in obligatory service for foreign powers."[7] Here, as in the statements of the BvW and other groups, are the pledges of loyalty to the Federal Republic, the struggle for soldiers' rights, and the maintenance of camaraderie and tradition, albeit in more millennial language.

Despite the apparent similarity of their goals, each veterans' organization developed an easily recognizable organizational ideology to justify its existence. Especially as the number of organizations mushroomed in 1951 and 1952, carving out a niche became a Darwinian necessity, particularly for the larger groups. Groups like the DAK shared the concern of the BvW, Stahlhelm, and Großdeutschland for maintaining camaraderie, supporting needy veterans, and clarifying missing in action (MIA) cases, but they and several other organizations went further in elaborating their self-images and perceived contributions to society.

The DAK's particular idiom was especially interesting because it was based so strongly on the unit's experiences during World War II. The group's newsletter, *Die Oase* (The oasis), declared that the DAK members "want to honor and to hold high what we learned and experienced, and to be now, as we were in Tunisia, brave and honorable, fair also in the fight on the economic and political level. Now as then we want to help in the spirit of camaraderie and share with those who have less—whether they be former Afrikaner or other suffering people."[8] An open letter in a later issue struck a similar note when it claimed that the organization did not discuss political matters such as rearmament but rather "attempt[ed] to maintain those virtues that were so generally exemplary, in human terms, in the desert."[9] This image of the former Africa Corps as a unit that fought fairly and with compassion was a compelling one for its members. The Africa Corps benefited greatly from being held in generally high esteem by former adversaries as well as from its association with Field Marshal Erwin Rommel. Rommel's brilliant victories in the desert earned him the admiration of his foes. His tangential involvement in the 20 July assassination plot and his eventual death at the order of Hitler provided him with an untarnishable historical image.

The DAK trotted out the image of Rommel and its legacy of fairness in battle whenever possible. It printed frequent stories about Rommel in its newsletter, including one with the intriguing title "Would Rommel Have Been with Blank [in the Defense Ministry]?," which criticized the newly formed Bundeswehr and the Defense Ministry for favoring former General Staff officers in their leadership positions.[10] The selection process, the article claimed, ignored the obvious leadership qualities of a man like Rommel, who never held a staff position. Rommel had become the point of reference for these veterans, the symbol and embodiment of what they felt had been best about the Wehrmacht. Rommel, the DAK argued, "was a soldier with 'civic courage,' whose love for his country was based on truthfulness and an essential linkage with the native soil and with eternally vibrant nature.... Erwin Rommel—a *miles fati*—remains the embodiment of good, clean, German soldierdom."[11] Rommel's widow, Lucy, frequently appeared at the DAK's meetings and fundraisers, cementing the group's association with the war hero. Nearly every photo, brochure, or publication of the DAK in the late 1940s and early 1950s featured Frau Rommel prominently, standing by the group's chairman or presenting an award or prize to a member. Significantly, however, her place in the organization was as a symbolic link to her dead husband rather than as an active participant. One member of the VDS who attended a DAK meeting in 1954 even called Frau Rommel's presence "disturbing" because she occupied such a large place in the proceedings.[12]

Former Africa Corps soldiers carried another idealistic "banner," also theoretically based on their wartime experience, proclaiming their concern for the "reconciliation of peoples." This element of their ideology exploited the still popular idea that the war in North Africa had been a "war without hate," during which the combatants, according to the editors of a series dedicated to World War II, never sank to the levels of barbarity common on other fronts, despite the severity of the fighting.[13] The DAK hoped to use this legacy to "build bridges with our former enemies and to see that the old wounds slowly form scars," as the group's chairman, former general Ludwig Crüwell, said at the annual meeting in 1956.[14] In 1953, the local DAK group in Trier sponsored a "Family Christmas Festival," which, "in the spirit of true reconciliation ... gained special meaning for both the members and the public at large in that for the first time soldiers of other powers participated in a German Christmas Festival." As unlikely as it seems that these were the *first* foreign soldiers ever to have spent Christmas in Germany, some fifty to sixty French and American soldiers and their families accepted the Trier group's invitation, causing one speaker to laud the occasion as a milestone in the history of international relations.[15]

The Western allies legitimated the DAK's claim to be an agent of international reconciliation. Speaking at the DAK's annual meeting in 1956, the British general Sir Richard Gale took the opportunity to express his pleasure that German and British troops were now defending Europe together, giving them the chance to renew the camaraderie that they allegedly had shared in the North African desert. "I am convinced," said General Gale, "that this meeting, as a meaningful contribution to West European unity, will strengthen the feeling of comradeship between German and British soldiers as well as between our peoples."[16] Although his speech contains some confusion as to who had been and who was still a soldier, General Gale nonetheless subscribed to the DAK's idea that its existence contributed to international peace and the defense of Europe.

The former Africa Corps soldiers also believed that their unique contact with the North African people gave them a particular obligation to advocate friendship between Germany and North African nations. Articles in *Die Oase* frequently recalled their supposedly congenial relations with the natives. One Egyptian general (Naguib) supported their belief when he improbably stated that "Field Marshal Rommel and the German Africa Corps were the beacon on the road to freedom for [the Egyptians]."[17] The "obligation" that these former soldiers derived from their wartime experiences in North Africa was somehow to promote peace, freedom, and mutual understanding between Germans and the peoples of that region. How this obligation was to be translated into action remained vague, but the prominent place occupied by Egyptian affairs in their newsletter attests to the strength of their identification with the land where they fought.

For the DAK, the drive for reconciliation even extended to areas in which the Africa Corps had not seen action, such as Southeast Asia. Richard Salchow, an Afrikaner doing ethnological studies of Thailand, urged "more understanding for the peoples of Asia" in a 1954 article in *Die Oase*: "The current situation and the future demand more factual knowledge and understanding of the people of Asia on the part of a wider public among us." An ethnologist must, Salchow believed, promote such understanding by reaching a nonacademic audience: "If I now and again report here [in *Die Oase*], then I do so on the basis of a rational consideration that precisely the circle of comrades of the former German

Africa Corps offers the best possibility for such an effect." The mere proposal that some sort of international understanding was involved apparently convinced both the writer (after "rational consideration") and his audience that the DAK was uniquely qualified to tackle the issue.[18]

Other groups shared with the DAK a geographically based focus on international relations. The members of the former First Panzer Division usually devoted the majority of their newsletters to reminiscing about their experiences during the war with articles like "Tanks between Warsaw and the Atlantic," but on at least one occasion, they felt obligated to forget the old wounds and "come to a new relationship with the peoples of the Balkans, to [our] former enemy, Yugoslavia." In 1957 the group's chairman admonished his readers to "draw up new plans of attack that can lead to a new beginning! To make our most honorable effort to find a new relationship with Yugoslavia and its neighbors, with reserve and unprejudiced justice on the basis of our earlier good relations, means to win the future for Europe!" and—the general added significantly—"therefore for our German homeland as well!"[19] It seems doubtful that the involvement (diplomatic or otherwise) of the men of the First Panzer Division in the Balkans would have helped much since Tito, the leader of Yugoslavia in 1957, had made his career fighting the Wehrmacht and its Slavic allies in the Balkans. The people with whom the First Panzer Division had earlier had "good relations" were not those in power in Yugoslavia.

Like the members of the First Panzer Division or the Africa Corps, former soldiers of the Großdeutschland division selected a defining ideology that reflected the history of their unit—namely, its elite status and service on the Eastern Front. The soldiers of Großdeutschland claimed to have special knowledge of Soviet communism and therefore to be immune to the effects of Soviet propaganda. "In these times of social conflict and democratic rules," wrote one former soldier in Großdeutschland's newsletter, *Die Neue Feuerwehr* (The new fire brigade), "even the KPD [German Communist Party] has its supporters, especially among those who never saw Russia, whose experiences do not originate on the battlefields of Russia. Their watchfulness will first be aroused when they are given the opportunity for some thorough 'sightseeing.'" The soldiers who fought in Russia knew better, the article continued. "For us the KPD is like a red cloth to a bull! [German soldiers] are the greatest enemies of the KPD because they have seen the land of its origin; and they will remain its enemy so long as German soldiers do not allow their memories of forgotten days to be blown away!"[20]

In language reminiscent of Adolf Hitler's infamous "fight to the last man" orders, Großdeutschland promised to counter the "red ideology" with a "clean, clear, and German attitude, to take not a single step backward, what is more, to fight [that ideology] wherever we find it!"[21] The particular instance of communist activity that provoked the above outburst is illustrative because it indicates the types of local struggles between veterans' organizations and their opponents that must have been fairly commonplace, at least in the early 1950s, when rearmament was still a volatile political issue and the KPD was not yet outlawed.[22] According to accounts in *Die Neue Feuerwehr*, the KPD in Nuremberg had threatened to destroy the restaurant of a Herr Kellerman if he allowed the local Großdeutschland affiliate to meet there as scheduled. The threat of violence prompted the organization to seek police protection, but when members arrived at the police station, they found the police better informed about the whole matter than the organization itself. On the night of the meeting, if one believes the soldiers' account, the streets outside of Kellerman's restaurant were filled with uniformed and plainclothes police officers, supported via radio link by a special reserve unit armed with water cannons and tear gas grenades.[23] One wonders how a group that received such treatment from the police could claim to be defamed and treated like a social pariah. Nevertheless, such incidents led Großdeutschland to feel justified in citing its special enmity with the forces of communism and to urge its membership to combat the leftist foe.

Unlike the DAK, whose slogans of peace and reconciliation had a more positive ring, Großdeutschland expressed a great deal more bitterness over its treatment at the Allies' hands. The members felt offended when they were not consulted by the government when it sought to establish a usable tradition for the Bundeswehr.[24] Their newsletters also printed more resentment-laden material relating to the issues of pension rights, prisoners of war and war criminals, and the soldier's public image.[25] They cried foul in 1956, for example, when a French officer who had ordered the execution of three alleged Nazis near the Alsatian town of Appenweir in the spring of 1945 was sentenced by a French court to "a relatively light prison term." Because of a special French amnesty agreement, the officer was released immediately after being sentenced. The court found his co-defendants innocent since the officer had taken all responsibility for the execution and they were therefore "only following orders." "We do not wish to express feelings of bitterness," wrote members of *Die Neue Feuerwehr*'s editorial staff, "that a crime of French soldiers against Germans has found no expiation." But they were bitter, despite their protestations to the contrary, and the article continued with a none too subtle slap at the French military: "Eleven years is a long time, and if French military justice can act no more quickly, then punishment does not represent real atonement because the deed lies so far in the past."[26] The veterans were bitter that there was a double standard of justice in France since German soldiers still sat in French prisons for what they felt to be crimes similar to that of the French officer. Großdeutschland fed upon this sense of injustice and nurtured a deep resentment toward the Allies for their treatment of veterans after the war. Similarly resentment-laden articles on the trial of General Manteuffel in the late 1950s confirm this sense of injury.[27]

Großdeutschland, as its name implies, also strongly advocated German unification. Throughout the 1950s, the leadership used the Großdeutschland newsletter to remind the members of Germany's division. The editors of *Die Neue Feuerwehr* filled its pages with stories decrying the lack of progress toward reunification and urged their readers to make the most of historic opportunities such as the 1953 uprising in East Germany.[28] Großdeutschland frequently published articles or statistics on the situation in Berlin, still the capital in the minds of these "Greater Germans."[29] The newsletter featured several articles on the East German uprising and almost invariably called the German Democratic Republic "Central Germany" in memory of the eastern provinces lost to the Russians and the Poles after World War II.[30] It even suggested, albeit indirectly, that the Western Allies, especially Britain, had an interest in keeping Germany disunited for economic reasons.[31] Such attitudes, though voiced privately by a number of the leaders of other organizations in the postwar period, never found their way into the pages of the publications of the VDS, DAK, or other mainstream groups.

By way of contrast, the organizational ideology developed by a quite different type of veterans' group, the Association of Former Prisoners of War (Verband der Heimkehrer—VdH), is illuminating. Founded in 1950 when two older organizations merged, the VdH practically denied by its organizational ideology that it was a soldiers' organization at all, though over 50 percent of its members were veterans.[32] The name alone indicates its distance from groups like the BvW or the VDS, as does the fact that its chairman in the early 1950s was not himself a former soldier.[33] Like some of the more "traditional" veterans' groups, the VdH addressed the issues of war criminals, rearmament, the trials of captivity, and the need for a revitalization of Germany and its youth, but there were several differences in its approach. For one thing, speakers at VdH meetings were Bundestag representatives, ministers, and only rarely prominent soldiers.[34] Most telling was the VdH's nearly universal omission of former ranks from the names of its members, speakers, and anyone else whose name appeared in their paper who had been a Wehrmacht officer.

The VdH also took greater pains to address its nonveteran members, especially women. Its newsletter, *Der Heimkehrer* (The returnee), featured frequent articles relating to the particular plight of women and mothers in postwar Germany, such as "The Women Got a Raw Deal," appearing in November 1954.[35] *Der Heimkehrer* also printed advertisements for washing powder, margarine, and illustrated books, items that were obviously directed at a female audience.[36] Advertisements in general were a rarity in the other organizations' materials, and those that did appear were often for more "masculine" items such as commemorative armbands and war memorabilia. Even *Der Heimkehrer*'s format distinguished it from other newsletters. It was a large, well-illustrated newspaper, while the other newsletters, when they were printed at all and not merely mimeographed, were of leaflet or at best magazine size and usually lacked photographs.[37]

One must be careful not to overstate the differences between the VdH and the more traditional soldiers' organizations. As noted, some of the VdH's goals were similar to those of the other organizations, especially after most of its material demands had been met by 1954, and the VdH joined with other groups on various committees and projects.[38] Still, the VdH remained remarkably nonmilitary in character, despite the composition of its membership.

Creation of the VDS

The formation of a large number of veterans' organizations in the course of 1951 and 1952, despite the similarity of their goals and ideas, created uncertainty and disappointment among many former officers, particularly those who for years had been fighting for the existence of their own organizations. With the renewed interest in German rearmament catalyzed by the Korean War, the stakes became much higher in the game that Hansen and his associates had been playing prior to 1950. Everyone involved saw great potential for influence and gains on the part of former soldiers because of the government's need to consult and court veterans. For this reason, Hansen jealously guarded his group's position as the most influential and largest body of organized former soldiers. That statement is not intended entirely to disparage Hansen's motives because he and his comrades in the BvW certainly favored the unity of former soldiers in an idealistic sense as well. Given the former officers' views on the importance of social cohesion and their distaste for "party politics," one can see how the apparently increasing fragmentation of organized veterans would disturb them at a level deeper than their own organizational egotism.

For some time, Hansen and others had been toying with the idea of forming a single veterans' group in Germany that would provide an organizational home for all former soldiers, Wehrmacht or Imperial Army, officer or common soldier, either individually or corporately as part of a tradition society. In the late spring and early summer of 1951, the call went out among prominent former officers and the leaders of several existing soldiers' leagues soliciting proposals and planning meetings to discuss the creation of a unified organization. Months of correspondence among Hansen, Frießner, Manteuffel, Lt. Gen. Erich Dethleffsen, and others resulted in a meeting on 9 September in Bonn, at which representatives from the larger soldiers' organizations would create an umbrella organization.

In the spirit of revival prevalent in 1951, the aims of this new organization were as ambitious as those of the other recently founded groups, such as Stahlhelm. The new soldiers' group, wrote Dethleffsen, who was influential and well connected, would not only represent former soldiers' interests, but would also contribute to the security and the future of Germany by reminding Germans that "the interests of the individual must be placed beneath the interests of the community and that only the bringing together of all efforts in a common cause can lead to success."[39] Somewhat later, Frießner drafted a speech entitled "Purpose and Goals of the League of German Soldiers" that embodied the same spirit. Frießner lamented that immorality ruled contemporary Germany. The VDS, like Stahlhelm, would change Germany by providing a positive example and "moral rearmament."[40] Frießner's statement, like Dethleffsen's, confirmed the organization's idealistic role as the keeper of soldierly values and the safeguard of Germany's future.

Hansen, Dethleffsen, Frießner, and the others who had a hand in creating the VDS consulted extensively with the federal government, the opposition parties, and unions before acting on their plans to create a unified veterans' organization. Members of the Blank Office were in continual contact with prominent soldiers and closely followed the events that led to the September meeting. Hints exist that the government was somehow steering the developments to ensure that the organization that emerged was sufficiently pro-Western and politically reliable. In an intriguing letter from Axel von dem Bussche to a Herr Gerhard Günther in August 1951, Bussche wrote that "as far as [he] knew, Admiral Hansen in Kiel was charged with organizing the unification of existing, or rather, newly forming, soldiers' organizations," though how official Hansen's commission was remains unclear.[41]

The government's interest stemmed from a dual desire to have a handle on the seemingly endless number of veterans' organizations by creating a single, politically diverse and reliable group and to use the more potent voice that a single large organization would have in the ongoing negotiations with the Western Allies over German rearmament. Kielmansegg in fact admitted the government's interest on both counts to Dethleffsen in a meeting on 31 August 1951, when he said that Theodor Blank would welcome a veterans' group that would back the government in its negotiations or even force the government to present conditions to the Allies.[42] Dethleffsen felt he was not only being informed of the government's position, but was also being milked for any information he might provide on the political reliability and loyalty of Hansen, Frießner, and the other potential leaders of the proposed VDS.

Dethleffsen was also in frequent contact with the Blank Office, and he solicited its opinion on the subject of an umbrella organization several times, especially where dealings with the political parties and unions were concerned.[43] Kielmansegg, with whom Dethleffsen frequently corresponded, recommended, among other measures, that Dethleffsen speak to SPD leader Schumacher about plans for the proposed group and that the soldiers consider electing a union official, such as Christian Fette, to the new organization's board. The effort to ensure the political reliability and acceptance of the VDS was a mammoth one, with nearly every step carefully prepared in advance.

As noted, on 9 September 1951 in Bonn, representatives of the major (and some minor) veterans' organizations met to create a unified organization. Representatives came from Hansen's recently renamed BvW, now the German Soldiers' League (Der Deutsche Soldatenbund—DDBS), Stahlhelm, the League for the Defense of Former German Soldiers (Schutzbund ehemaliger Deutscher Soldaten—BDS), DAK, Großdeutschland, and members of the airborne troops, Waffen-SS, and even the transportation corps. Details had been worked out in preliminary meetings though slight differences of opinion about the organization's name and competition between Hansen and the BDS marred the assembly. After a lengthy speech by Frießner, who had been nominated as chairman, the representatives chose the name Verband Deutscher Soldaten for their group, elected a board of directors, and the VDS was a reality.[44]

The petty issues that had divided the groups during the summer faded into insignificance because of the storm surrounding the first press conference of the VDS's new chairman, Frießner, which took place on 22 September before both foreign and German reporters in Bad Godesberg (near Bonn). As chairman, Frießner had so far been quite successful in cultivating the group's public image and had scored public relations victories by extending a conciliatory hand to both Schumacher and union leaders on behalf of German soldierdom.[45] Frießner no doubt felt that he possessed the necessary tact to handle the press as well, but the VDS was taking no chances. In preparation for the first press conference, a former colonel named Wechmar briefed Frießner on what to expect. Wechmar, the press liaison for the VDS, had a son who was a reporter who would be present at Bad Godesberg. Therefore, Frießner had reason to suspect that he would be facing a somewhat sympathetic crowd.

Wechmar's primary advice was to be forthcoming and to answer all of the reporters' questions in order not to provide "any room for unnecessary doubts." Wechmar even asked his son immediately to pose questions on some sensitive subjects, such as the 20 July coup attempt, so that these questions would come from a friendly source.[46]

Despite this friendly aid, however, Frießner was unable to make the impression he desired. Shortly before the press conference, he confided to Manteuffel that "good instincts and tact" would be required to handle the growth of their new organization and that "[e]very derailment detracts from the cause."[47] Frießner called the "cross-examination" at the press conference "worse than at Nuremberg," and he was simply not up to such a challenge. In his effort to be forthcoming, Frießner, among other things, condemned the 20 July coup attempt as murder, declared the 1939 attack on Poland justified, and blamed the Allies for the division of Germany and strength of the Soviet Union. Even Frießner's own accounts of the press conference indicate the magnitude of his blunders. On the outbreak of the war against Poland, for example, Frießner said, "At that time [before September 1939] we were informed by the press and radio about the goings-on in the [Polish] corridor, about the persecution of the German minority by the Poles, and about [the Polish] atrocities. Politics was no longer adequate to clear up these matters. Then the long arm of politics, the Wehrmacht, had to step in. So it came to war."[48]

As though this stance were not clear enough, a *Manchester Guardian* reporter asked Frießner whether he was of the opinion that the start of the war had been justified. Frießner replied, after a short pause, "Yes." Frießner's "train" not only derailed; it collided with loaded tanker cars in a busy train station.

Frießner should have understood that these were unacceptable opinions for the self-proclaimed representative of German soldierdom to hold. His ineptitude in front of the press is further corroborated by the fact that even months and years later, he could not understand why everyone was so upset by what he had said. He tried to excuse the above passage by claiming that in saying the attack had been justified, he meant only that the soldier must obey the state leadership when it gives an order. He never seemed to suspect that by citing the stories of Polish atrocities and persecution—largely invented by the Nazis—

that he was supporting Hitler rather than defending his fellow soldiers. Instead, Frießner blamed an innately hostile foreign press for the storm of reactions to his statements, claiming that they were part of a plot to weaken the VDS and further tarnish the soldier's image.[49]

The negative reactions were widespread. Peter von Zahn, in his radio program, "From Near and Far," summarized Frießner's comments best and typified the general criticism of the press conference. If any general ever displayed a severe lack of diplomatic skill, said Zahn, it was Frießner. "As he poured out his heart there, a few other things fell out that were better left in," Zahn told his listeners. "The Americans were made to understand that it was not they but the Germans who were to be thanked that the Russians did not now stand on the shores of the Atlantic. . . . The opponents of Hitler among the former soldiers the general labeled 'murderers.'" Zahn was particularly shocked by Frießner's unwillingness to denounce Hitler's murder of Rommel, a fellow general.[50] Two days after the press conference, another radio program, "From Day to Day," compared Frießner in his public debut to "the proverbial elephant in the porcelain shop." His lack of tact in discussing the origins of the war and the 20 July coup attempt disappointed but did not surprise the commentator, who expected no less from a former officer.[51]

Not only in the press did such negative reactions appear. The government and politicians across the political spectrum voiced their disappointment and disapproval of Frießner's comments. Erwin Schoettle, Social Democratic representative of Stuttgart in the Bundestag, called the press conference "an unhealthy development that would cause new discord among [the German] people," while Ernst Mayer (Free Democratic Party—FDP) said that Frießner's blunder was bound "powerfully to renew the resentment that [the Federal Republic] had managed to diminish over the past few years."[52]

The federal government's official response took a similar form when the Federal Press Office issued a statement that distanced the government from the VDS while at the same time trying to justify its previous support of the effort to unify the veterans' organizations. The government had hoped, the press release reported, that the union of the soldiers' groups would not only help them represent their own interests, but would also bring them a clearer understanding of democracy and awaken "more understanding for our state and its mission." Without actually referring to Frießner, the government expressed its dismay at the statements of "certain speakers" of the VDS that could not be reconciled with that group's promises to stay out of "political matters." "Through statements such as those, the danger of disunity among the Volk has arisen and the struggle for the German people's image in the world has been made much more difficult."[53] Here "political matters" and "political engagement" seem to be code words for any discussions about the Third Reich or responsibility for the war, but what was really at stake was the issue of loyalty to the democratic government of West Germany, which was in the midst of negotiating rearmament with the Allies and depended on a certain homogeneity of opinion among its representatives. Since the government had so obviously been grooming the VDS to be the mouthpiece of soldierly opinion on rearmament, statements such as Frießner's were catastrophic for Adenauer's efforts to convince the Allies that German soldiers could be reasonable and reliable partners in European defense.

Even within the VDS's ranks there was shock and disappointment at Frießner's comments, as their hopes of unity and influence were dashed and their position became less tenable with each sentence he spoke. The chaos in the VDS in the aftermath of the disastrous press conference centered in part on the decision of Donat, long-time leader of first the Emergency Groups and then the BvW in Württemberg and Baden, to leave the VDS and restrict his organizations to purely economic matters. Donat's stance emerged slowly in the fall, as he first called for the immediate resignation of Frießner; only later, when that resignation was not forthcoming, did he begin the process of complete withdrawal from the VDS. On the basis of a special congress that he convened in December, Donat claimed that the majority of his members, although wishing for some sort of umbrella organization for all veterans' groups, believed that because of Frießner, the VDS could no longer serve as such an organization.[54] Other groups in the south, especially in Bavaria, joined Donat in his rebellion, charging that the leadership of the VDS had lost touch with the common members and that the organization's goals could be expanded only at the cost of further economic gains.[55]

With his traditional soldier's sensibilities and notions of comradeship, Frießner simply could not believe that fellow soldiers would treat each other the way Donat was treating him. "Things have gone so far," he wrote, "that without having heard me personally, people are spreading all sorts of resolutions to the four winds, demanding my resignation." Unable to fathom this behavior, Frießner concluded that the officer corps was "approaching the abyss with gigantic steps."[56] Such disunity among people who allegedly valued solidarity and comradeship above all else was forever undermining the soldier's strength and image, Frießner believed.

In reality, however, Donat's challenge was less to the VDS's principles than to Frießner's leadership. The goals of his Württemberg/Baden group argue more for a lower public profile in order to prevent fiascoes that might further damage the soldier's image and complicate the group's efforts to regain pensions. The charge that Frießner entertained political aspirations was more of a stick with which to flog a rival leader than an indication of major differences of opinion over the goals and proper conduct of a veterans' organization.

The VDS board met hastily on 14 October provisionally to confirm Frießner as the chairman until another general meeting could be called in Hanover in January 1952. Increasing pressure from all sides forced Frießner to declare his resignation on 10 December 1951.[57] The VDS remained in a state of chaos until the January meeting, at which the group merged with the BvW and named Hansen its chairman. Donat called off his rebellion at that meeting and joined the reorganized VDS/BvW.[58] The new group expressed its desire to be "a true union of the VDS and the BvW . . . a general soldiers' organization that encompasses all career and noncareer soldiers alike and that wishes to provide a home for all those who are not included in other soldiers' organizations with specialized platforms."[59] (For brevity and clarity, we shall continue to refer to the group as the VDS.)

The VDS goals were nearly identical to those of the other veterans' groups founded earlier that year. Hansen's new group, like the old, demanded the "public, final, official end to the defamation [of the soldier] by the Federal Government," in addition to the release of all prisoners of war and the innocent "so-called war criminals" and the recognition of officers' pension rights.[60] Though it professed to be a universal soldiers' organization, the VDS never bridged the gap between soldier and officer and became (and remains) largely an officers' club, with membership hovering at about 80,000–100,000 career soldiers.[61] Other groups, such as the DAK, Großdeutschland, and several war victims' associations, tied themselves once again to the VDS, but only loosely. The hopes for a truly unified organization vanished forever.

The VDS and Soldierly Values

The VDS, which appealed primarily to career soldiers and was a general rather than a unit-based veterans' organization, did not rely on wartime experiences to construct its organizational ideology because the careers of its members varied greatly. Rather, it claimed to be the repository of soldierly values in general and stated as its purpose the transmission of these necessary values in the new West German democracy. One former soldier summarized the motives behind the VDS's creation as the desire "to win back the moral substance of German soldierdom so that it is available for the good of the state and especially for the foundation of a defense contingent."[62] The BvW prepared the ground for this stance by lobbying for the reestablishment of "soldiers' honor." Hansen in particular had taken the offensive on this matter, asserting (as noted) that by definition only civilians could be "militarists" and that the traditional political "neutrality" or "unpoliticalness" of soldiers was in fact the guarantee of order and stability in any society.[63] The threats of radicalization and the loss of "valuable Germans" to the East that Hansen identified were part of this developing ideology of service and the indispensability of soldierly values that reached its fullest expression in the VDS. As the DAK had reconciliation and Großdeutschland had anticommunism, so the VDS had "service to the Volk."[64]

Prominent West German politicians supported the VDS leadership in the belief that "soldierly values" were indispensable to the Federal Republic's nascent democracy. Adenauer himself said during a speech before the Bundestag in December 1952 that "it must be our goal . . . to amalgamate the moral values of German soldierdom with democracy."[65] The leaders of the VDS were so pleased to hear even a Social Democratic Bundestag representative confirm their belief that "precisely the democratic state can least afford to do without the lofty values of true soldierdom" that they printed the passage from the representative's speech twice in their newsletter.[66] After Frießner's *faux pas*, the government was not necessarily willing to entrust the transmission of those values to the VDS, but it nevertheless supported the group in testifying to the inherent worth of certain soldierly traditions.

Despite Frießner's debacle, Hansen, as the refounded VDS's chairman, persisted in his efforts to make his group the Federal Republic's "official" veterans' organization by ingratiating himself with the government and particularly the provisional defense ministry under Theodor Blank. In April 1952, in a meeting with Blank and Heusinger, Hansen and his representative in Bonn, Linde, not only broached the subjects of the release of war criminals and the restoration of pensions, but also explicitly addressed the question: "How can the [VDS] help the Blank Office?" Hansen proposed that the VDS could provide both ideological and material support for the nascent defense ministry by serving in an expert advisory role, especially in the areas of education and the future army's structure. The notion of "ideological support" was left strikingly vague in the notes on the meeting, but whether because of the self-evidence of that support or its insignificance is unclear.

Failing some sort of official recognition, the VDS nevertheless attempted in 1953 to gain a voice in the selection process for new officers by posing as the occupational representative of former soldiers, not unlike a union. Hansen officially requested that the VDS be represented on the PGA, the board that screened officers for the new force. He made the request "because the [VDS] is generally recognized as the occupational representative of career soldiers, and [because] this capacity is disputed by no one, there can exist no fear that other veterans' organizations can justifiably claim to be disadvantaged by the participation of the [VDS]."[67]

Blank was no doubt aware that Hansen's claims bordered on the outlandish, given the territorial struggles among veterans' organizations that followed Frießner's press conference. He politely rebuffed Hansen's request, claiming that he could give no answer at the moment, and invited Hansen to come to Bonn to discuss the matter privately.[68] At this meeting, Blank declared his desire to people the PGA with "former soldiers and civilian dignitaries who command respect among the general public." He regretted being unable to include the VDS as "one among many soldiers' leagues" (a direct slap in the face of Hansen's universalistic claims) but insisted that the board's composition would be to the VDS's liking. In any case, Blank continued, the VDS would not want to become involved in the "intrigues" associated with the selection process.[69] It was not an encouraging meeting for Hansen, as Blank not only dismissed the VDS's claims to be the occupational representative of former soldiers, but also refused to be moved by Hansen's predictions that not enough former soldiers would volunteer for the new military contingent if certain preconditions (such as the release of war criminals and the complete reestablishment of pensions) were not met.

Still the government persisted in its desire for the soldiers to create some sort of unified organization, though perhaps not with the name VDS. According to Dethleffsen, an official of the Chancellor's Office approached him regarding the future of the many veterans' organizations and asked him to organize a meeting of the senior officers involved to discuss the topic.[70] DAK leader Crüwell received a similar request from Federal Interior Minister Robert Lehr.[71] The final unification of all soldiers' organizations, including the revived Kyffhäuserbund, never came to pass. Nevertheless, the issue of some sort of meaningful union among soldiers' groups inspired both hopes and acrimonious exchanges for years to come.[72]

The negotiations surrounding the creation of a unified group indicate that form more than substance separated the various mainstream soldiers' organizations in the first ten years of the Federal Republic. The organizations shared the same ideological background. They unanimously paid homage to a pantheon of military heroes such as Ludwig Yorck von Wartenburg, Gerhard von Scharnhorst, August von Gneisenau, and (most recently) Rommel. They all praised ad nauseum the "soldierly values" of loyalty, bravery, responsibility, duty, and discipline.[73] Members of the VDS often advocated German unity as strongly as did Großdeutschland and preached the spirit of international cooperation as fervently as the DAK. Nevertheless, each group considered certain ideological realms to be uniquely its own. As the DAK considered fairness and reconciliation to be the products of the Africa Corps campaign in the desert, so Großdeutschland saw its immunity to communist influence arising from its intimate knowledge of communism gained on the battlefields of the Soviet Union. While each developed its particular organizational ideology and invariably charged the other groups with being too political, there existed a remarkable similarity among the organizations in terms of their desire to construct a common platform, preserve comradeship, and somehow serve Germany by providing a moral example to the German people.

Associational Life

In order to claim moral leadership and shape society as they hoped, the veterans' organizations needed members. To attract members and to mobilize them for the cause of German soldierdom, the organizations of the early 1950s promised economic gains through the recovery of pensions, job placement assistance, intellectual stimulation, and—above all—comradeship and the renewal of the close bonds forged in wartime. Groups such as the VDS, DAK, and Großdeutschland constructed massive human networks connected by newsletters, meetings, and the sense of common experience and purpose embodied in each group's organizational ideology. All of this activity amounted to the creation of what some historians have labeled a "military subculture."[74]

In terms of sheer volume of newsprint expended, by far the topic of greatest concern for the organizations was the reestablishment of pensions. VDS newsletters almost invariably included a section entitled "Pension News" that detailed all the latest changes in the status, requirements, and current levels of pensions and pension payments.[75] For the uninitiated, the news items in this section are nearly impossible to follow, given the level of detail and legal/bureaucratic jargon that they contain. Any VDS member who cared to keep abreast of the developments in the pension and welfare programs of the Federal Republic found his group's newsletter more than adequate for that purpose.

Economics were not, however, the sole concern of these organizations. With few exceptions, pension and other economic matters were nested in the middle of the newsletters somewhere. The newsletters almost invariably began and ended with statements of ideals, exhortations to close ranks, or political and social commentary of some sort. No doubt the soldiers' notions of honor compelled them to be more circumspect in their economic dealings. It would appear uncouth, after all, if pension concerns were splashed all over the front pages, however much those concerns formed the core of many organizations' missions.

By mid-1951, these economic matters, while still occupying a prominent place in the veterans' organizations' activities, were diminishing in importance. As noted in chapter 1, the passage of the Law Relating to Basic Law Article 131 in 1951 brought the largest groups of those entitled to pensions within the Federal Republic's welfare net so that the urgency and claims of hardship gradually disappeared. There were still significant elements of the system to which veterans objected, such as the continued absence of pensions for some long-serving noncommissioned officers and the provisions limiting the number of wartime promotions that would be recognized, but these were relatively minor points once the government officially recognized its obligation and ability to provide for former Wehrmacht career soldiers.

As outgrowths of Hansen's Emergency Groups, the later soldiers' organizations also saw mutual aid as one of their responsibilities. They distributed aid to needy families of former comrades, especially at Christmastime, and newsletters proudly reported the organizations' successes in providing coats and other gifts, especially to families with many children.[76] The Kyffhäuserbund dreamed (in vain) of recovering its former property from the federal government and making such charity its primary contribution to the cause of German soldierdom. The DAK sponsored a considerable aid program within its organization, named (of course) the "Rommel Social Program" (Rommel-Sozialwerk). The Rommel Program, among other activities and charities, built houses in which Africa Corps veterans and their families could live cheaply, all funded by the contributions of members and the generous sponsorship of the Volkswagen corporation, which donated automobiles as prizes for the DAK's fund-raisers.[77]

In the minute but developing military subculture of the early 1950s, the organization newsletters served as a marketplace for jobs and products of interest to the former soldier. The VDS lobbied the government (albeit with little success) to make certain civil service jobs available to soldiers, and when such jobs became available, they were frequently listed in the group's newsletters. The VDS also implored its members to aid each other by notifying their local branch when they planned to retire so that their vacancy might be made available to a former comrade. One of the local branch office's primary functions was to serve as a job search network.[78] Typical job notices included listings in public service (such as with the federal railroad or the post office) or for salesmen to peddle anything from insurance to champagne, needles, or fire extinguishers.[79]

Nor were the job offers directed only at men. A few of the notices sought women, usually for domestic service, but in a few cases as assistants in doctors' offices or saleswomen for "household articles."

Advertisements that appeared in a few newsletters often played on the soldier connection for increased business. In January 1953, one VDS newsletter carried an ad offering lower life insurance rates to VDS members.[80] A similar ad in a later issue offered linens and bedding at favorable prices to former comrades.[81] An advertisement for "Oasis Coffee" in the DAK newsletter in 1954 was perhaps the most blatant example of such an appeal to the bonds of the past.[82] Though the advertisements were not always directed exclusively at former soldiers, as an ad for nylons in one newsletter indicates, the vast majority of the material was specifically male-oriented and heavily laden with the language of comradeship.[83]

Some officers, however, worried about what sort of image of their subculture was being presented by the content of such advertisements. The officers' concern for public relations is evidenced by Donat's fear that some ads for wine, coffee, lotteries, and similar "luxury" goods might create the impression that officers lived in such comfortable circumstances that they had no need for pensions. The particular example that prompted Donat's observation was an ad for wine that read, "What I learned among my comrades as a lieutenant is now paying off: I know the best wines!" "The socialists will never give up once they read that," concluded Donat. "This verse is water through their mill because it is precisely in these circles that it is claimed that officers for the most part bummed around, drank, and looted."[84] Though former officers were the intended audience for such publications, the leadership suspected that the newsletters served as a showcase for officers' concerns and opinions. That the socialists might be reading them meant that there was a propagandistic element to the newsletters as well.

As indicated by their statements of goals, many veterans' organizations actively supported the Red Cross in its effort to clarify the cases of soldiers missing in action. It became a primary expression of comradeship dutifully to file past the huge tables full of photographs laid out at meetings, hoping to recognize a face and provide clues to the fate of a missing soldier. With more than thirteen thousand German soldiers still being held by the Soviets in 1950 and over one million men still missing, such efforts kept the memory of the war alive in the hearts and minds of veterans.⁸⁵

Once rearmament became a political issue in the Federal Republic, "soldiers' opinion" took on a new importance, and the veterans' organizations stepped in to entify and express that opinion. Part of the effort consisted of keeping members informed on important political and cultural issues. The VDS and other organizations reviewed films, recommended books to their membership, and even provided small libraries or reading rooms at some of their offices, which were supplied with works on military history, defense issues, and a significant number of biographies, usually of famous military commanders. The lectures sponsored by the veterans' organizations fall into a number of categories. One regional VDS branch between 1952 and 1954 sponsored at least eight lectures that dealt with such topics as current defense issues, world politics and communism, and the history and goals of the VDS and its predecessor, the BvW.⁸⁶ Similarly, the VDS branch in Frankfurt over roughly the same period sponsored at least twenty-nine lectures on those same topics, with the majority (fifteen) devoted to European and German defense issues.

The Society for Defense Information (Gesellschaft für Wehrkunde—GfW), which frequently sponsored lectures and conferences, also sent representatives to other lectures on rearmament or topics of interest to soldiers to assess their impact.⁸⁷ Much of this information found its way back to the Blank Office as a report on public opinion. One such report evaluated the effect of a lecture by a former lieutenant colonel (von Zydowitz) entitled "Wehrmacht—Yes or No?" The GfW, as semiofficial propagandist for West German rearmament, was concerned to monitor, and when possible counter, any efforts by opponents of rearmament to influence public opinion. Zydowitz's lecture was precisely the kind that the GfW (and presumably the government) feared most, for a variety of reasons. The lecture, according to Jobst von Cappele, a member of the GfW in Bremen, was a polemical tirade against the government, the occupying powers, the soldiers' organizations, and the tradition societies. Zydowitz's arguments were especially dangerous because they were "extremely simple, unrealistic, and *emotional.*"⁸⁸ The GfW and the government feared the audience's reaction to Zydowitz's statements because he was a former officer and therefore "ought to know such things" when it came to rearmament and national interests.

Cappele's remarks betray the lack of faith that many government officials and former officers alike had in the political acumen of most Germans. Lectures such as Zydowitz's were dangerous, Cappele believed, "because the speakers mostly direct themselves at groups that have neither formed a political opinion nor are in the position to form one."[89] "Unpolitical Germans" were susceptible to radical arguments. Therefore, the government and many veterans' organizations sponsored lectures to both combat the negative effects of such speakers and impress their own views on the presumably pliable electorate. That both sides placed so much faith in (and that the establishment so feared) "emotional" propaganda is no doubt a legacy of the Third Reich.

For similar reasons, the VDS kept tabs on the effect of speakers among audiences of former soldiers. One particularly interesting incident occurred when a Herr Teich, from the communist-sponsored Leadership Circle of German Soldiers (Führungsring deutscher Soldaten), made a speaking tour of the Ruhr region in late 1952, in a "dogged and persevering" effort, as the VDS spokesmen put it, "to gain a foothold in the industrial area" of West Germany.[90] A local VDS leader upset Teich's plans by convincing the owner of the local hotel to cancel Teich's reservation of the hotel hall at the last minute. Teich continued his tour, however, speaking before small and uninterested crowds. Despite his apparent lack of appeal, the VDS considered him worth monitoring, so it sent contingents to several of Teich's lectures to engage him in discussion and presumably expose his propaganda for what it was. At Teich's final appearance in November in the town of Gelsenkirchen, the local VDS arranged a showdown that erupted in a "fierce exchange of words" and ended with the audience leaving the auditorium in protest. Having thus achieved victory, the former officers praised Teich's delivery, calling it outstanding in style and dialect, complimented the cleverness of his lectures, and pronounced him to be a danger for those uninitiated in the arts of communist propaganda.

Former officers were as concerned with Teich's style and delivery as with the content of his speeches. In fact, there seems to have been a striking similarity between what Teich had to say and what the former officers had been complaining about for years—namely, their poor treatment at the hands of the Allies. VDS members were careful, however, to distinguish between that "factual" element of Teich's message and the communist propaganda that Teich hoped to spread. One VDS member noticed the transition not so much in what Teich said as in the force and emotion behind what he said. While the members of the Blank Office had criticized Zydowitz for his overly "emotional" use of patriotic themes such as national honor and love of country, they recognized that it was precisely the sort of rhetoric that appealed to former officers and made speeches like both Zydowitz's and Teich's dangerous. The former officers in the VDS identified with and labeled as "reasonable" Teich's patriotic (and even occasionally anti-Western) statements. However, they, like the government, feared Teich's use of emotion, especially in light of their belief that the Western democracies lacked idealism, something to pit against the East's "emotional" appeal. They merely applied that pejorative to different elements of Teich's speech. Ironically, the lectures sponsored by the veterans' organizations themselves seem to have been exactly the dry and uninteresting monologues that had the smallest chance of countering the emotional diatribes of men like Teich.

The most popular and prevalent justification for the veterans' organizations was the group meeting, with its attendant social and recreational possibilities. Most organizations sponsored both local monthly meetings and national yearly conferences, usually in some resort area. National meetings invariably included the placing of a wreath at the local memorial for fallen comrades, a speech, and a meeting of delegates from the local groups. They also included concerts and dances, church services (if held over a Sunday), more speeches by politicians or prominent figures, sports of some kind, and a farewell playing of taps, often followed (preceded and accompanied) by the prodigious consumption of alcoholic beverages.[91]

One such meeting was the congregation of the Fourth Panzer Division in Bamberg in July 1953, which former captain Heinz Karst of the Blank Office described as a true "people's festival," attended mainly by common soldiers and noncommissioned officers and cleverly and "stylishly" organized by former tank general Heinrich Eberbach.[92] The primary function of most such congregations was the restoration of old bonds of comradeship, but the Blank Office hoped for more. At the meeting, Karst interviewed both officers and common soldiers about their attitude toward European unification, the occupying powers, and reenlistment in any new West German army. He was able to establish to his satisfaction that most former soldiers were willing to reenlist. Though Karst regrettably noticed a tendency toward nationalism among certain participants, he urged in his report that neither the unifying power of such meetings nor the opportunities for propagandizing that they presented be underestimated.

The course of such meetings often reflected each particular group's organizational ideology. For example, the DAK, which always touted the fairness of its battles in the desert and which adopted reconciliation as its postwar motto, sponsored a soccer match against a representative unit of the British Eighth Army (the Africa Corps' counterpart in the North African Campaign) during its annual meeting in 1953 in Hanover.[93] This sporting contest was clearly meant to mirror the spirit of sportsmanship with which the Africa Corps and the Eighth Army had waged war in 1942.

That the organizations were anxious collectively to prove their loyalty to the Federal Republic can be surmised from both formal and less formal but not less striking actions—for example, the VDS's insistence that the Federal Republic's flag be flown at any function where the group was officially represented.[94] The DAK faced the problem of the unsuitability (indeed the illegality) of its old symbol, a palm tree growing out of a swastika. To solve this problem while retaining as much of the former symbol as possible, the DAK's leaders adopted the symbol of a palm tree growing out of the Iron Cross. This image served their purpose doubly well since it not only removed the offending symbol, but also replaced it with the embodiment of both soldierly tradition and the new West German Bundeswehr.[95] Such attempts to retain tradition while adapting to the new situation in Germany are illustrative of the effort by many veterans' organizations to keep past comradeship alive and to preserve for the future what they saw as the valuable traditions of military service.

It appears that the soldiers often resented the intrusion of "outsiders" into their circle of comradeship, which, according to some sources, bridged the gap between officer and common soldier. A Blank Office official who attended the first official meeting of the DAK in 1951 wrote that his overall impression of the participants was that they were "a group of reliable, often simple people who demand substance above and beyond their small daily obligations. Because they only partially forge a similar human bond in their current surroundings, they look to their former commanders with an almost moving trust."[96] Because of this bond, the soldiers present objected to any implication that they were not unified as comrades. According to the report submitted to the Blank Office, the soldiers refused to distinguish among officers, noncoms, and privates when asked to do so by the press. "Not for the first time were they, as privates first class, sitting here next to their generals," they insisted.[97]

Some doubt is cast on how truly deep this "moving trust" ran, especially in light of the angry letters early organizers received from former soldiers and the popularity of the film *08/15*. Nevertheless, for those who bothered to join groups like the DAK and in the spirit of their conventions, expressions of comradeship were commonplace and an important element in the veterans' organizations' daily life.

The dryness of the organizations' lectures and speeches was no doubt compensated for by the lively atmosphere of their meetings and the literal "wetness" of those events. Alcohol played an important role in maintaining comradely bonds and was a centerpiece of organizational life.[98] An amusing story that hints at the amount of alcohol consumed at these meetings (as well as the role these meetings played in the lives of veterans' wives) appeared in the June 1955 issue of *Die Oase*. Under the title "(Please Don't Be Angry) Tales Told out of School," the editorial staff reported that the wives of the Heidelberg men had decided to hold their own meetings. "It has already occurred," the article revealed, "that the lady 'Africans' have returned home long after their husbands were peacefully sleeping. A noteworthy emancipation, which has positive aspects for the men as well: No more tongue-lashings after a well-provisioned monthly meeting."[99] The women's meetings were surely equally well provisioned (if not better), and one can imagine that the wives took great pleasure in their independence. Apart from the women's "emancipation," the passage clearly indicates that alcohol played an important perennial role in these veterans' organizations.

The notion of comradeship was important not only on a personal level, but on an organizational one as well. Comradeship became equated with democracy since it allegedly represented a unity across rank, class, and political boundaries. When, in the aftermath of the Frießner press interview, many groups tried to distance themselves from the VDS, Hansen tried to keep the organization together by recalling the bonds of comradeship shared by the members, both during the war and during the struggle to regain their pensions.[100] For the DAK, of course, the comradeship, like seemingly everything else positive in the members' lives, began in the desert. "Just as in the desert the ties of comradeship stood above rank," read the program for the DAK's annual meeting in Hanover in 1953, "so it remains now as the good ethical foundation of democratic action and belief in our new organization."[101]

The equation of comradeship and democracy forms a remarkable parallel with the soldiers' earlier equation of comradeship and the National Socialist "folk community" (*Volksgemeinschaft*). As Manfred Messerschmidt explains, the Nazi concept of a folk community was "particularly adaptable to military principles of subordination" because it merged the individual into a "supra-individual body." "This concept made possible a dismantling of the social barriers between officers and soldiers and the propagation and often the practice of a 'comradeship' felt as very modern." The military should be, according to then commander in chief Werner von Blomberg, "the last stage of education in the service of the *Volksgemeinschaft*."[102]

Thus unified, represented, and espousing their own version of democracy, the former officers and soldiers of the veterans' organizations of the early 1950s hoped to affect Germany's future. All of the elements of their organizational life, from matters of purely economic representation and job placement to the search for missing comrades to the beer and sausages of the monthly meeting, embodied what the former soldiers defined as comradeship. Comradeship meant not only democracy; it meant unity, and unity, even by the government's own admission, meant influence.

The veterans' organizations that formed in the course of 1951 and 1952 reflected the desire of many former Wehrmacht officers to preserve the comradeship and the soldierly values of the past. They hoped also to take advantage of the waning criticism of soldiers by organizing to represent their interests and pass on the legacy of their experiences to the future. The idealism—the hope that their efforts would somehow renew or revitalize Germany, which is so apparent in the goals and organizational ideologies of those groups—clearly not only suggests the cynical conclusion that the majority of the career soldiers' material demands had been met by that time, but also reflects the officers' increasing confidence in their place in society and their desire to contribute to the reconstruction of Germany.

By 1953, former officers and their organizations had learned the language of democracy and had gone to great lengths to cooperate with the Federal Republic's own variation of *Gleichschaltung* (coordination). "Democratic principles" and "democratic action" reigned supreme, at least in the pages of their newsletters and the speeches of their chairmen. Theirs was a democracy based on their terms, however—on the foundations of comradeship, loyalty, service, and above all unity. Both within and among the organizations, the former officers (and many common soldiers as well) proclaimed their cohesion and resoluteness, even if the vehement differences of opinion, the seemingly unending variety of organizations, and their inability to unite in the VDS often belied their claims. Equally fervently they declared their dedication to West German democracy, even if their idea of democracy and what "West Germany" ought to be frequently differed from the mainstream.

3

Service to the Volk:
Traditions and the Lessons of Captivity

In defining the missions that would guide their postwar organizations, former career soldiers often turned to the traditions and slogans that they had learned during their military education and careers as officers. Veterans found among these traditions a rich source of catchwords and phrases, historical interpretations, and rationalizations that they could employ after 1945 in order to prove their loyalty and value to Germany and to the West. Essential to their understanding of themselves and their postwar mission was the notion of service to the German people. The army served the nation, they believed, not only by providing for the country's defense, but also by exercising its strength of character and remaining "above the fray" of party politics.

In justifying their material demands after 1945, therefore, organized veterans developed a "corporate ideology" that asserted the need for a healthy "soldiers' estate" to serve as a moral example for society. For reasons of both public relations and their own consciences, former officers cast themselves as the most valuable and selfless servants of the German people. In the context of an increasingly stable and prosperous postwar democracy, this self-image helped to ease the former officer corps' transition into the new society. Anxious to contribute and with few viable alternatives to the Western-oriented and democratic Federal Republic, former officers engaged in a competition to prove their loyalty to the state. The officers' desire to serve forms a marked contrast to their attempts (covertly and overtly) to undermine the Weimar Republic in the period following World War I.

The willingness—indeed eagerness—of most former career soldiers to contribute to the reconstruction of postwar Germany was intimately linked to their experiences as officers. Their understanding of military traditions and the relationship of both the Reichswehr (Weimar army) and the Wehrmacht to the state fundamentally shaped their attitudes. Their experiences during World War II reinforced and added a sense of urgency to their postwar mission. Officers had traditionally seen themselves as servants of the people in times of peace as well as war. They felt that as soldiers, they had special qualities and had special insights from the war that would be invaluable if West Germany were to face the postwar challenges and resist the perceived threat of communist aggression.

Education and Tradition

The military's belief in service was the product of a long tradition within the officer corps. Military men from Scharnhorst to Hans von Seeckt (Reichswehr commander in chief, 1920–1926) insisted that selection criteria for the officer corps be based on character and personality in order to protect Germany. Former officers made this traditional idea of "service to the *Volk* (people)" a central element of their arguments for the reinstatement of both their pension rights and public prestige. Service was also a key component of their conception of democracy, similar as it was to the National Socialist idea of a folk community.

Many leaders of postwar veterans' organizations were educated in the years around World War I. During this turbulent time, the officer corps' loyalties were in flux. With the revolution and fall of the Hohenzollern monarchy in 1918, the officer corps "lost not only the focus of its loyalty, which made possible its seeming distance from the decisions of politics; it lost at the same time the basis of its social self-image as the occupational group closest to the throne."[1] "With God for King and Fatherland" had been the military's motto in the nineteenth century. As it was, some members of the officer corps had grown increasingly disenchanted with Wilhelm II, whose "cowardly" abdication dashed any hopes of a restoration in the 1920s.[2] To complicate matters, the officer corps was unlikely to grant its loyalty to the new Weimar Republic, founded under the auspices of the military's traditional domestic enemies, the Social Democrats.

An agreement reached in 1918 by the provisional government's Social

Democratic leader, Friedrich Ebert, and the army's first quartermaster general, Wilhelm Groener, secured the military's service in the short run, but the pact failed to solve the long-term issue of the outright hostility of many former officers toward the government that then ruled Germany. Many officers, hoping at least for a more conservative and nationalist regime if not for the monarchy's return, were repelled by the notion of serving the new republic. Many of the lucky few accepted into the much diminished Reichswehr of the 1920s served only grudgingly. Their suspicious (and doubtless somewhat jealous) former comrades labeled them "Noske-hounds" to disparage their service to the new republic and its Social Democratic minister of defense, Gustav Noske.

Seeckt the "father of the *Reichswehr*," recognized this problem of loyalty and strove to save his beloved army from destruction. He decided that just because the traditional order was collapsing, the army did not have to follow suit. In order to keep the military's traditional structure intact under the new system, Seeckt created a new concept of duty to replace the officer corps' former link to the monarchy.[3] What had once been service for "King and Fatherland" became service to the nation, regardless of the form of government. By this clever tactical step, however, Seeckt decided that the military's traditions were more important than the "legal system of the society in which the Reichswehr lived and worked"—a dangerous precedent for the future, given the system that would govern Germany after 1933.[4]

The tenuous peace established by the Ebert–Groener agreement could therefore be maintained. The existing army provided for the state's security, and the often republic-hating officer corps contented itself that it was doing its duty to the nation. In fact, despite the officers' antipathy to the regime, Seeckt's attitude toward service under the republic allowed many conservative officers to turn the mere fact that they served into a virtue, an act of selflessness and sacrifice.[5] Seeckt even expressed his pride that "on more than one occasion, unhealthy plans [for the republic's overthrow] ran aground on the prudence and insight of a General Staff officer."[6]

Officers had long believed that they served more than the nation's military needs, and the Reichswehr's leaders were no exception. Seeckt hoped that the officer corps would become the "School of the Nation" and serve not only to protect Germany (a difficult task, given the Versailles Treaty's restrictions), but also to preserve the values officers believed necessary for the country's continued moral health. Seeckt wrote in 1919: "One thing no peace treaty, no enemy can take from us: manly spirit. To ensure that our people never lose this [trait] is our primary mission. . . . Bursting the bounds of the army, [the General Staff officer] will sow the seeds of manly spirit in all circles."[7]

By claiming to have only the nation's interests at heart, the military propagated the myth of its apolitical nature. "No one wants to affect the personal beliefs of the individual," Seeckt said, "or his internal position on the many issues of the day. No one asks about the political convictions of the individual. No one demands approval for deeds for which the individual does not carry the responsibility." In Seeckt's famous formulation, "[soldiers'] honor is uncompromised so long as we do our duty."[8]

Interestingly enough, officer candidates officially were left to their own devices when it came to outright "political instruction." The reading rooms of the officers' clubs allegedly contained issues of even the communist newspaper, *Rote Fahne,* so that young officers could form their own opinions on "the many issues of the day."[9] No doubt peer pressure and the rigorous selection process for candidacy meant that few if any officers expressed anything other than contempt for the *Rote Fahne*'s ideas, but publicly the army's policy on political instruction maintained the myths of political neutrality and service to the Volk.

The key to maintaining the army's role in society lay, Seeckt believed, in maintaining the officer corps' homogeneity. The size limitations set by the Versailles Treaty actually increased Seeckt's power to maintain that homogeneity. The reduction in size of the officer corps to around four thousand men (its pre–World War I strength had been about twenty thousand, not including the reserve officer corps) meant that Seeckt could select candidates based on precisely the characteristics (occupational, political, and other) that he thought were most desirable. Seeckt continued the established practice of recruiting from only the "desired circles" of the population by establishing educational criteria for officer candidacy and then altering them in order to recruit officers mainly among the nobility, the middle class educational elite, and families with a tradition of service in the officer corps. The proportion of recruits drawn from these backgrounds (which was still as high as 38 percent in the 1960s) reached its zenith in 1926 under Seeckt at around 90 percent.[10]

Acknowledging the importance of education for a modern army, the Imperial Army's leadership, led by the educational reformer Eduard von Peucker, had made the *Abitur* (slightly more advanced than a U.S. high school diploma) a requirement for officer candidacy in 1871. The Abitur remained a requirement until 1958. In the years before 1914, however, never more than two-thirds of the officer candidates had attained that level of education. The head of military education lamented in 1909: "Think how many personalities there are whose strengths lie more in praxis than in theory, who, however, as soldiers are entirely able to stand the test!" With so many officer positions to be filled and so few applicants meeting the educational requirement, therefore, the army saw it as no great misfortune if a candidate had not passed the Abitur, "so long as character is not lacking."[11] Because of the size limitations on the officer corps in the 1920s, Seeckt was able to raise the educational requirements and still fill open positions with "men of character" from among the desired segments of the population. For Seeckt, however, the insistence on education served largely as an excuse for his strict maintenance of the homogeneity of the corps.[12]

The notion of character came to represent the positive qualities supposedly exhibited by officers and became an integral part of their self-identity, (along with the virtues of camaraderie, selflessness, the willingness to accept responsibility, loyalty, courage, and a sense of honor, as noted above). The official guidelines for officer education issued in 1922 stressed that the emphasis should be on the creation of "strong-willed, responsible, reliable men."[13] "Character" thus became an ideological catchword for the officer corps, symbolizing their usefulness to the German people, their imagined status as role models, and their spiritual separation from the evils of the modern industrial world.[14] The officer corps' elite consciousness remained intact throughout the 1920s, (despite a relative lack of power, either military or political), and "character" played a significant role in maintaining it.

Most officers during the Weimar Republic supported the republic for pragmatic rather than idealistic reasons.[15] The fledgling Reichswehr gleefully suppressed communist uprisings in Berlin and the Ruhr but elected judiciously to hold its fire in the face of a clear threat to the republic's existence during the Kapp putsch in 1920. When Gen. Walther von Lüttwitz and Wolfgang Kapp launched the putsch against the government in March, Seeckt in no uncertain terms declared the army's neutrality in the conflict, despite the provisions of the Ebert–Groener agreement made barely a year earlier. "Troops do not fire on troops," Seeckt told an emergency war council assembled by Noske. Should former comrades fire on one another in Berlin, Seeckt asked? He immediately answered his own question: "When the Reichswehr fires on the Reichswehr, then all comradeship within the officer corps has vanished."[16] Seeckt then went into seclusion for the next few days, avoiding any contact with the putschists and refusing to take any responsibility, despite his frequent diatribes on the importance of an officer's integrity.[17]

The Kapp putsch's failure convinced Seeckt that the military could not, for the moment, flout the people's will and establish its own order in Germany. The putsch also revealed, however, that most officers defined their loyalty in terms of the military above all else and felt more responsible to preserve the memories of comradeship at the front than to preserve the republican government. Seeckt effectively created a "state within a state" by isolating the Reichswehr from the political ideals of republicanism and insulating the military against efforts at reform. Increasingly throughout the 1920s, this isolation turned to outright hostility toward the republic, especially among the military's higher leadership. Once Kurt von Schleicher took over for Seeckt after the latter's illegal contacts with the Soviet Union were revealed, the Reichswehr leadership increasingly sought to circumvent the few parliamentary controls on its actions and procurements. These trends were only exacerbated when Schleicher became chancellor for a brief period in the early 1930s and actively undermined the basis of parliamentary government by aiding the development of the so-called "presidential dictatorship" that preceded Hitler's assumption of power in January 1933.

The appointment of Hitler as chancellor in that year is a crucial event in the history of the officer corps. For obvious reasons, former officers in postwar West Germany sought desperately to absolve themselves of responsibility for Hitler's seizure of power. It is true that some officers, particularly those in the army's upper ranks, felt nothing but disdain for the "Austrian corporal" and little but contempt for many of his ideas.

The attitude of Weimar president and former field marshal Paul von Hindenburg, still the focus of the army's loyalty, epitomized the elitist discomfort that some officers felt for National Socialism, which seemed to them not too far removed from Bolshevism.

The Reichswehr's isolation within the state, its alleged political neutrality, and the increasing hostility of its leadership to the Weimar Republic enabled many officers comfortably to accept the appointment of Hitler, however. Even those apathetic toward the ideas of National Socialism relished the thought of increased career opportunities that Hitler's rise to power portended. The Reichswehr's limited size meant limited chances for advancement within the officer corps. Hitler's rhetoric of a revitalized Germany promised a larger army, and Hitler quickly reassured officers of his intentions when he eliminated the military's principal National Socialist rivals, the SA, in the "Night of the Long Knives" in June 1934. By providing technical assistance in some instances or, more often, by inaction in the face of the numerous murders perpetrated on that night, the Reichswehr and its leadership fatefully cast their lot with the National Socialists. In 1935, Hitler ordered the introduction of conscription, followed quickly by the remilitarization of the Rhineland in 1936. The prevalent belief within Germany during the 1930s that Hitler was a brilliant statesman and that the regime's mistakes or unseemly acts were the fault of radical elements within the Nazi Party contributed greatly to officers' indifference toward the violence or injustices occurring under Hitler's rule.

The personal oath that officers swore to Hitler in 1934 is also of paramount importance in understanding their attitude toward the Third Reich. When Hindenburg died in August, Hitler combined the offices of chancellor and Reich president in himself. Technically officers were still bound by their oath of December 1933 to serve "people and Fatherland at all times," and yet they (and every soldier in the Reichswehr) swore a new oath on 2 August 1934 that read as follows: "I swear by God this sacred oath, that I will yield unconditional obedience to the Führer of the German Reich and Volk, Adolf Hitler, the Supreme Commander of the Wehrmacht, and, as a brave soldier, will be ready at any time to lay down my life for this oath."[18]

Officers would later argue on the basis of this oath that they shared no responsibility for the behavior of SA or SS thugs and that action on their part against the regime was therefore impossible. Ensconced within their own commands, without the responsibility or the right to vote (see below), too many officers heeded the words of Hitler, "I cannot demand from you that you define your specific position relative to our movement, but none of you have lost your position of duty relative to the National Socialist state."[19] These words would have sounded familiar to anyone who had heard Seeckt's speech only a few years earlier (and cited above) on individual responsibility and attitudes toward the Weimar Republic. The oath's wording makes clear that officers supported the Nazi regime. They were therefore deeply implicated in its misdeeds.[20]

Officers found it important in the postwar period to claim that they had had nothing to do with Hitler's appointment. They were fond of reminding anyone who would listen after 1945 that they had been forbidden to vote during the Weimar Republic, and therefore the civilians were to blame for "electing" Hitler.[21] The army, they argued, remained a haven from Nazism well into the war, and as an institution the military was "coordinated" only late in the war, primarily in the aftermath of the 20 July conspiracy.

Despite what many veterans would claim after 1945, the Nazi leadership required that officers conform to the ideals of National Socialism. Conformity in the officer corps as a whole became more prominent as time progressed and Hitler's expansion of the army and his manipulation of its leadership positions took its toll on the influence of older, more traditional officers. The 1936 guidelines on political education and instruction for the Wehrmacht make clear that the notion of political neutrality was nearly impossible under a regime like the Nazis'. "The officer corps of the Wehrmacht," the guidelines read, "can fulfill its leadership role in the state and among the people only if it is spiritually united in possessing the National Socialist world view, which guides the life of that state and people, as a personal belief and inner conviction."[22] Nearly three years later, the army reminded its officers that "no one should be allowed to surpass the officer corps in the purity and sincerity of its National Socialist worldview.... It goes without saying that the officer will behave in every situation according to the principles of the Third Reich, even when such principles are not set down in legal regulations, decrees, or service guidelines."[23] Whatever forms of resistance may have been present within the officer corps, the military's leadership nevertheless enforced conformity with the outlines of National Socialist doctrine with such statements. Moreover, the Wehrmacht's leadership incessantly proclaimed its unshakable faith in the Führer's "genius" and its appreciation of the "miracles" he worked for Germany.[24]

Despite the high degree of ideological commitment and penetration, on a certain level, the military conducted business as usual. Although the massive and sudden increase in the officer corps in 1935 necessarily involved a loosening of the strict recruitment standards (not to mention the fact that the expansion was steered by Hitler, who was anxious to increase the prevalence of National Socialist loyalists in the army's ranks), officers still preached the need for character and unity within the corps.[25] Military education policies in the Third Reich stressed the importance of molding officers with "character, with heart and loyalty"— in other words, "steel-hardened, strong-willed men of prominence."[26] Officer candidates were to be instructed in the "eternal foundations of military leadership," the decisive influence of great leaders, and the importance of spiritual, as opposed to material, factors in waging war.[27]

National Socialist ideas about the importance of will and the Führer's personality cult were indeed similar to the elitist ideas about character propagated by the officer corps. As much as some officers later protested that their ideas were diametrically opposed to the Nazis', during the 1930s, many preached the identity of National Socialist ideas and the traditions of German soldierdom. Hitler had, according to the army's official stance, successfully "reminted the profound lessons of the front fighter" in the National Socialist world view.[28]

Ironically, Hitler's war destroyed the fabled esprit and ideological unity of the officer corps. The massive expansion of the 1930s hamstrung military leaders' efforts to recruit only from among the desired circles that had traditionally supplied young officers.[29] Clear favoritism from Hitler regarding promotions further skewed the military's upper ranks and encouraged ideological conformity among the rest. Finally, massive casualties provided a further powerful nazifying influence on the officer corps. As its ranks filled with younger and younger men who had spent more of their adult lives in Hitler's Germany than in any other, the officer corps, like the army itself, came in many ways to reflect the character of German society.

Despite their incessant references to their ability to make responsible decisions, the officers' focus on their careers and their own areas of technical responsibility within the Wehrmacht relieved many of them of any sense of *joint* responsibility for what occurred outside their own narrow sphere. Such a concept was not included in their definition of character. "Our honor is uncompromised so long as we do our duty," Seeckt had said.[30]

Hitler's reliance on the SA and the SS ingeniously relieved the military of being the state's sole executive force. No longer as responsible for maintaining domestic order as they had been during Weimar's early years, officers could delude themselves that they provided solely for the defense of the Fatherland. Their domestic influence would be, as it had always been according to them, purely positive and idealistic; they would spread the "manly spirit" of which Seeckt had spoken in 1919. Those facts, combined with the military's rhetorical independence from the state—repeated so fervently by Seeckt when the Weimar Republic was an unattractive object of loyalty—meant that most former officers honestly felt little connection with the crimes committed during the Third Reich. The most common excuse heard in postwar Germany was "I didn't vote for Hitler," and in the case of career soldiers, that was strictly true. Their personal oath to Hitler, their service in the military of his regime, and their silence in the face of his brutality, however, make former officers as a group at the very least responsible by association.[31]

The officers educated before 1945 carried into the period after the war a strong sense of the importance of will and personality and a desire to prove their value to Germany that greatly affected their willingness and ability to adapt to their new situation. As noted, given their experiences and training, former career soldiers not surprisingly grasped at these ideas of service and "character" in order to ingratiate themselves with the postwar powers in Germany. By emphasizing their indispensability to a healthy and stable Germany, they clearly hoped to overcome their continued "persecution" and isolation within society.

Captivity

If their training as officers prepared veterans after 1945 to speak the language of "service to the people" and instilled in them a faith in certain values, the experience of captivity that nearly all former officers endured in the immediate postwar years also reinforced their urge to serve the German people. Like their experiences of postwar demilitarization, captivity embittered former officers, but it also filled many with a sense of mission and purpose. They desired to improve Germany so as to make their lost months or years "count."

Captivity occupied a central place in the memories of nearly all former officers during the period 1945–1955. Though historians as well as former prisoners insist that there was no common story, no single "prisoner of war experience" to which all captives could refer, shared reactions to captivity certainly existed, especially among officers, whose education, training, and social background made them a relatively cohesive group. Conditions varied not only from captor nation to captor nation, but from camp to camp within each nation and according to the circumstances and duration of capture. Prisoners received varying rations, performed different types of work for varying amounts of time, endured vastly different accommodations, and lived in different social milieus, depending on the accident of their assignment to a certain camp. Many prisoners described their camps as tightly knit communities of fate, while others told of Gestapo terror tactics by their "comrades." Some soldiers were taken prisoner in 1940, others in 1945. Some were released in 1945 or 1946, some in 1955 or 1956. And significantly, officers were treated differently from enlisted men. Despite the variety of experiences, however, most officers returned with a sense of mission and a willingness, even a need, to contribute to the reconstruction of Germany.

In order to establish a basis for understanding the impact of captivity on officers, one must examine the general pattern that imprisonment took for both career soldiers and enlisted men. There existed two major categories of captivity: the Soviet and the Western. German prisoners of war in Soviet camps faced tremendous hardships. They worked harder, were held longer, and had less contact with the outside world when compared to their comrades in the camps of the Western Allies.

Captives in the Soviet Union

Estimates of the number of German prisoners held by the Soviet Union during and after World War II vary widely. Even the definitive study of German prisoners of war conducted by Erich Maschke in the 1960s only narrowed the range of possibilities to between 3.15 and 3.46 million men. Of those, approximately 1.1 million died in captivity, leaving (again approximately) 2 million to return to Germany, some as late as 1956.[32] The astonishing mortality rate, as well as the long duration of imprisonment, were two defining characteristics of captivity in the Soviet Union.

According to the Geneva Convention regarding prisoners of war, higher-ranking captured officers could not be compelled to work for their captors. The Soviet Union, however, was not a signatory of that agreement and was able in most cases to extract some form of labor from officers. The Soviets distinguished at first between "subaltern" (captain and below) and "staff" (major and above) officers and forced only the former to perform manual labor. Using cunning and coercion, however, the Soviets convinced many staff officers "voluntarily" to perform some sort of work. "Those who do not lay down their medals and volunteer for work are fascists," said one Soviet camp official in greeting his new charges, "and we do not send fascists home."[33] Indeed, many officers acquiesced most eagerly. "Better to keep ourselves occupied here in the camp with night watch or a little clearing work," thought more than one officer, "than to be dragged outside," where the heavy work was being done.[34] Many were simply happy to be alive, having expected much worse treatment from the Russians. They worked merely in the hope that that situation would not change.

Significantly, many officers had a positive attitude toward work. They faced a difficult problem because they often believed that manual labor was demeaning, yet idleness was equally stigmatized.[35] "We cannot just sit around here while someone in Germany must pitch in at the hard work of reconstruction. The more that the Russians see we are willing to make good our wrong-doing, the more we prove ourselves as democrats, the sooner they will send us home."[36] "We lost the war," wrote one officer. "We would in any case have to pay, and when we volunteer for work here, we are paying a sort of reparation." He wanted to ensure that he and his comrades had "the moral right to say that we have not just shoved our hands in our pockets but rather have given our homeland, which certainly has it worse than we do here, a sign that we are prepared to pay the consequences."[37]

Work for many officers was a way of breaking up the monotony and loneliness of camp life.[38] For noncommissioned officers and common soldiers, of course, the luxury of assigning a higher purpose to what was for the officers in effect voluntary (or half-voluntary) work did not exist. For them, it became an issue of how to do no more work than necessary and yet avoid punishment for a lack of productivity. Eager workers were stigmatized as collaborators, while failure to perform usually resulted in confinement or curtailed rations, which given the already poor state of the prisoners' diet, could prove fatal.

Many generals captured by the Soviets seemed to have fared reasonably well. An account of the life of 250 generals in a camp near Cerncy between 1943 and 1948 shows them receiving 2,800 calories a day (more than residents of Berlin received in 1948); performing only voluntary gardening; and being entertained with sports, movies, and a library. In fact, according to the polemic report, one would never had guessed that the men had at one point been responsible for the Wehrmacht's conduct if it were not for the fact that the vegetable and fruit gardens were divided into "fronts" (each with its own "commander"), the tomato vines and bean stalks were "dressed" (as in ranks, dressed for inspection), and men constantly addressed each other in the third person as "Herr General."[39]

The distinction between officers and soldiers ceased to exist in any case after 1949, when the Soviets began prosecuting the remaining German prisoners as war criminals. By 1950, some 13,500 prisoners, now "war criminals," remained in Soviet hands.[40] War criminals, whether former officers or not, did not share the exemption from work that applied to captive officers, so any officers remaining in the Soviet Union after 1949 worked. But by 1949 the situation of most captive soldiers was also improving significantly, so that work became less of a life-threatening burden. The endless shuffling from camp to camp and the outbreaks of infectious disease that had decimated the prisoners' ranks in the first months and years of captivity became less common. Most camps had at least minimal facilities for shelter and health care. Prisoners began to receive packages from Germany fairly regularly that supplemented their meager rations.

Nevertheless, imprisonment was not a pleasant experience, especially for former officers. The prospect of a twenty-five year sentence (meted out to all thirteen thousand or so of the prisoners remaining after 1950) was demoralizing enough, and the time spent in a Soviet prison before being released back to the POW camps was traumatizing. "What I, as a civilized Western European, had spiritually to live through is indescribable," one officer reported. "My entire life I have had a clean record and I could not believe that I, as an officer who had only fought for his country, should now be shoved in among Russian murderers, bandits, and criminals."[41] The vast majority of German prisoners were placed in cells with other Germans, so this particular officer's experience was atypical. Yet the feelings of hopelessness and injustice that he conveyed were common enough. Especially for this small core of captives condemned to remain in the Soviet Union for years after 1949, the legacy of captivity was bitterness and a sense of having lost years of their lives.

Of central importance to the prisoners in the Soviet Union, both before and after the convictions of 1949, were the antifascist organizations (Antifas) sponsored by the Soviet government; they were only thinly veiled communist propaganda schools.[42] Like captivity in the Soviet Union, the role and character of the Antifas changed over time, as did German reactions to them. During the war's early years, especially before the Sixth Army's surrender at Stalingrad, most soldiers strongly resisted Soviet efforts to form an anti-Nazi group among the prisoners. Prisoners captured early in the war tended to be younger and therefore presumably more influenced (through the schools and the Hitler Youth) by the ideas of National Socialism. Also, given the Wehrmacht's generally successful operations during 1941 and 1942, those taken prior to Stalingrad had high morale and were disproportionately members of submarine or air force units possessing an elite consciousness that made the Soviets' effort to convert them more difficult. Standard procedure, which could of course not be followed in many cases, was that newly captured prisoners immediately be interrogated and, if not overtly hostile, asked to sign a statement urging their fellow soldiers to desert. Such signatures were then copied onto leaflets that the Soviets would distribute over the German lines.[43]

During this early period, the Soviets took pains to isolate officers from their former subordinates, both physically and mentally. Attempting to win over the working-class elements within the Wehrmacht, Special Committee on Political Administration of the Red Army (GPURKKA) and other Soviet agencies tried to convince working-class soldiers that just as capitalists led workers astray, so too did officers mislead common soldiers, forcing them to fight a war that was against their best interests.⁴⁴ The Soviets even tried to promote suspicion between officers and men by spreading the rumor that the better treatment of officers in the prison camps was a result of money sent covertly by the Nazi government via Sweden.⁴⁵

The vast majority of soldiers, officers and conscripts alike, remained unmoved by Soviet efforts, however. Only some 5 percent of the thirty thousand Germans captured during 1941 took part in an election to select delegates to an antifascist conference at the end of that year. A few select recruits were sent to special Antifa schools to be trained in propaganda techniques, but most soldiers looked down upon the Soviet programs as enemy efforts to undermine morale at the front.⁴⁶

The stubborn resistance on the part of German prisoners to cooperate with Antifa movements led the Soviets to change their tactics, especially with regard to officers. In 1942, the Soviets began courting officers more fervently by directing their appeals at officers' concerns. They told officers that their oath was to the German people and that therefore their duty lay in ridding Germany of the madman Hitler.⁴⁷ Antifa groups were not working for the destruction or division of Germany, the Soviets claimed, but only for the elimination of Hitler and the return of freedom in Germany. Interviews with soldiers captured at Stalingrad made it clear to the Red Army that not only would German soldiers surrender only once it became clear their situation was utterly hopeless, but also that they usually surrendered only when ordered to do so by their officers. The Soviets therefore decided to convert German officers to the antifascist cause.⁴⁸ Nevertheless, until 1943, never more than ten percent of all German prisoners became involved in antifascist activities, and the proportion of active officers remained even lower.⁴⁹

After Stalingrad, Soviet efforts to form antifascist groups met with more success. In order to make their efforts at converting German soldiers more attractive, the Soviets in July 1943 established the National Committee for a Free Germany (Nationalkomitee Freies Deutschland—NKFD), with the avowed principles of ending the war, overthrowing Hitler, and building a "viable democratic order" in Germany. The Antifas receded into the background or were eliminated. With a black, white, and red flag as its symbol and led by German prisoners trained at the antifascist schools set up during 1941 and 1942, the NKFD had some success recruiting among the rapidly increasing numbers of captured soldiers. Especially for the common soldiers attending the lectures and signing the NKFD's declarations grew more appealing because the extra rations and better treatment accorded to those who cooperated with the NKFD could mean the difference between life and death. Participation in the NKFD's activities was still stigmatized. Though the total number of prisoners participating in the NKFD rose over the years, the number of prisoners rose even faster, making those won over by the Soviets more of a minority with each passing month.

The NKFD was even less successful in recruiting officers. The original NKFD leadership contained not a single high-ranking officer. In an effort to counter this failure by appealing to the officers' corps spirit, the Soviet government on 12 September 1943 founded the League of German Officers (Bund deutscher Offiziere—BdO). Though some prominent generals were won over by a combination of the clear inevitability of Germany's eventual defeat and Soviet promises to leave the German military intact, the BdO's recruitment efforts failed to attract many adherents from the officers' camps.[50]

While increased rations and better treatment may have prompted some common soldiers to join the NKFD, for most soldiers and officers alike, complying with the wishes of the Soviet enemy was unthinkable. As one prisoner recounted, most Germans rejected the Soviet Antifas not because of any commitment to Nazism, "but simply because the captive [was] against his captor. . . . Above all, . . . what was going on there with corruption, and with these Russian guards, . . . [was] indescribable, and that brought all that [opposition] out."[51]

For officers, participation in the NKFD was tantamount to fraternizing with the enemy. Even Count Claus Schenk von Stauffenberg, who himself committed treason in 1944, rejected the NKFD's methods and principles, saying, "What I am committing is high treason [*Hochverrat*]. What [the NKFD members] are doing is committing treason [*Landesverrat*]."[52] For some prisoners, reaction against the methods of Soviet indoctrination was so strong that Diether Cartellieri has claimed that only in Soviet captivity did many soldiers first discover their sympathy for National Socialism![53]

Until the war's end, Soviet successes in forming a group of antifascist German soldiers were extremely limited. The capitulation of Germany on 8 May 1945, moreover, made even these minimal efforts obsolete since two of the NKFD's three stated goals (overthrowing Hitler and ending the war) had been accomplished with little help from German antifascist groups in the Soviet Union. There remained only the goal of creating a viable democratic system in Germany, and for this task, the Soviets developed a policy similar to that instituted by the Western Allies after May 1945: denazification.[54] To carry out this policy, the Soviets gradually dissolved the NKFD and BdO and revived the other antifascist groups that had existed before 1943. These groups (which had continued to exist during the intervening years in many cases) were more avowedly communist than the NKFD or the BdO had ever been. Their goals, as stated on 3 January 1946, were to identify both Nazis and potentially sympathetic prisoners in the camps, provide antifascist education, and "free the masses of prisoners from anticommunist influences."[55]

Like their Western allies, the Soviets attempted to screen prisoners to determine the extent to which they still subscribed to Nazism. Antifa screening committees could veto a prisoner's scheduled return to Germany if he were found still to be under the influence of National Socialism. No data exist on the exact number of prisoners thus rejected, but because prisoners judged other prisoners by sitting on the screening panels (unlike in Western Europe), the rancor generated by the procedure lingered for years after the war. Not only had some prisoners licked the Soviets' boots for better rations and easier work, so the charge went, but now they sat in judgment on their fellows who had shown character and remained immune to the siren songs of the Soviets.

The experience of captivity in the Soviet Union furthered a process of disintegration in the officer corps that had been going on for years. Issues of survival, work, collaboration, and loyalty tore at bonds of comradeship already weakened by the casualties of war and the Nazis' ideological demands. Yet in other ways, the experience of Soviet captivity confirmed many officers' prejudices, especially their anticommunism and their belief in the importance of character. According to many officers who returned to West Germany, those who showed character survived, while those who did not either perished or, even worse (according to the officers), fell before the Soviet propaganda blitz.

Soviet Antifa programs solidified the eventual division of Germany by providing a small yet active and trained cadre for the administration of the Soviet zone while simultaneously alienating the vast majority of prisoners and ensuring their hostility to the Soviet Union.⁵⁶ For most prisoners returning from the East and for their former comrades living in the Western zones, the Soviet Union was the object of hatred. The suffering, the tales of corruption, and the memory of the hundreds of thousands of soldiers who died in Soviet captivity made any cooperation with the Soviet Union or its later client state, the German Democratic Republic, an impossibility.

Captives in the West

The experience of German prisoners in the camps of the Western Allies was vastly different from that of their fellow prisoners in the East.⁵⁷ Soldiers under the Western Allies' supervision were not generally worked as hard nor kept as long. Still, many soldiers faced a wait of some two to three years even beyond 1945 before they were released. One must also distinguish among the various Western nations when discussing the conditions, both material and spiritual, under which the captives lived. Soldiers captured earlier in the war—in North Africa, for example— were often shipped to remote destinations to be held until the war's end. Many prisoners taken by the British remained in the Middle East or were sent to other areas of the British Empire. The U.S. Army set up camps all over the United States that held thousands of prisoners until they were sent to France or Britain in 1945, pending their return home. Britain hosted hundreds of thousands of prisoners in addition to those sent by the United States. Once liberated, France assumed responsibility for large numbers of prisoners, who immediately were put to work repairing the damage caused by the war and German occupation. Most prisoners interned in Britain and the United States arrived to find their camps already constructed and an infrastructure for their care in place. In France, however, because of the damage done by the war and the relative suddenness with which the bulk of prisoners arrived there, POWs often had to labor for weeks or months before they had shelter, toilets, and kitchens. Then the real work began.

As Kurt Böhme writes in his work on prisoners' experiences in the West, the life of the prisoner in France was characterized throughout by work and still more work. This fact, combined with the generally poorer nutrition of the prisoners in France, meant that prisoners spent less time wrestling with their consciences and more time worrying about survival than their comrades in American or British camps. One prisoner wrote in the journal of a French Catholic organization that the nature of imprisonment in France led to a preoccupation with one's own well-being, a consequent breakdown in morals, a desire for sheer entertainment rather than religious instruction, and an unwillingness to delve into matters political. Especially strong, he claimed, was the desire to keep following orders. "The prisoners were accustomed, as soldiers, to carry out orders—although they often did it with reluctance and curses, they carried them out anyway. This system of orders and 'blind obedience' gave their life stability."[58] Officers, too, were accustomed to taking (not just giving) orders, and as human beings, they too felt the pressures of their survival instinct. Many officers undoubtedly also sought, at least subconsciously, the relief from responsibility that their captivity provided.

Britain and the United States placed a much greater emphasis on the prisoners' cultural life. Although prisoners in France were entertained and educated and prisoners in Britain and the United States certainly labored, the experience of former officers in the latter two countries was distinguished by the "reeducation" efforts of the Allied governments rather than by work.[59] Britain and the United States established entertainment and educational programs intended to provide benefits beyond a mere distraction from the dreariness of camp life. As the war drew to a close, and especially after May 1945, both the British and U.S. officials were concerned to eradicate Nazism, which they saw as a sort of disease infecting the German people. To combat this disease, they instituted a program of reeducation. Though officials in the United States had fewer hopes for such a program among their prisoners because of the relatively short duration of their stay, German POWs in the United States had access to a wide variety of educational and cultural materials aimed at preparing them for a career or ridding them of Nazism's stain.

The American general in charge of German prisoners of war, Archer Lerch, hoped to fight the effects of Nazi propaganda with a little propaganda of his own. He saw how the Nazis used film, plays, and other methods to spread their ideas, and he drew on that experience. In order to combat the stereotype (transmitted by Hollywood movies) that America was a cultural vacuum, Lerch provided camp administrators with guidelines instructing prisoners in the quality of the American arts. Lerch hoped to debunk Germans' notions of racial supremacy by allowing the prisoners to compare "Aryan" with "Jewish" or "Negro" performers. "If the German prisoners could hear the quality of American symphony orchestras and performers," Lerch wrote, "they might lose a little of their supreme belief in Germany as the seat of all culture."[60] In October 1945, the Office of the Provost Marshal General produced a pamphlet entitled "Music in America" and delivered it to POW camps throughout the United States. "The purpose of this pamphlet," read a note enclosed with each copy, "is to acquaint the German prisoners with the benefits of a democratic way of life as revealed in the cultural growth and freedom of expression in American symphony orchestras."[61]

The British were even more concerned with reeducating their charges than the Americans. The Foreign Office's Prisoner of War Division supervised the more mundane provisioning of the POW camps, as well as the cultural and educational care of the prisoners. Like the Americans, the British provided English-language instruction to interested prisoners, as well as workshops, lectures, and classes on a variety of subjects, ranging from Roman archaeology to economics, baking, theater, and painting. Prisoners were sometimes entertained in surprisingly high fashion. The program of cultural events at an officers' camp in Britain contained enough Mozart, Chopin, and Goethe to please even the most discriminating of upper-class palates.

In Britain, this reeducation took on an even more strongly moral tone than elsewhere. The British set up Screening Committees to rate the prisoners according to their political sympathies, as well as their general human qualities, such as reason and compassion. Much like the Soviet Antifas, the committees were explicitly concerned with identifying politically and morally reliable prisoners to use as aids and role models in the process of cleansing the other inmates of their National Socialist ideas. Once it became clear that the Third Reich was going to collapse, the Screening Committees also hoped to single out certain willing, correct-minded prisoners for repatriation so that the reconstruction of Germany could begin under the most auspicious circumstances possible.[62]

In this setting, many officers first faced their own consciences regarding their service for the Third Reich. In August 1945, an official of the Prisoner of War Division submitted a lengthy report on the mood of the officers held in one British camp that clearly illustrates how imprisoned officers wrestled with Nazism.[63] According to the report, British reeducation efforts were "a spiritual necessity" for their "childish" and confused charges. The report suggested that thanks to reeducation, many prisoners were finally becoming aware of "the moral decay of National Socialism, the lies and omissions of the propaganda, the mass hysteria of the Volk concept." Few prisoners had grappled with National Socialist doctrine on an intellectual level. Most had simply "reacted to the stimulus of mass excitement and mass fear that ensured that one avoided moral critique and emphasized the superficial virtues of a militaristic way of life." The report noted a pronounced generation gap, with younger, intelligent officers hungry for factual information, while older officers tended toward moral judgments of National Socialism. The report's author lamented that this rejection of National Socialism came so late, but he judged it to be "honest and true."

Despite the willingness of many officers to abandon National Socialism, most were unwilling to examine more closely their own role in the Third Reich. Instead, they clung fanatically to the supposed power of their personal oath to Hitler. That oath combined with a defensive attitude, fostered by their captivity, to produce among many officers a rigid insistence on the correctness of their behavior, at least initially. In the assessment of one British captor, younger officers lacked any "social-moral standpoint" from which to judge the crimes of the Third Reich. Older officers "knew what it was all about" and were therefore afraid to face their own responsibility. Young and old alike referred to their oath as a defense.[64]

This single report reveals many of the themes that determined the behavior and attitudes of German officers in the postwar period. Like the defamation the officers believed they were experiencing, their captivity encouraged a defensive attitude. They believed that they alone were being punished for the actions of Hitler and all Germans during the Third Reich. They recognized, albeit slowly in some cases, the evils of National Socialism but remained unconvinced of democracy's virtues. Yet in the postwar world, there existed few alternatives for the Germans because of their innate anticommunism. According to the British assessment, the officers were "the products of a social upbringing and a military tradition that predisposed them to fear communism." Despite their intelligence, their exaggerated fear of communism clouded their judgment and led them to "readily agree with any propaganda that supports their tendencies. A group among them confess openly that they joined the [Nazi] Party because it was an active opponent of communism."[65]

Above all, as was the case with the prisoners held by the Soviets, former officers wished to improve themselves and contribute to the rebirth of Germany. The psychological shock of captivity meant that "the smallest token of positive aid or encouragement [brought] forth a surging reaction of thankfulness and also a lively willingness to contribute." The above cited British camp observer detected among the officers an "enormous activism," a "new interest in religion," and "a sort of renaissance of all things aesthetic." Classical music concerts evoked in the former officers the "awe of the old Italian scholars in the face of the newly-found Greek manuscripts, and exactly like the medieval scholars, they are conscious of this respect."[66]

Given their training and their faith in the tradition of service to the Volk, many officers responded positively to the notion of contributing to the rebirth and reconstruction of Germany. In this way, the desires of the reeducators and the prisoners overlapped. Even given the British observers' tendency to exaggerate or to be overly self-satisfied with their successes, prisoners undeniably desired not simply to return home, but also to contribute. Evidence of this desire appeared not only in British reports, but also in the newspapers of the prisoners themselves. General Lerch issued an appeal shortly after the capitulation of Germany reminding his charges that their nation was at a crossroads and needed clear-thinking and honorable men to weather its crisis. "You owe it to your country," he admonished them, following that with the threat that those who did not genuinely convert to the ideals of freedom would return to Germany as prisoners and not as free citizens.[67] One group of prisoners responded to this appeal in their camp newspaper, *Der Ruf*, by acknowledging their nation's need for the "physical, intellectual, and moral energy" of former soldiers. "In the belief that Germany desperately needs us, that it must rely on the service of its sons and the will to rebuild," the soldiers vowed, "we commit ourselves to the address of the Provost Marshal General, we commit ourselves simultaneously to our people, whom to serve we recognize as our highest duty, also in the future."[68]

Among the prisoners, the sense of wasted time was palpable. They were concerned that they would be left behind. *Der Ruf* had earlier asked its readers, "Will you be able to answer succinctly: 'I did not knuckle under. Here I am. I can do that. Where should I begin?' Or will you stand aside and let others work, work on the reconstruction of your homeland?" In the effort to find some meaning in their imprisonment, they saw it as their duty to keep themselves and their comrades healthy. "We must always ask ourselves," the article insisted, " 'can we keep pace with our homeland?' If we can answer this question in the affirmative, then our captivity will have acquired its deeper, creative meaning."[69]

In fact, some prisoners—and not just those held in the West—took away from their captivity a deeply felt sense of mission. Most undoubtedly returned to West Germany with a negative opinion of the Soviet Union, a fact that is key to understanding the enthusiasm of many officers for a democratic Federal Republic. Many also returned with an unshakable, if not uncritical, faith in democracy and the West. While this yen for democracy may be a reflection of the struggles of Soviet captivity, it is still significant. Former prisoners spoke of the "weaknesses," "mistakes," or "childhood illnesses" of democracy, but they professed a belief in it nonetheless. "On the whole," wrote one prisoner, "the opinion was widespread that the future of our people depends largely on finding the appropriate balance between democracy and socialism."[70] That the undoubtedly horrible and taxing experiences of captivity in the Soviet Union filled even a few former prisoners with such a profound, indeed improbable, sense of what it meant to live in the "Free World" played a large role in ensuring the Federal Republic's success as a democratic state.

Postwar Effects of Education and Captivity

One of the major effects of former officers' captivity, as noted, was to increase their desire to contribute, but this constructive determination did not necessarily imply any genuine reckoning with the past. The officers' reflective exercises so often observed by the British ended short of repentance or recognition of responsibility. A list of guidelines for his fellow inmates written by Johannes Frießner in 1946 embodied the spirit of contribution without necessarily counseling, or exhibiting any signs of, self-examination. Along with admonitions not to aid "the enemy" or denounce one's fellow officers, Frießner commanded his comrades "Never [to] forget that you are a German!" and that "the unsurpassed achievements of [the Wehrmacht] and the entire German Volk" were not in vain. The Wehrmacht had "kept its honor despite it all," he insisted; therefore the captives had no cause to be ashamed of their ideals. "The point is," wrote Frießner, "with clear perceptions positively to construct a new future."[71]

The implication is strong in these guidelines that Frießner's fellow prisoners, the entire army, and German people had no cause for self-examination as a result of the war. The references to the Wehrmacht's honorable and valiant achievements, to the war not having been for nothing, and his obvious pride at being both German and an officer clearly indicate that Frießner was not experiencing the self-doubt and moral self-examination that the British official reported witnessing in the report cited above. Further, his use of the somewhat archaic term *Stand*, or "estate," to refer to his occupational group; his concern for the army's honor and achievements; and his reference to the "enemy" even in 1946 indicate that Frießner was still deeply influenced by his background as a traditional officer.

After the officers returned home, one sees evidence of the sense of mission instilled by their captivity, often independent of the experience of moral conflict that was so evident in the writings that emerged from the POW camps in newspapers like *Der Ruf*.[72] Nevertheless, one also detects another common effect of imprisonment: resentment. The longer the captivity, the stronger the feelings of discontent and anger—first, at being forgotten, despite the enormous efforts of many organizations to provide prisoners with some connection to their homeland, and second, at the hypocrisy of the captor nations and of fellow Germans. As noted, many former soldiers and officers resented the fact that they alone were being punished for the crimes of the Third Reich, while most Germans enjoyed their freedom and—increasingly in the early 1950s—the Federal Republic's prosperity.[73] The verbal abuse many Germans heaped on the former officer corps immediately following the war compounded the officers' bitterness.

Despite the bitterness, the desire to contribute predominated for many prisoners. "The most bitter disappointment for the returnee," a discussion group at the Evangelical Academy in Loccum concluded, "was the feeling of having come too late and no longer being needed."[74] In practical terms, the returning prisoner often had difficulty finding a job. In a spiritual sense, for the prisoner who had languished in a prison camp for years or labored rebuilding France or the Soviet Union, not to contribute to the reconstruction of Germany in some way was an additional burden. At the Evangelical Academy in Guntershausen in 1950, Frießner reminded his listeners that he and his fellow soldiers were positive and future-oriented and wished "to contribute to the achievement of mutual understanding in mutual appreciation and respect among the various mentalities and peoples." "We do not want to stand still and always look backwards, nor do we want to do mere busy work; rather we want to build anew, in conjunction with the other European peoples, our shared home, in awareness of our shared fate and for the good of the European idea."[75] Busywork is exactly what many soldiers, even officers, had been doing during their captivity. This passage is indicative of the desire spiritually to contribute to the future of Germany (and occasionally Europe as well) rather than dwell on an often embarrassing past.

Officers also attributed a variety of other effects to their time as prisoners of war. They often saw their captivity as a test of character, which either qualified or disqualified them to contribute to the new Germany. "We are all here subject to a constant trial of our human values," wrote Hans Diester, a former military judge with the rank of major, "in which more than one begins to fail."[76] Soldiers assumed that the trials of imprisonment revealed a comrade's essential nature, and their descriptions of fellow inmates' behavior illustrate many of their beliefs about themselves and the officer corps. One former prisoner claimed that soldiers did not concern themselves with their comrades' political views, faith, or social status. They judged a fellow inmate solely on the basis of "whether he was a good guy and especially whether in the tough situations of Soviet captivity and a heretofore unknown psychic and physical terror, he showed character."[77] Such statements betray the officers' common assumption that a true "front community" had existed in which all soldiers were equal, independent of class, politics, or religion, but they also expose the officers' equally common faith in an elite of character.

Many officers remembered their captivity as a sobering experience during which the negative qualities of some prisoners came to the fore. Many evidently failed the test of character. In one chapter of his unpublished manuscript, "A General Experiences Hitler and Nazism," Hans von Donat betrays many of his own class prejudices while calling his imprisonment an eye-opening and depressing experience. The number of prisoners addicted to tobacco particularly struck Donat. "This poor self-discipline struck a not insignificant percentage of former high- and low-ranking soldiers. Birth, occupation, estate played no role." Even his fellow generals committed ignoble acts in order to satisfy their cravings. "The sum of these highly regrettable manifestations showed the true character faults of the Germans, because this was simply lack of character in its most severe form. For these people one had committed one's life to exhausting labor. It was a depressing observation."[78] Donat obviously felt that occupation and birth should determine a prisoner's behavior. Frießner also mentions the "intellectual and moral failure of individual members of my occupation; yes, I must unfortunately also admit even many of my own peers [presumably his fellow generals] during and after war, in captivity and in free life."[79] Of course Diester, Donat, and Frießner considered that they had weathered their captivity admirably and therefore were qualified to voice their opinions.

For prisoners of the Soviet Union, captivity was also a rite of passage.[80] Why certain people withstood the mental and physical rigors of captivity better than others remains a mystery, but one former major did not hesitate to offer his theory. He blamed the decline in corps spirit and unity within the officer corps that had already begun prior to the war. "Jealousy and vanity, expedient egotism and callousness, and so-called 'ideological reliability' had become paramount over modest fulfillment of duty, moral irreproachability, unconditional objectivity, and truthfulness."[81] In other words, officers had strayed from the values that had defined their self-image for centuries. Compounding the problem, according to the major (and other officers as well), was the fact that Hitler's rearmament and the war had given epaulets to many men who in reality were "adequate corporals, but never officers" and that these men had collapsed under the strain of captivity once the prestige provided by their rank was taken away. Another soldier saw his captivity as a life-changing event, claiming that only he who has experienced captivity can truly value freedom.[82] For those who stood up to the test of captivity, it became the central, defining experience of their lives. For better or for worse, most returnees, especially those from the Soviet Union, were undeniably changed, some bitter and broken, some proud and thankful.[83]

An image of comradeship, the bond between officer and soldier within the Wehrmacht, also emerged from numerous accounts of captivity. The same major who had shamefully reported that many soldiers failed the moral test of captivity lauded the camaraderie and equality in the camps, despite the hardships. "One saw the regimental commander, the General Staff officer, or the higher Wehrmacht civil servant next to the simple soldier, the weathered old 'front soldier' next to the member of the logistics branch or the reserves."[84]

Another account of the bond between soldier and officer came from the Soviet Union. Hans Lempp, a company commander whose command was encircled by the Soviets in 1944, surrendered to a group of approaching Russian tanks. A Russian sergeant said to him in broken German, "Comrade, war kaputt, Hitler kaputt," and after having disarmed the Germans and identified Lempp as the commanding officer, he pointed a pistol at Lempp's head and said, "Officer kaputt!" In his account, Lempp faced the prospect of death stoically, only to be saved momentarily by a corporal in his group who tried to convince the Russian that "This officer, good!" In the meantime, a lieutenant of the Russian infantry had arrived and recognizing the plight of his fellow officer, convinced the sergeant to allow Lempp to live. In his frustration, the Russian sergeant demanded that Lempp relinquish his fine officer's boots and stored them in his tank. Then the Germans set off for the collection camp with their commander in bare feet. One of his men, a farmer from Swabia, offered Lempp his shoes, claiming that he had grown accustomed to walking barefoot on the family farm as a child. Touched, Lempp refused the offer "instinctively," adding, "I had the feeling that I should, due to a new-found inner truth, lead my external life exactly as the Russians intended."[85]

The common soldier's almost childish innocence in offering his shoes and the refusal by the noble and stoic officer make this story sound apocryphal and indeed, in the context of the meeting of the Evangelical Academy in Bad Boll where it was told, almost biblical. Nevertheless, this story of the comradely link between commanders and subordinates while in captivity appears frequently in other forms, giving it ideological significance quite independent of the story's veracity.

Such stories, whether mythical or not, reinforced the officers' views of their place in society and their value to it. That such bonds between soldiers and their commanders existed is without question, but whether they could be termed "prevalent" is doubtful given the accounts of tension between officers and soldiers inside the camps. In the Soviet Union, many prisoners suspected the Russians of actively promoting the hatred between officers and soldiers that usually just simmered in the background.[86] According to some accounts, most officers lacked any feeling of responsibility for their comrades, were too concerned with their own survival, and were therefore cursed by their fellow prisoners. Only the true "front officers," who had "suffered, struggled, and bled" along with their soldiers were accorded any measure of respect.[87]

Especially in Britain and the United States, special camps were established that housed only officers, so that contact with former subordinates would have been minimal in any case. An article from *Der Ruf* illustrates the alienation of many officers, especially those schooled in the traditions of German soldierdom à la Seeckt. As prisoners in the United States became aware of the horrors of Nazi concentration camps through pictures and films distributed by the Americans, Gen. Jürgen von Arnim, the ranking German officer in the United States, issued a declaration proclaiming himself and the officers held in his camp in Clinton, Iowa, innocent and ignorant of such crimes. Not surprisingly, he rejected the whole principle of collective guilt and insisted that "on the contrary, the German Wehrmacht constantly conducted itself in battle according to the applicable rules of war and staked its honor on treating prisoners of war decently."[88]

The response of the editorial staff of *Der Ruf* indicates how isolated Arnim and those who thought like him really were. The editors charged that General Staff officers had known all along about the realities of the concentration camps, reminding Arnim that some officers had tried to object. With keen insight, they reasoned that most had remained silent because "they believed, as soldiers, that they bore no responsibility for actions outside their own military sphere, even though they were the only power in the state apart from the [Nazi] Party."[89] Arnim, they argued, missed the point. No one implied that he was directly responsible for such acts, but denying responsibility was counterproductive. Better to face the facts and admit a sort of passive guilt, so that such horrors would never be repeated.

All sorts of lessons were assumed to have come out of the mass experience of captivity of around eleven million former soldiers. In interviews conducted in the 1950s and 1960s, former captives suggested that they had learned to accept personal responsibility for their actions and to strive for social peace and justice. In the political arena, they saw the necessity of breaking down confessional and class barriers in Germany, some form of supranational cooperation, and the clear rejection of "Soviet conditions." An appropriate blend of democracy and socialism was the answer for Germany—not communism. One aristocratic former officer claimed to have learned the importance of living with people of all classes.[90] This impressive list of supposed benefits is to some extent the product of the years intervening between the actual captivity and the time of the interviews. The fact remains, however, that former officers felt themselves changed, schooled, even chastened by the experience.

In sum, many officers emerged from captivity with a sense of mission. They wanted desperately to contribute to the physical and moral reconstruction of Germany. Years of training and service in the military had made them accustomed to being a respected, powerful, and active force in society. Their inherent patriotism, combined with months or years of captivity, increased their drive to rebuild their homeland.

In many cases, however, this activism represented an escape from, rather than a confrontation with, the past and the officers' responsibility for the Third Reich's crimes. The Allies' actions often discouraged the moral self-examination they hoped to provoke. By practically singling out the military for discipline—especially through imprisonment and the denial of pensions—they created within many officers a sense that German soldierdom alone had atoned for its sins of the preceding years. The irony (and, some insisted, hypocrisy) of the Allied internment of a group of people in order to teach them about freedom was not lost on the prisoners. How was a soldier supposed to have recognized the injustice of his actions, one observer asked in 1955, when he himself was suffering an injustice?[91]

The bitterness and resentment many soldiers felt at being singled out for punishment had two effects. First, it often prevented soldiers not from wanting to serve their nation, but from realistically examining their past. Like the defamation they experienced in public life, their punishment helped to create a defensiveness among them that shielded them from criticism, both justified and unjustified. Second, resentment was primarily focused on the Allied (especially democratic) governments that had imprisoned them, making many soldiers suspect that "democracy" was more of an ideological slogan than a reality worth achieving.

Their education and class background, as well as their experiences in wartime and in captivity, clearly influenced the ideas and proposals that former officers brought to the political arena of the late 1940s and early 1950s. The often cited soldierly values that they claimed Germany so desperately needed in the postwar era were precisely those that Seeckt and other military leaders had sought in their recruits for decades. Character, as defined by those leaders, remained the primary criterion for judging the value of a person, whether officer or politician. As we will see in the following chapters, the political alternatives that emerged from the former Wehrmacht officers (or from the parties they supported) combined a focus on character, patriotic urges to contribute, and the lessons of captivity to produce a unique blend of right-wing nationalism, pan-Europeanism, elitist oligarchy, and civil-rights democracy. These soldiers maintained (if partly in self-defense) that their one desire was further to serve the German Volk by providing a moral example, a "soldierly conscience."[92]

4

Unpolitical Soldiers: Veterans, Politicians, and Military Reform

Despite their desire to serve, organized veterans still faced the issue of how and where to contribute. The attitude of many former officers toward politics in the late 1940s and early 1950s was stereotypically hostile. "Politics" in the vocabulary of German soldierdom, was quite simply a pejorative term applied to the activities of parliamentary deputies who in some way opposed the veterans' organizations' wishes. The charge of political activity was often wielded as a weapon in fraternal disputes among those organizations as well. Nevertheless, most former career soldiers were aware that by organizing to restore their rights and their honor, they themselves were engaging in "politics." Some soldiers even became effective lobbyists in their capacity as representatives of the VDS or the other veterans' organizations. Within their organizations they fought for (pseudo-)democratically elected positions, developed policies and platforms, and campaigned among the general public for support of those policies.

They viewed their contributions to the political scene as expressions of national interest, however, rather than as the desires of any single constituency. Not that such a tactic is uncommon in politics in general. Rudy Koshar identifies this tendency among bourgeois parties as a whole in his study of Marburg.[1] Soldiers merely took such an attitude to an extreme. In the spirit of "service to the Volk," former officers placed their expertise at the disposal of the German people by theorizing about the ideal nature of government, as well as offering advice on specific issues of the day. Officers constructed their own ephemeral political alternatives at the same time that they were engaged with the mainstream political parties and the government in formulating policy and legislation.

In particular, former officers desired to have an impact on the plans for rearmament that circulated in the Federal Republic after 1949. They immediately recognized the benefits that would accrue to experienced soldiers if the Allies created a West German defense force. Once it became clear that the United States desperately wanted a West German army to help defend Europe in the wake of the Korean War, veterans' organizations had a bargaining chip in their struggle to regain soldiers' pensions and restore the honor of German soldierdom. Beyond the material benefits inherent in pensions and renewed employment, former career soldiers sought to restore the influence of the military and military values in German life and society.

Soldiers and Politics

The disenchantment of many former officers with both Nazism (which had betrayed its soldiers and was responsible for the destruction of Germany) and democracy (which had imprisoned them) led officers to seek political alternatives. The alternatives they proposed were founded in their notion of service to the people. Former soldiers could best serve the German people, many believed, by remaining above the fray of party politics—a "national soldierly conscience," as one officer put it.[2] Officers involved themselves in a variety of movements and groups and, despite their common aversion to party politics, frequently joined political parties in order to do their part for the rejuvenation of Germany.

As so often happened, officers looked back to the army's tradition-rich past for the origins of this commitment to Germany rather than to any one political party. The military's noble task—to protect the Fatherland—had united all Germans since the institution of conscription, argued former lieutenant general Smilo von Lüttwitz. No matter what a recruit's age, class, or confession, Lüttwitz claimed, "as soldiers they forgot party disputes, class struggle, self-interest, let themselves be seized by the great common mission of the Germans. This clearly visible, unifying bond became a tradition among us—especially in times of war." This great tradition of "service, the inner bond of camaraderie, the selflessness and loyalty" of the soldier "originated in German history and was the spiritual and moral prerequisite for the foundation of the army."[3]

To the group of organized former officers, soldierdom and politics simply did not mix. Politicians, in their view, were the representatives of special interests, not of Germany as a whole, and were therefore unfit to make the necessary decisions in Germany's time of crisis and reconstruction.[4] Because they assumed politicians were dishonest dealmakers, most former officers viewed politics as incompatible with their honor, and their organizations uniformly abjured political activity. Most officers realized at some point that the mere existence of their organizations was a political act.[5] The abjuration of politics in their bylaws generally meant only a strict *party* political neutrality and reflected the officers' dislike of politicians and parties. Maintaining an apolitical stance also diffused the suspicion among the Allied governments and the public that the military sought influence over the government, such as it had wielded in the days of the Kaiser and World War I.

In the period before the Federal Republic's establishment in 1949, former officers' spokesmen proposed a variety of political reforms, aimed mostly at eliminating the discord among the German people caused, as they saw it, by class warfare and party politics. There were even efforts to reestablish the rhetoric of a "front community" that was so prevalent after World War I. Joachim von Ostau, whose name appears frequently in the post-1945 era on right-wing political leaflets and treatises, circulated a letter among his associates and "like-minded friends" that appealed to the unity not of the trenches this time, but certainly of the Russian steppes, the deserts of Africa, and the hedgerows of Normandy.[6] "Contrary to the current party- and class-hatred," Ostau reminded his readers, "out there on the front there was no difference between factory-owner and worker, Catholic or Protestant, Bavarian or Prussian, . . . and this spirit of soldierly unity should be carried over into the work of peace."[7] In the view of Ostau and many former officers, the current party system in West Germany was simply a revival of the failed methods of the Weimar Republic, the fate of which was so well known.[8]

Some of the most elaborate ideas concerning the former soldier's role in the Federal Republic's political life came from Gert Spindler, an industrialist and former major in the reserves whose money and energy made him influential among former officers. Spindler sponsored frequent meetings attended by soldiers, government officials, and others, and he published a newspaper, *Der Fortschritt* (Progress), which he tried unsuccessfully to transform into the VDS's official organ.

Among Spindler's many projects and fully in keeping with the officers' predilection for "movements" rather than parties was the Tatgemeinschaft freier Deutscher (Free Germans' Action Community). The Tatgemeinschaft's program was a strange mixture of Christian, elitist, social Darwinist, pan-European, and nationalist thought. "Our political, social, moral, and economic life is shaken to its very core," one of the group's leaflets began. Only the "principles of the Christian-formed occidental culture" such as human rights and the protection of the individual could bring about the group's dream of "an organic upward development of [the] Volk."[9] Such consistently vague language unfortunately litters the programmatic statements of the Tatgemeinschaft and similar organizations.

To achieve this organic growth, the Tatgemeinschaft proposed the formation of local groups that would constitute an "elite not of the spirit or of the intellect, but of conviction." Because these groups would be formed in local communities, where everyone knew everyone else personally, it would be impossible for anyone to be dishonest in one's intentions or convictions. Each person's "achievements in his career would be immediately recognizable, as would his social and upstanding behavior. The chaff will thus be quickly separated from the wheat. Career political dealmakers will no longer find a place." Once these small groups establish themselves, "the hitherto existing procedure of power battles among organized interest groups will be dissolved. In their place will step the progressive, organic construction of our country."[10]

This strange mixture of quasi–National Socialist notions of social Darwinism, an organic Volk, nationalism, Western Christian culture, and an almost Leninist notion of a small elite cadre of actors was not uncommon. A similar mixture appeared in a flyer distributed by the Deutsche Union (German Union) entitled "What Does the German Union Want?" Like the Tatgemeinschaft, the German Union advocated the civil rights of the individual versus authority and saw the "creative personality" as the decisive factor in the European community's spiritual and cultural development. Like Ostau, the German Union's leaders saw their enemy in party bureaucracies and the "bankrupts" from the Weimar Republic who were again erecting their "Phantom Democracy."[11]

Even after the elections to the first Bundestag in August 1949, the rightist critics expressed their disdain for the party system. Hans von Donat kept files on many of the parties in Germany and his home state of Württemberg. One of the groups whose efforts he frequently praised was called the Deutsche Gemeinschaft (German Community).[12] Based in Braunschweig and one of few such movements to have enjoyed any electoral success, this group actively solicited the participation of former soldiers, especially officers, and made the veterans' organizations' demands, such as the reestablishment of pensions and an end to defamation, its own. The headline of one of the German Community's leaflets provides a sense of its political prejudices: "Total SPD-State? . . . Cold Civil War and the Two-Class State—Intensifying of the Class War—The Union Commands the State . . . Communist Infiltration of the SPD . . . Class Means More than Volk!—The Decayed Middle-Class World of Parties Is Not Up to the Danger—Powerless Bonn."[13]

Without even bothering to put together a sentence, the German Community's leadership declared the current party system in general, and the Social Democrats in particular, unfit to rule Germany. In Donat's words, the group directed its efforts against the bureaucracy and the waste and corruption in administration on behalf of all those who had been denied their rights.

Former officers also hoped to contribute to the rejuvenation of Germany outside normal political channels by providing a moral example, as they believed they had done for centuries. Frequently, they expressed their desire to "wake the people out of their lethargy and interest them in the fundamental questions of our life" such as defense against communism.[14] Harkening back to their service in wartime, the officers in the VDS called for Germans to follow their example and participate in a "moral rearmament."[15] Especially the youth, one former tank general asserted, needed the moral example of their elders.[16] "In all our actions," the officers proclaimed, "we want to keep it just like we did in the war: All for Germany!"[17] The Wehrmacht traditionally had been, they insisted, "the bulwark of order," a condition sadly lacking in contemporary Germany. During a meeting of the Evangelical Academy at Guntershausen, Frießner appealed to all former soldiers to help in rebuilding the "level of order, the moral platform" that the soldierly values of reliability, consciousness of responsibility, a model lifestyle, and camaraderie had once made a reality in Germany.[18] Finally, most officers agreed that any veterans' organization must place its idealistic beliefs ahead of its material concerns. These universally recognized idealistic foundations of soldierdom would lead Germany and its people out of their current crisis by teaching them the value of honesty, responsibility, and correct behavior. In short, what Germany needed was more character.

The parallels between the rhetoric of the former officers' moral–political campaign and that used by the National Socialists in the 1920s and 1930s are inescapable. Their nightmare visions of socialist- or communist-incited class warfare could have been taken from any number of National Socialist diatribes against their enemies on the left. The constant references to the rebirth or rejuvenation of the Volk are clearly analogous to the Nazi slogan, "Germany, awake!" The scorn heaped on the Federal Republic's ineffective and cowardly party bureaucrats as direct descendants of Weimar politicians clearly resembles the Nazis' vilification of the "November criminals." Even their pan-European ideas stem more from a Goebbelsesque crusade against Bolshevism than from any deep feelings about cooperation among European nations. In their desire to be a "bulwark of order" or a "moral basis" for society, the advocates for the former Wehrmacht often "breathed the spirit of restoration," as one contemporary observer phrased it. "In its bombast, this [desire to be a bulwark of order] cannot deny its origins in the vocabulary of a Führer's birthday speech."[19]

Nevertheless, one cannot simply dismiss these proposals as the mere efforts of National Socialist devotees to reestablish their Reich clothed in the necessary robes of peace, freedom, democracy, and pan-Europeanism. The proposals of these groups sometimes included concrete suggestions for the reconstruction of Germany. The German Union's program, published in the wake of the Basic Law's passage in March 1949, addressed some of the political issues arising from the new West German constitution. It proposed direct democracy in the form of a referendum to decide fundamental issues concerning the electoral system, the houses of parliament, and federal and state finances. These movements and "communities of deed" appealed directly to the former officers' patriotic, elitist, activist, antiparty, and antibureaucratic tendencies. Many officers, even those who thoroughly repented their association with Nazism, looked to the programs of groups such as the German Union or German Community for the salvation of Germany. Former officers hoped by their example to produce a moral renaissance.

Veterans and the Mainstream Parties

The rhetoric of unity, morality, service, and nationalism carried over into veterans' contacts with the larger political parties such as the Christian Democratic Union (CDU) and the SPD. Even though most former officers seem to have preferred the CDU or FDP in national and local elections, they frequently iterated their belief that *all* groups must be united in order for Germany to survive. While Hansen stressed the importance of CDU victories when writing to his associates, in a letter to Konrad Adenauer in 1948, he advocated the unification of all Germans in a common front. While praising the CDU for its efforts on behalf of Wehrmacht veterans, Hansen believed the recovery of Germany required "the bringing together of all powers to the right of the SPD." "In this connection, I do not wish to leave unmentioned that I have in mind the incorporation of the SPD also into a common front against external enemies as the highest goal of an internal political nature."[20] Unity across class and political conviction and closing the ranks against external enemies remained important rhetorical devices for Hansen and his associates in the postwar world, as they had been for Seeckt in the 1920s. Of course, in previous eras, external enemies did not always reside outside the borders of Germany. Bismarck as well as Hitler, albeit in different ways, targeted "enemies of the Volk" and used such campaigns to forge domestic unity.

The veterans' vocal mistrust of political parties did not dissuade them and their organizations from trying to manipulate both official and public opinion through careful lobbying and the press.[21] Hansen and his associates circulated ideas and traded stories of successful and unsuccessful strategies. Since Hansen lived in Kiel, he focused most of his attention on the British zonal government and German officials in the north. He wrote letters to anyone he could find, masterfully appealing to the charity of British churches and the sense of fairness of British officers and playing on the communist nightmares of British politicians. Leaving no stone unturned, Hansen also lobbied German administrative officials and party leaders, hoping to wring from them commitments to the officers' cause. He found a willing partner in a few newspapers, especially *Die Welt* and the local paper, *Kieler Nachrichten*, which frequently published his letters. Soon, he was exchanging political notes with veterans all over Germany. The interesting exchanges hint at the officers' sophisticated lobbying methods and range from analyses of foreign and German public opinion to letters outlining strategies tailored for individual political parties to general historical treatises on the Nuremberg trials or the officers' role in the Third Reich.

The Korean War was a turning point in the German military's fortunes. After June 1950, the remilitarization of West Germany was a foregone conclusion, and remilitarization meant a rise in the fortunes of former officers, whose pension demands had to be met in order to win their support for the new West German army. The veterans' organizations of the early 1950s used the threat of a Korea-like invasion to their advantage. However, while the Korean War might have represented a turning point in the international acceptability of a West German military contingent, the watershed in the veterans' minds had occurred much earlier. With the breakdown of the Allied Control Council in 1947 and the overthrow of the democratic coalition government in Czechoslovakia in early 1948, veterans' leaders increasingly used the Soviet threat and the demands of the Cold War in their arguments for the rehabilitation of the German soldier.

In a 1948 letter to Sir Brian Robertson, military governor of the British zone, Hansen emphasized the necessity of securing the support of former officers for the defense of Europe. "I always believed," he wrote, "that the real danger for my country, for Europa [sic], for the whole world was and still is in the East." That danger had only increased thanks to Soviet gains in the war and would increase further if discrimination against Wehrmacht soldiers continued. To promote such divisions within Germany "makes it very difficult, if not impossible," Hansen warned, "for any honest former German soldier to feel himself obliged to join the nations of Western Europa and the civilized world to establish the solidarity of mankind and to safe [sic] the old Western civilization and culture."[22] Hansen expressed himself more succinctly in a letter to a British parliamentarian in which he wrote, "There is enormous danger that valuable Germans definitely decide for the East because they cannot any longer trust British policy."[23] This letter accompanied an article entitled "Who Will Defend the Democracy?," which somewhat sarcastically reminded its readers that demilitarization officials were unlikely to contribute to the defense of democracy in the Western zones.[24] Both of these letters were written more than two years before the communist invasion of South Korea and indicate that the veterans well understood the implications of the ensuing Cold War rivalry for their cause.

The early veterans' leaders also developed sophisticated strategies for dealing with German political parties. Hansen began lobbying the major parties in Schleswig-Holstein almost immediately after their foundation. Letters to the SPD and CDU throughout 1946 and 1947 referred to the suffering of the ex-soldiers and their families (especially elderly soldiers and widows) because of the unjust treatment they received from the Allies. Hansen hoped to gather support for the reestablishment of pensions by degrees by first committing the parties to grant pensions to older veterans. He constructed logical, if not flawless, arguments concerning former officers' innocence of the charge of militarism and emphasized both the necessity of harnessing the power of veterans to the reconstruction of Germany and the danger of driving them into opposition. Hansen made similar arguments once the national government was formed in 1949. In congratulating President Theodor Heuss on his election, Hansen stressed the danger of radicalization inherent in denying former soldiers their rights.[25] This carrot and stick combination of promises of rewards and threats of radicalization characterized the policy of veterans' organizations toward political parties and the government throughout the late 1940s and 1950s.

Most political parties responded to the appeals of Hansen, Donat, and others with cautious assurances of support. Several letters from the CDU expressed support without committing the party to any particular stance or identifying it with the veterans' organizations. One such letter carefully phrased the CDU's support for a reestablishment of soldiers' pensions by grouping the soldiers with other needy war victims. "Be assured that Herr Adenauer . . . is resolved to bring all his influence to bear so that the claims of the war victims and other impoverished members of society are satisfied."[26] A few weeks later, a CDU official agreed in principle that career soldiers deserved pensions after an appropriate investigation of their background. Even the SPD, from which Hansen and others expected little, expressed a generally favorable attitude toward former officers. An early letter from the SPD executive committee in Schleswig-Holstein apologized for the excesses of demilitarization but insisted that such a process was necessary. "Naturally not all career soldiers are militarists, and still they must now carry almost the entire burden." Other victims of the Third Reich had legitimate grievances, the letter continued, and they had to be accommodated as well. The SPD promised to work for the satisfaction of everyone's needs.[27] The local SPD branch was slightly more encouraging when it admitted that the nonpayment of pensions was in many cases unjust, especially in the case of older officers, in effect granting its support to the first of Hansen's goals, the reestablishment of pensions for the elderly.[28] Such responses convinced Hansen that his step by step lobbying approach was bearing fruit.

The parties on the right were less wary of being identified with the soldiers' cause. The FDP in particular strove to make itself the voice of the former soldier, and it counted a number of former officers among its representatives in the Bundestag.[29] Other more marginal right-wing parties, like the short-lived German Union and German Community, made the demands of veterans' organizations part of their political platforms.[30] Not surprisingly, the former career soldiers reciprocated and viewed the parties of the right far more favorably than they did those on the left. Hansen wrote in 1948 that he and his fellow officers "had every interest in the CDU emerging from every election as strong as possible" since the CDU was more sympathetic to the officers' concerns.[31]

While the charters of the BvW and other organizations uniformly contained commitments to political neutrality, this did not preclude exhibiting resourcefulness in their dealings with political parties. In preparation for discussions with members of the Bundestag in 1950, Rudolf Veiel, a friend of Hans von Donat, drafted a list of guidelines based on his prior experiences with the various political parties (and, one might add, his prejudices against most of them). This detailed document consists of specifically tailored arguments designed to play on the sympathies of the specific parties. For the parties more inclined to lend a friendly ear to soldiers' concerns, like the FDP and the right wing of the CDU, Veiel counseled the iteration of established rights and financial feasibility. The former officers' right to pensions was old and had been recognized in principle, he insisted. The money for such pensions existed since the number of potential recipients would be small (about 194,000), since civil servants were about to receive a raise, and since the property of the Wehrmacht (some DM 5 billion) had become the property of the Federal Republic. The SPD and the left wing of the CDU were more likely to argue that other war victims must be taken care of first and that the Wehrmacht, being to blame for the war, must suffer the consequences. Veiel's suggested arguments therefore stressed former soldiers' miserable conditions, their inability to find work due to the boycott, their innocence in the outbreak of the war, and the Wehrmacht's role as a bastion of resistance to Hitler.[32]

More telling than Veiel's rhetorical tactics are his suggestions for dealing with the parliamentarians. The picture he paints of politicians is not flattering. In Veiel's opinion, politicians could be categorized into one of three groups: they were either Nazis (anxious to divert attention from their crimes by using the military as a scapegoat), ideologically shackled socialists (giddy at the prospect of weakening the military), or money-grubbing civil servants (worried that granting pensions for former officers might lessen their own chances for a raise). Sympathy, he argued, could only be expected from members of the old imperial parties or from representatives who had themselves been officers or were from families with a military background.

Thus organized and armed for battle, the former career soldiers embarked on their decade-long struggle to reestablish both the honor and the rights of the German soldier. To the veterans' leaders, the two notions of honor and rights were inextricably linked. Certainly there was more to the prevalence of idealistic arguments about honor and values than a purely unselfish desire to preserve morality. The concentration on defamation and idealistic goals did have a unifying effect. More ex-soldiers were willing to support a group that fought for an ideal than one that simply wanted money from the state, and men like Hansen were keenly aware of this fact.[33] Diehl indicates that many of the other war victims' associations in postwar Germany similarly developed idealistic platforms that underlined the uniqueness of the group's values and the necessity of enlisting those values in the service of the new state.[34] Another reason for the predominance of moral or idealistic goals in the early organizations' charters was the former officers' shared belief that Germany needed not only soldiers, but also a viable soldierly ideology. So while their campaign for the reinstatement of their pensions proceeded along lines similar to the efforts of other social groups to establish their claims on the state's welfare resources, former officers believed that they were carriers of a great tradition, with all the responsibilities to the future that that implied. In defaming German soldierdom, they believed, great damage was being done to the fabric of society. Their insistence on the importance of honor, discipline, and bravery, especially for a democracy confronted by the Cold War threat of an aggressive Soviet Union, made the veterans' organizations unique.

Rearmament

Allied officials publicly broached the idea for a West German security force as early as 1948.[35] Later, in a famous interview printed by the *Cleveland Plain Dealer* on 3 December 1949, Konrad Adenauer lent his support to the idea of creating an armed force within the recently founded Federal Republic of Germany. Foreseen as a counterpart to the East German Kasernierte Volkspolizei (KVP), this small-scale force could, Adenauer believed, firmly establish West German sovereignty in the international community, as well as make a meaningful contribution to European defense.[36] But by mid-1950, no real progress had been made. In May 1950, possession of arms in the Federal Republic was still illegal (by order of the Allied High Commission), and the SPD had recently proposed a law imposing enormous fines and a jail sentence on anyone "undertaking to coerce a German into 'war service.' "[37]

The major impetus for rearmament was the reaction of the U.S. government and its European allies to the invasion of South Korea by the Soviet-backed North Koreans on 25 June 1950; it had a serious impact on Western attitudes toward the Cold War. The attack on South Korea denoted, for American analysts, a radical shift in Soviet policy from economic and political wrangling to outright military confrontation. The "lesson of Korea"—namely, that the Soviet Union would use its puppet-state allies to wage proxy wars against the West—was immediately applied to the European theater. As early as 4 July, the United States considered plans for a West German police force along the lines of the East German KVP. By the end of 1950, serious multilateral discussions among the Western Allies addressed the possibility of a West German contribution to a European army.

Although these plans were ostensibly subject to the approval of the members of the North Atlantic Treaty Organization (NATO), the United States' strong support made the outcome practically a foregone conclusion. French efforts—such as the Pleven Plan/European Defense Community (EDC)—to keep the Federal Republic out of NATO and to inhibit German control of any future European army were undercut by the Federal Republic's understandably firm opposition. The diplomatic twists and turns that characterized the EDC's rise and fall and the eventual incorporation of the Federal Republic within NATO are well outside the scope of this project. Relevant, however, are the effects that the various proposals to arm the Federal Republic had on former officers and their perceptions of their role within the state.

In 1955, Wolf von Baudissin called the creation of a new military a "test of strength" for West Germany's nascent democracy.[38] Rearmament was also a test of the well-established veterans' organizations' strength and the unity of former officers because rearmament was the reality behind the officers' flights of fancy concerning politics and the contributions that soldierly values could make to society.

After all of the warnings issued by Hansen to the effect that former officers would not support a new army if their demands were not met, few knew whether those threats would be made good. To reenlist or not was a difficult choice for those concerned. Competing with their patriotism and sense of duty were memories of their service under Hitler and fears that soldiers would again be "misused," this time by the Americans or their allies. Also, many former career soldiers, in the absence of a military career option, had found rewarding positions in other fields and were understandably reluctant to give up their hard-won positions. Former colonel Hans von Luck recalled being asked to reenlist. He was an experienced tank commander who had fought on nearly every front during World War II and would therefore have been a welcome addition to the Bundeswehr. Several issues gave Luck pause, however. He had found a new profession and was doing quite well financially. Moreover, the recruiter could not guarantee a suitable placement for Luck because "ranks of colonel and above need approval from the political parties [sic]." This requirement aroused Luck's suspicions. "I have no wish to find myself back as a parade-ground commander all of a sudden, just because my face doesn't fit somewhere," Luck explained with some sense of bitterness. Not trusting that "politics" would not disadvantage him somehow, Luck declined.[39]

Bitterness and even contrariness over their treatment during the early postwar years also turned many against the idea of rearmament. Between 1949 and 1955, while tens of thousands of former officers and noncoms wrestled with their private decisions, the veterans' organizations labored to mold public opinion on the subject and to parlay the uncertainty about the government's military plans into political capital for their constituencies.

The institution that played the crucial role in formulating West German rearmament policy was the Blank Office. Theodor Blank was a prominent Christian Democrat who had previously dealt with labor union issues. In August 1950, Chancellor Adenauer gave Blank the daunting task of leading "the negotiations with the Allied High Commission concerning the accommodation of additional Allied troops and the task of addressing the general question of the security of the Federal Republic."[40] In October, Adenauer formalized this position and granted Blank the obfuscating title of Chancellor's Deputy for Questions Relating to Increasing the Number of Allied Troops in Germany.[41] Actually, Blank was replacing Gerhard von Schwerin, who, as the head of a semisecret division of the Chancellor's Office that had supervised earlier rearmament preparations, had infuriated Adenauer by meeting privately with journalists to discuss rearmament plans.

Schwerin's dismissal illustrated the delicate nature of the proposal for a West German army. Domestic and international opposition were enormous. French opposition has already been mentioned, and the Soviet Union naturally protested vigorously against the arming of America's client state. While Soviet opposition was understandable in power-political terms, it seems to have played a relatively minor role in discussions of the structure of the army. More important was the attitude of West Germany's allies. Ulrich de Mazière indicated in a seminar discussion in the early 1970s that the Blank Office (of which he had been part) was forced to avoid making too many concrete plans lest it appear too eager—not to the Soviets, but to its allies, particularly the French.[42]

On the domestic front, the Social Democrats spearheaded the opposition to rearmament, arguing not only that it would mean the permanent division of Germany, but also that it would divert much needed funds from economic reconstruction and social programs. The SPD was later joined in its protest by several nonsocialist trade unions and certain leaders of the Evangelical Church.[43] Finally, the West German public, particularly the youth, was vehemently opposed to the creation of an army. "*Ohne mich*" ("Count me out" or "Without me") became the rallying cry of young men expressing their unwillingness to serve in the proposed armed forces. This attitude led to numerous instances of unrest, reported in the press, and even one occasion, mentioned by Gordon Craig, on which Blank was pelted with beer mugs at a meeting in Augsburg.[44]

This summary does not do justice to the strength and sincerity of the opposition movements within Germany and abroad, but it should give the reader some sense of the government's isolation on the topic of rearmament. The irony is that the fervent opposition accomplished little. The SPD was never able to harness the power of the opposition to rearmament and translate it into electoral success. The effect of the opposition was, however, to make officers more self-conscious and to force upon them a rather one-sided confrontation with the past and the historical legacy of German armed forces.

Former Officers and Rearmament

Even before the Korean War made the issue more urgent, former soldiers discussed among themselves the possibility of rearmament and its impact on veterans. As early as November 1949, Erich Dethleffsen collected his thoughts on the matter in an essay entitled "Thoughts on the Attitude of the German Generals in Case of a German Rearmament Demanded by the Western Allies." Dethleffsen identified three basic suppositions that conditioned the former generals' response to such a request. First, former generals must recognize eventually that they had a duty to maintain "occidental culture and civilization." They had the advantage that the Allies recognized in the German military a staunch and experienced bulwark against communism, but they must avoid merely providing cannon fodder for the European armies. The great opportunity for the former soldiers lay in properly exploiting the need for a German military in order to advance their political and economic agendas. To do so, however, would require a certain reserve in supporting rearmament. They did not want to appear as "bloodthirsty militarists . . . whose loftiest aim in life is to shoot holes in other peoples' stomachs." They should instead emphasize that they were tired of war, but do so without needlessly advancing the cause of pacifism in Germany.

Dethleffsen also insisted that officers should downplay their efforts to regain their pensions and end the defamation of German soldierdom so that it would not appear in foreign countries as though the German military was gaining the upper hand in politics once again. The army must be the tool of the state, Dethleffsen stressed, to be used to assert Germany's independence, and not merely the tool of the Western Allies. In this, Dethleffsen's ideas were similar to Konrad Adenauer's plans for regaining German sovereignty. Adenauer also wished to use rearmament as a political lever to gain some degree of independence for his West German state. To accomplish his aim, Dethleffsen noted that responsible, reliable former soldiers, economically independent and politically informed, must prepare the way by educating others.[45]

During the tense summer of 1950, prominent former generals quickly stepped in to provide the education to which Dethleffsen referred. In September, Hasso von Manteuffel, Heinz Guderian, and Kurt Dittmar had formulated six elements they wanted to be included in the West's "dowry" for the coming "military marriage of convenience." Three of the elements related to command issues, providing for German corps commanders and representation on the supreme commander's (that is, Bernard Law Montgomery's) staff. One demand was military and nationalist: "recognition of the Elbe instead of the Rhine as the line of defense." The final two elements were long-standing demands of the military subculture within the veterans' organizations: the provision of adequate pensions for soldiers and their families and the transfer of convicted war criminals to German jurisdiction.[46]

The *Manchester Guardian* commented that "a German general with 'Eastern experience' would not be a bad addition" to European defense.[47] The *Guardian* chose not to highlight the implications of the generals' statement, which included the demands for equality and semisovereignty that were the cornerstones of Adenauer's policy, as well as the pension and war criminal demands later adopted by the veterans' organizations. Nor did the newspaper comment on the notion of "forward defense" along the Elbe (eventually instituted by NATO). The marriage of convenience that the generals proposed would be largely on West Germany's terms.[48]

Simultaneously and often independently, other veterans' leaders were coming to the same conclusions. Johannes Frießner, upon his release from prison after the Nuremberg trials, became actively engaged in lobbying for the release of his fellow inmates. He recognized that the Korean War could redound to the benefit of those "so-called" war criminals (as he always referred to them). On 15 August 1950, his associate, Hans Korte, agreed with Frießner that "Korea and such, and especially the unavoidable, pressing need to help Europe, that is to rearm, should in my opinion be helpful and accelerate the process."[49] At meetings of former soldiers all over Germany, a strange sort of optimism spread, mixed with fear of the consequences of a Soviet invasion. Rearmament could mean the end of their postwar struggles.[50]

Because of the auspicious situation, former officers pursued the subject of rearmament with a remarkable intensity. In December, a flyer circulated by former major general Heinrich Claes and former police colonel Hermann Müller-Brandenburg entitled "The Reputation and Right of the Former German Career Soldier" added yet another voice to the rising chorus calling for pensions and the recognition of soldiers' rights as the quid pro quo for reenlistment. The sooner the officers' rights were recognized, Claes and Müller-Brandenburg argued, the greater the benefit for the state. Wehrmacht veterans would be indispensable experts in the defense of Europe against the Soviets. "But how can the state expect the former career soldier to place himself at its disposal gladly and filled with good will," the veterans asked, "so long as they are still defamed and their well-earned rights have not been reestablished?"[51]

The demands of Manteuffel, Guderian, Frießner, and Claes quickly became the standard cry of former soldiers who refused to be "the silent tools of a foreign military and political will, neither as slave-battalions nor as [prison guards]." Former officers all over the Federal Republic declared that they would serve only when Germany was an equal partner in the Western alliance and the war criminals were free.[52]

Relying on the tried and true methods developed in the late 1940s during their struggle to organize, Hansen and the other veterans' leaders used thinly veiled threats and the government's fear of radicalism to create a basis for further negotiations. Noisy, if not necessarily radical, demonstrations against rearmament, such as the one during which Blank was showered with beer mugs, caused concern among parliamentary leaders. Hansen was aware of these concerns.[53] He and other leaders made every effort to make it clear that the resolution of their social concerns could help to "increase their willingness to serve."[54]

Groups like Hansen's were always crippled, however, by their patriotism and by the widespread notion that German soldiers were champing at the bit to serve in the military again. Such ideas no doubt shared a great deal with the defamatory sentiments that filled Germany's newspapers in the early postwar years concerning militarism and the Wehrmacht's responsibility for World War II. As a result, the veterans' organizations had to tread the fine line indicated by Dethleffsen between shirking their self-proclaimed duties and appearing too bloodthirsty. Hansen formulated the position of the early BvW (and many former officers in general) concisely in a December 1950 letter to a female member. "We stand between two poles," Hansen wrote. "We must be ready to secure the peace, freedom, and life of our people. We must also demand, however, that every instance of defamation disappear and that full equality be reestablished before we can join in the common occidental defensive front." Hansen knew that patriotic veterans could not simply stand by while their country was in danger, however. "In the dire emergency of our Volk we are here," he added. "We are ready. That is clear. We need not talk of that much more."[55] Hansen nevertheless talked about it for years to come, though his position stayed largely the same.

Into 1951, the position of "yes ... but" remained the dominant one among former officers. Most discussions of the rearmament issue therefore began with the officers' affirming their willingness to serve in the interests of the epic struggle (as they saw it) then playing itself out in Germany. However, the initial declaration of principles was universally followed by a quid pro quo of some sort. German equality was a constant matter of concern, but veterans' leaders knew that they shared that concern with Adenauer, who, they understood, would devise the final policy. "In any case," one officer insisted, "the more forcefully soldiers pressure him in this sense, the more difficult it will be for him to decide for a 'yes' before the question is addressed."⁵⁶ Not only do such statements suggest a certain political savvy on the part of the former officers (in understanding, for example, Adenauer's democratic–autocratic style of rule), but they also indicate the power that former officers felt they possessed after 1950.⁵⁷

The same combination of moralizing and threatening, promising and demanding, remained the mainstream veterans' organizations' policy until the Bundeswehr's foundation in 1955 brought the speculation concerning rearmament to an end. In May 1955, Hansen addressed one last plea to Adenauer for the satisfaction of the VDS's demands. He called it "unbearable" that Germans be asked to serve shoulder to shoulder with the soldiers of nations still holding Wehrmacht veterans captive. The postwar defamation of the Wehrmacht and the denial of pensions also rankled. Hansen could not resist pointing out that "the Verband Deutscher Soldaten—perhaps the only German veterans' organization to do so—has fought for military readiness. That has not prevented, however, the sons of former career soldiers from having doubts about a state that failed to fulfill its obligations to their fathers."⁵⁸ Those sons, the recruits needed to fill the new army's ranks, would draw their own conclusions.

Still, while expressing bitterness over their treatment since 1945, former officers desired rearmament. They threatened to remain uninterested and they made their demands, but soldiering had been these men's lives. The opportunity to serve their Fatherland once more had a great appeal, even among those who met with some measure of economic success during the early postwar years. Older officers especially, for whom reenlistment was not an option, wished to affect the course of rearmament and so make their contribution to the revival of Germany as a sovereign nation. Those sorts of issues and emotions, combined with the palpable sense of threat from the East, helped to win many former officers for the cause of West German rearmament. For most soldiers, even as early as 1950, the question of rearmament was moot; there remained only the (still significant) "how and when."⁵⁹

Despite their reservations, many former officers cooperated with the government in its effort to reconstruct the German army. One such officer was Dethleffsen, who not only wrote the 1949 article that laid down one of the earliest formulations of soldiers' demands, but who also became one of the Federal Republic's most active lobbyists for rearmament. Dethleffsen had been involved in educational matters in the Wehrmacht, and the newly formed Blank Office solicited his opinion both formally and informally on several occasions regarding the structure of education and instruction in the proposed new army. Dethleffsen corresponded regularly with the Blank Office's military advisers, Adolf Heusinger, Hans Speidel, and Johann Adolf von Kielmansegg, as well as with prominent soldier-politicians like Manteuffel; the leaders of veterans' organizations, like Hansen and Frießner; and publicists—namely, the *Frankfurter Allgemeine Zeitung*'s Adelbert Weinstein.[60]

Dethleffsen established a reputation as a lucid and impartial thinker on a subject that often sent other officers into paroxysms of anxiety or anger. His articles and speeches on the German soldier's postwar situation, the importance of military education, or the social and economic elements of rearmament almost uniformly contained keen insights into the realities of the period. Nevertheless, Dethleffsen exhibited the strange blend of idealism and faith in moral factors that characterized former officers' writing at the time. A speech Dethleffsen gave in 1951 at St. Paul's Church in Frankfurt am Main indicated both his ability clearly to state the central issues of the rearmament debate among former officers and the degree to which the debate was imbued with quasireligious ideas of rearmament's importance. He reminded his listeners that ultimately the defense of Germany was in everyone's interest. Any specific preconditions lost their significance if veterans asked themselves, " 'Should I take up arms for my Volk and the future of my children?' Then the answer comes much easier."

"I will admit to you," Dethleffsen later wrote of the speech to a friend, "even if I did not say so in St. Paul's Church, that I am actually of the opinion that one should not link the question of Werl and Landsberg with the political decision [for rearmament]." To do so would confuse morality (a principled stand on the war criminals issue) with political bargaining (over military policy).[61] In making such a statement, Dethleffsen hit upon the one element of the rearmament issue that linked it so closely to the former officers' ideas of politics. Rearmament, like politics, was a question of morality and ethics for many Wehrmacht veterans. To reduce such an important issue to the political level and—worst of all—to entrust its resolution to politicians seemed to be a mistake. Therefore, because of their renowned sense of patriotism, responsibility, and apoliticalness, the veterans and their organizations felt called upon and uniquely capable to comment on the government's plans and to propose their own solutions.[62]

Some groups, like the Society for Defense Information (Gesellschaft für Wehrkunde—GfW), were explicitly formed "independently to address all questions of German defense legislation and defense politics" and "to interest individuals and public, cultural, and economic organizations in questions that relate to the German armed forces."[63] Other, more traditional veterans' organizations shared these goals and hoped by their contributions not only to secure their economic demands, but also to create the proper "moral atmosphere" for rearmament. Not surprisingly, what exactly the correct moral atmosphere was remained decidedly unclear.

Plans for Rearmament: Creating a "Moral Atmosphere"

Defense Minister Theodor Blank spoke before the VDS's Flensburg branch on 12 July 1956, saying the following in conclusion to the former soldiers present:

> I need you! You see, we have traveled a long, difficult road together, the older ones through two world wars, the younger through the last great war. We have both had to accept the difficult years after 1945. We must begin to do our duty despite the bitterness. We can only do that, however, when we can be sure of the help of the old soldiers. Even if not every old soldier can be a soldier again, the soldierly mission remains the same. The new German Bundeswehr will, as much as possible, repay its debt of gratitude to the old soldiers. Not only will it take in as many of the capable officers and noncommissioned officers as possible, but it will also offer a [means for] existence to the handicapped soldiers to the extent that it can. We will have an open heart for your cares and needs. We know that there remains much to be made good for the German soldiers. We need your expert advice, we need your good wishes, your positive support.[64]

No doubt good wishes and positive support were more welcome than expert advice in Blank's mind, given the problems his office had during the early 1950s with the demands and protests of groups like the VDS. Nevertheless, his statement reveals much about the government's attitude toward the established veterans' organizations during the development of the West German armed forces between 1950 and 1955. On several occasions, the government solicited the opinions of former officers regarding plans for rearmament.

In the years before 1955, veterans' leaders essentially took the government at its word, offering (sometimes) their support and good wishes and (more often) their advice and criticisms. Not only were former officers anxious to parlay the government's need for former soldiers into a bargaining chip in their pension fight, but they were also concerned that the Bundeswehr be staffed with the "right" soldiers and imbued with the proper spirit. Former admiral Konrad Albrecht circulated a leaflet in December 1950 addressed to the U.S. President that illustrated his comrades' concern for both their own situation and the ethos of the new armed forces. In petitioning for the release of Admirals Erich Raeder and Karl Dönitz, Albrecht insisted that "in order to ensure German cooperation, it is necessary to create the appropriate moral atmosphere and that nothing could be more helpful in this than restoring the two admirals to liberty."[65]

Albrecht's fear, shared by many of his comrades, was that without the proper guiding spirit, the new army would become a haven for bitter, unprincipled, even reactionary former soldiers. They recognized the danger that some soldiers, unlike Hans von Luck, may not have benefited from Germany's "economic miracle" and would hide their bitterness or their true feelings about democracy and the new army until they had already enlisted. One group of former soldiers believed that without the recovery of their honor, rearmament should not even be discussed. They recognized the reality of the situation, however. "Many who saw rearmament as a way out of unemployment would jump at the chance."[66]

Erich Dethleffsen, too, indicated that economics would undoubtedly play a role in the decision of many old soldiers to enlist. In "The Current Spiritual and Social Situation of Former Officers and Noncoms," Dethleffsen warned that reliable officers would for the most part have found good jobs in the civilian sector and would be reluctant to take a severe cut in pay, despite their desire to serve. Bitter, unrepentant former soldiers might pretend to overcome their objections to the reform measures proposed by the Blank Office in order to get good jobs that they were unable to find as civilians. Dethleffsen was aware that too many soldiers believed that changing the form was enough when, in fact, the army's spirit had to be renewed.[67]

Former officers were unable to separate their ideas about honor and character from their material demands or from the resolution of the war criminals issue. They did not see themselves as hypocritical or self-serving when they insisted on the satisfaction of their demands in exchange for their service. Only the restoration of "justice," as they defined it, could ensure that honorable soldiers would join the Bundeswehr. Simply saying "without me" would not be a viable option if an army were founded prior to the satisfaction of the soldiers' demands. Too many unprincipled veterans would reenlist anyway and occupy the positions of power. The key was to ensure that *"upstanding* and *brave* people [gain] control of the new army . . . men who are dedicated not to move until the honor issue is resolved." The new army, they believed, would be the perfect position from which to launch an offensive to restore justice.[68]

Concentrating on the moral issues of rearmament also allowed veterans to maintain the facade of being purely "unpolitical." Some organizations, in an effort to remain unpolitical, therefore expressly denied any involvement with concrete plans for rearmament and claimed to focus instead on the purely moral elements of the defense contribution. The DAK claimed not even to discuss rearmament, but rather solely to "attempt to maintain those values that were so exemplary in the desert—on both sides."[69] Their contribution to the new armed forces, insisted Crüwell in 1954, would be "only spiritual."[70] Indeed when a government official and former general Speidel spoke out against the "without me" attitude at a DAK meeting in 1956, a veteran screamed out in disgust, "We are not a propaganda company for the Bundeswehr!"[71]

Of course, DAK members could not resist commenting on the form and functions of the Bundeswehr, especially when it came to useful traditions to which the new army could refer. They most often held forth their "beloved Rommel" as the model of modern leadership and soldierly values, and the DAK cast its vote on the side of preserving military traditions whenever such issues arose. Despite the DAK's protestations of disinterest, its newsletter's editors wrote in 1956, "We want to help furnish the new house of the Bundeswehr." "The house must rest on the foundations of the old soldierly values of bravery, obedience, fulfillment of duty, and comradeship," the article proclaimed, without suggesting how such traditional values of duty and obedience could be reconciled with the efforts of the Bundeswehr's reformers to rethink the foundations of command.

The VDS, too, was ambivalent about its direct involvement in propagandizing and recruiting for the new German military. As mentioned above, the VDS was anxious to have official links to the government and to serve as the occupational representative of career soldiers. But at other times, the VDS, in trying to maintain its stance "above parties," fervently denied any such activity. In a circular to the various branches, the VDS's chief lobbyist, Kurt Linde, worried about a flyer that claimed the VDS would accept enlistments for the EDC at its meeting. "The League offers advice to those interested, it informs its membership about the goals and composition of a European Defense Community," Linde admonished, "but it must also avoid the appearance that it is conducting or sponsoring a sort of screening or preparatory procedure [for Bundeswehr recruits]."[72]

The motivations for such a carefully worded stance were manifold. In 1951, H.D. von Conrady recognized that any lobbying for conscription or the new army in West Germany would not only be unpopular with the public, already bled dry by two lost wars, but also within the VDS's ranks because of the perceived defamation campaign after 1945. German soldiers calling for rearmament would be certain to reawaken the Allies' fears and hinder the struggle for the Federal Republic's equality within the circle of Western powers.[73] Nevertheless, the VDS and other organizations clearly hoped to influence the course of developments. At a meeting of the CDU's Committee of Former Career Soldiers for Wehrmacht Issues in Bonn in June 1955, one delegate asserted the VDS's undisputed obligation to comment on the legislation necessary to establish the Bundeswehr. The perceived functions of the VDS, according to those present at the meeting, would be threefold:

1) Foreign–political: The United States and other foreign countries would closely watch statements by soldiers and look for evidence of the Federal Republic's trust in soldiers. Reactionary or radical statements by former soldiers could have a huge negative impact.
2) Domestic: The German public would be watching as well. While the veterans' organizations largely sided with the coalition parties (the FDP, CDU, and their partner, the Christian Social Union—CSU), any criticism of the proposed laws or treaties would put them on the side of the opposition and draw them into party-political struggles. Veterans' organizations were also in a good position to influence Germany's youth, though by what mechanism that would occur was unclear.
3) Organizational: The Bundeswehr could attract up to 50 percent of the VDS's membership; therefore, the VDS needed to retain those soldiers after they enlisted.

The group concluded by relating the VDS's commentary on the proposed bills (which at some level was a matter of organizational self-interest because of the consequences for its membership) to its oft-cited and high-minded mission of serving the German people. It should not automatically approve of rearmament in any form. The public would recognize any criticism for what it was: "a loyal contribution for the benefit of our entire Volk."[74]

As always, the veterans linked their ideas to the notion of service to the German people. As with their political and social ideas, former officers believed themselves capable of constructing a military force that would aid in the reformation of society by imbuing it with the soldierly values of loyalty, bravery, and a sense of responsibility. In principle, this placed them in agreement with the Blank Office, which believed that the Bundeswehr would provide a positive, democratic model of behavior to the German people. That the former career soldiers' claims about the need for honor and justice also served their own interests is undeniable. However, their demands for reform and their offers of expert advice were always more than a mere bargaining chip in their fight to regain their pensions. Contributing to rearmament was one of the ways in which former officers sought to serve the Volk. The issue thereby played an important role in their rehabilitation and adjustment to the Federal Republic.

Unfortunately for the former officers, the one bargaining chip that they unashamedly did use failed to be as powerful as they had hoped. As a result of early predictions that the number of volunteers would be far fewer than necessary to create an army, groups like the VDS hoped to establish themselves as recruitment centers for the new army and thereby gain some say in its construction. The VDS gathered from its membership letters stating the writers' willingness to enlist and then forwarded these to the Blank Office with the caveat that the former career soldiers would view their statements of intent as void if on the day of enlistment certain conditions were not satisfied. Hansen noted with satisfaction in 1952 that the German contingent of the EDC then being planned would need twenty-two thousand officers and eighty thousand noncommissioned officers, while only thirty-five thousand former career soldiers had volunteered by that point.[75]

The supposed strength inherent in this position proved ephemeral, however. In 1951, the Interior Ministry received over twenty thousand applications for the mere five hundred officer positions in the newly formed Federal Border Guard (Bundesgrenzschutz—BGS), which many at the time assumed would be the precursor to any new army.[76] The overapplication did not bode well for Hansen's hopes to wield power over the application process for the Bundeswehr. Indeed in June 1955, a former colonel Kurt Brandstädter (a member of the Blank Office) told a CDU gathering that his office had already received 135,000 applications for the Bundeswehr—roughly 40,000 from former officers, 80,000 from former noncommissioned officers, and 20,000 new applications.[77]

Creation of the Bundeswehr

Despite their increasingly obvious inability to affect the course of rearmament, former officers' leaders maintained their demands. Hasso von Manteuffel, now a Bundestag representative for the FDP, at a speech in Essen in 1954 demanded that the chancellor "restore the [pension] rights of the former soldiers in principle before the first volunteers for the new armed forces enter the barracks."[78] Though this passage reflects the weakening of the soldiers' position as the demand had changed to "in principle" from "in their entirety," the essence of the old soldiers' argument remains.

As late as July 1955, veterans' groups were still protesting the Bundeswehr's impending creation. The "Declaration of Protest against the Coming Entry into the New German Armed Forces" of the Bielefeld Soldiers' Circle (Bielefelder Soldatenring) reiterated Hansen's (and Manteuffel's) protest that new soldiers should not serve while former soldiers were still in Allied prisons. "The so often mentioned isolation of the Reichswehr was the consequence of the mistrust with which they were treated by the [political] parties. In the current negotiations in the Bundestag a mistrust shines through in such a way as newly to conjure up the same danger."[79]

Whether that danger would in fact be newly conjured was tested soon. On 12 November 1955, just one day after the anniversary of Germany's surrender in World War I, 101 men stood in a converted garage as the new defense minister, Theodor Blank, welcomed them into the Bundeswehr. Standing beneath a gigantic Iron Cross, the symbol of the new armed forces, Blank solemnly paid homage to the traditions of Germany's military past. Yet he took great pains to emphasize the new "citizen army's" democratic character, and few could escape the sense of a new departure in Blank's speech. The new spirit was even embodied in the decidedly un-German cut of the new soldiers' uniforms. Some commentators thought the assembled recruits resembled trolley-car conductors more than soldiers.[80]

The Bundeswehr's creation evoked criticism from former officers for a variety of reasons. Johannes Frießner objected to holding the historic induction ceremony in a garage. Former officers perceived further insult from the new uniforms. Frießner sarcastically remarked that the tailor had apparently not finished them. "They do not fit a German soldier and appear unsoldierly," he remarked. "If the events in Bonn on 12 November are truly what the press and radio of Germany and the world report—namely, an event of historical significance—then it was a bad beginning for our new army."[81]

Frießner approved of the adoption of the Iron Cross as the Bundeswehr's symbol, but his dismay over the uniforms shows that he, like many other former officers, missed the government's point. It had chosen the venue, designed the uniforms, and drafted the regulations that governed the behavior of Bundeswehr soldiers precisely to minimize the profile of the new armed forces and make them appear "unsoldierly." They were meant to be, according to the oft-used phrase, "citizens in uniform."

To avoid the charge of renewed militarism and ensure the future democratic nature of the Bundeswehr, the Blank Office adopted command principles known as "Innere Führung" or "Inneres Gefüge," which roughly translate as "internal leadership" or "internal guidance."[82] Official Bundeswehr publications variously describe "Internal Leadership" as an "idealistic goal," a "critical consciousness," "a program for a democratic army," a new way of conceiving of older principles of command, and a significant departure mandated by the nature of modern technology and ideological warfare.[83]

The variety of these definitions indicates the all-encompassing nature of "Internal Leadership." The most frequent justification for the concept was twofold. "Internal Leadership," the Defense Ministry explained, would enable the seamless incorporation of the armed forces into society and strengthen the soldiers' resistance to the novel forms of psychological warfare waged by communists by basing the military's command structures on democratic principles. The aim was to balance democratic freedoms with military authority. No one proposed that parliamentary procedures be adopted in the field. Rather, officers would command by means of respect, not coercion, and would serve as models of democratic soldiery. Attention should also be paid to the conscript's career goals, in order to smooth the transition from civilian to army life and back again. Ideally, the category of "career soldier" would all but disappear. Even the officers in that category should, while in the military, prepare for an eventual civilian career.[84] In principle, "Internal Leadership" would mean an end to parade drills and harsh treatment of trainees, a more relaxed barracks life, and an emphasis on self-discipline and responsibility in training. Practically, it meant an incessant flow of prodemocratic and anticommunist propaganda directed at the soldiers for the purpose of "spiritual armament."

While spiritual armament may have sounded appealing to them, the traditional veterans' organizations were bound to be ambivalent toward the new Bundeswehr and its guiding democratic ethos. Not only did the Bundeswehr's notion of "Internal Leadership" seem too vague and coddling to former officers, but also the new army proposed to do away with the concept of a career soldier by encouraging even its longer-serving officers to prepare themselves for civilian careers while in uniform. Veterans' groups by their existence also contradicted the principle of a "citizen in uniform." Groups like the VDS both consciously and unconsciously promoted the separation of their members from the majority of citizens.[85] By maintaining the old traditions and bonds of comradeship and promoting the esprit of the officer corps, they formed a group identity that clashed with the Defense Ministry's idea of a seamless transition between military and civilian life.

In the end the Bundeswehr struck a huge blow to the hopes of the VDS and the other veterans' organizations to maintain their membership. The vast majority of soldiers in the new army chose, after their period of service, to join the new Bundeswehrverband (Bundeswehr League) rather than the VDS. The VDS consisted not only primarily of officers (that had been decided in 1951 with the collapse of hopes for a unified organization), but also of Wehrmacht officers. Some veterans' leaders even suspected the government of practicing divide and conquer tactics, encouraging a large number of veterans' organizations so that each one would be powerless.[86] So much for the soothing words spoken by Blank at Flensburg. Older veterans were free to conduct their own affairs, but their expert advice was increasingly ignored and their influence would not be welcomed among the Bundeswehr's recruits.

The vast majority of former officers actively participated in mainstream political life in West Germany by being members of large political parties and special interest groups like the veterans' organizations. Koshar's study of the Marburg middle class in the decades prior to 1945 suggests that veterans' and other similar organizations gave their constituents "a chance to talk about political events, form contacts, and gain parliamentary skills" despite their claims to shut out politics.[87] In their dealings with the mainstream political parties, former officers often displayed considerable savvy. They tailored their arguments to suit certain audiences, appealed to the parties' desires for power by threatening to withhold their votes, lobbied for their material interests, and made deals with the government.

As Koshar's study proves, however, vital associational life does not automatically produce stable parliamentary democracy. National Socialism, not Weimar democracy, satisfied the Marburg middle class's yearning for a unified folk community.[88] The Nazis manipulated that yearning to produce a barbaric, genocidal system of rule. Yet despite its eventual corruption, the middle class's urge for spiritual national unity sprang from altruistic sources, from a "political passion and a sincere desire to rise above one's personal and corporate interest."[89] The veterans' organizations of the 1950s provided a framework for officers to express similar passions. The larger political context hindered their grasping for the radical solutions of the 1920s.

While expressing their passions, former officers betrayed their affinity for the vague ideological programs of marginal groups. These soldiers, imprisoned by the Allies and marginalized by postwar German society, maintained, partly in self-defense, that their one desire was further to serve the German people by providing a moral example, a "soldierly conscience." Despite their preference for movements and communities of deed, however, the political effects of their activism were negligible. Much like a nagging conscience, the bearers of the traditions of German soldierdom were content to peck away with their arguments about radical change at the remote edges of the Federal Republic's political consciousness, while they addressed their material demands through regular political channels.

Even in discussions of rearmament, former career soldiers with few exceptions (namely, those men who worked in the Blank Office) remained marginalized and out of touch regarding the developments that preceded the Bundeswehr's creation in 1955. Their ideas and proposals simply had too little in common with the West German government's desires or the possibilities of the postwar era. Former general Friedrich Wilhelm Hauck, in a speech at Bad Boll in 1952, insisted, for example, that the new army must have well-tailored and striking uniforms; otherwise a heroic death on the battlefield would no longer be possible. "If one makes the uniform into overalls, then death on the battlefield becomes an industrial accident."[90] Such ideas appealed to many former officers, the same men who fought for the right to wear the medals awarded to them during the Third Reich, but public or official acceptance of such ideas was unlikely.

There were undoubtedly some positive aspects of the former officers' participation (however marginal) in the rearmament debates. As was the case in the economic realm, government officials treated former soldiers with a degree of respect, even if many soldiers remained skeptical of the government's sincerity. Also, soldiers somewhat ironically took the same stance as the SPD toward rearmament by sharing that party's demand that only in the context of a total commitment to the defense of Germany was a military contingent meaningful.[91] No doubt such tacit agreement between former soldiers and the party of parliamentary opposition did much to break down the traditional antipathy between former soldiers and the Social Democrats. Promising as well was their basic affirmation of rearmament proposals. Even a "yes . . . but" answer indicated that former officers felt that the Federal Republic was worth defending.

Despite these positive experiences, however, the older former officers eventually faded even further from the picture once the Bundeswehr was formed. Even the Evangelical Academy in Bad Boll, which in the early and mid-1950s had so prominently featured the voices of men like Hauck and General Heinrich von Vietinghoff, by 1959 relied almost exclusively on Bundeswehr personnel and government officials to speak at its meetings.[92] The arguments made by career soldiers were restricted largely within the boundaries of their own subculture, where others like themselves felt a strong emotional attachment to honor, tradition, and the military's "eternal values."

5

A European Fatherland?
Anticommunism and European Defense

During the late 1940s and early 1950s, proposals for a pan-European federation or supranational governing body gripped the imagination of many West Europeans. European unification intrigued former officers, too, as did the promises of peace and protection from the Soviets that such plans held forth. However, as was the case with their ideas about politics and political parties, career soldiers often thought of European unification in ways, although not entirely unique to soldiers, at least largely determined by their experiences, prejudices, and desires for postwar Germany.

The military and political situation in Europe after 1949 allowed former officers to lobby and express their ideals in such a way that their tactics and their principles largely coincided. The threat of the Soviet Union and the European efforts to counter that threat played directly into the hands of the nationalist, anticommunist veterans. As noted, the occupying powers and the federal government occasionally sought the participation of former officers in the new plans for German and European defense, and those men and their organizations thereby gained a bargaining chip in their quest for the reestablishment of their "honor" and "rights." The former officers exploited the Allies' and the Federal Republic's fears in order to achieve their goals of better pensions, the release of the so-called war criminals, and the restoration of their honor.

The officers' support for the West and their willingness to defend Germany were not mere tactical considerations, however. Their deeply rooted social and political beliefs, sense of nationalism, and perceptions of history profoundly influenced their ideas. To the former officers for whom service to the Fatherland was the centerpiece of their self-image,

Germany's situation in Europe was extremely distressing. Germany's continued division, the Soviet Union's increasingly hostile attitude, and their perception of the Allies' unwillingness or inability to meet the Soviet threat prompted much hand-wringing among former soldiers. The lively debate within the Western zones concerning the role of Germany and a united Europe in resisting the growing menace of Soviet communism struck a powerful chord within the ranks of the former officers. In both their public meetings and their private letters, they incessantly appraised the desirability and feasibility of plans for German and European unification and rearmament, and they frequently formulated their own proposals.

As patriotic Germans, however, the former officers faced difficulties in discussing European unification. They were pleased that those in power in the late 1940s conceived of a unified Europe as an anticommunist alliance. The soldiers were not always willing to accept that the plans for union also included a tacit acceptance of the status quo and a reliance on other Western nations' good faith. Many former officers still harbored resentment for their captivity and the postwar measures against soldiers. Some took a page from Goebbels's handbook and blamed the Allies for the division of Germany, made possible, they believed, only by the aid given to the Soviet Union during World War II.[1] Nor could the former officers easily accept the division of Germany and the loss of its former eastern provinces. Their patriotism made them unwilling to serve in a "foreign" army and demanded not only a defense against further aggression, but also the recovery of territory from the Soviet Union.

The officers also discussed European unification and defense in idealistic terms. They felt that their primary contribution to both Europe and Germany would be a restoration of values such as forthrightness, bravery, and a sense of responsibility that were the particular province of soldiers. Europe could not be defended, they argued, without some principle to motivate its soldiers. They worried a great deal about the German people's alleged materialism and selfishness and German youth's apparent unwillingness to participate in their country's defense. Even more than Germany's military impotence, this "moral weakness," they feared, portended a social and ideological cataclysm that would dwarf the military catastrophe of 1945.

European Movements toward Unification

The backdrop for most of these discussions among the former officers was the widespread public and governmental interest in European unification and European defense. Walter Lipgens identified two common beliefs inspiring European integration after World War II.[2] The first, popular after 1945 in Western Europe, was that "'lawlessness in the relations between states that always creates wars' [could] only be overcome by means of federal systems and a merging of sovereignty under one common authority by popular vote."[3] The second prevalent belief was that Europe, suffering the devastating effects of two world wars, could compete on relatively equal terms with the two dominant superpowers only if it somehow pooled its resources and strove for common goals.

Resistance groups in Germany, France, and elsewhere stimulated these beliefs by publishing often detailed plans for such unification upon their emergence from underground. European governments and the United States stifled these early movements, however. The Soviet Union effectively vetoed any proposals in the direction of European unity, seeing them as fundamentally anticommunist and preferring to reestablish smaller nation-states.[4] Nationalists in both Britain and France, where Charles de Gaulle ruled in Bonapartist style for the first nine months after the war, also resisted any infringements on their sovereignty.

Within Germany, the infrastructural collapse (which made communications difficult at best) and the chaotic political situation meant that initial proposals for European unification were isolated and ineffective. Occupation authorities refused to license groups that advocated such ideas in the first months after the war, but the single month of June 1946 saw the establishment of four separate groups calling for the unification of Europe.[5] Other groups followed suit in the wake of public speeches by Prime Minister Winston Churchill and U.S. Secretary of State James Byrnes that called for a "United States of Europe" and promised to help the Germans "win their way back" into the community of nations.[6]

"The European movement in Germany," Lipgens writes, "was distinguished by a motivation that operated more strongly than in other countries and tended to give its utterances a philosophical rather than a political flavour." Even German nationalists viewed European unification "not as merely a matter of everyday politics but as a historical opportunity to escape from the predicament of the German collapse."[7]

Not until 1947 did the United States' Marshall Plan and a new policy toward regional security arrangements create the opportunity for Europe to integrate more effectively. Only then did the various West European governments, in conjunction with the United States, establish the institutions that eventually developed into the foundations of the European Economic Community, such as the Organization for European Economic Cooperation (1947), the Council of Europe (1948), NATO (1949), and the Common Coal and Steel Market (1953).[8]

Ideas about what exactly constituted European unification were in flux in the late 1940s and early 1950s. The sheer number of organizations founded within Germany and across Europe indicates both the enormous general popularity of the notion and the diversity of opinions. Former officers entered the discussions of European unification and defense as patriots, idealists, and as an interest group—a combination that made those discussions revealing studies of the soldiers' worldview. Many of these discussions took place in the Evangelical Academies of the German Protestant Church.

Soldiers' Conventions at the Evangelical Academies

The Evangelical Academies of the German Protestant Church played an important role in elaborating and documenting the interplay among the former officers' concerns for Germany, their self-image, and the public debates over European unification. At an early date, the Protestant Church identified itself with both the soldiers' plight and the movement for European unity.[9] Some of Gottfried Hansen's earliest contacts were church officials in both Germany and Britain. Beginning in 1950, the academies at Bad Boll (near Göppingen, east of Stuttgart) and Hermannsburg (north of Celle) sponsored "soldiers' conventions," with the intent of helping soldiers to confront the crises of conscience engendered by their service under the Third Reich and the defamation of the German soldier after 1945. The meetings often exploded those narrow limits and became forums for the discussion of rearmament, European unification, and the soldier's role in postwar society. Attended by prominent and common soldiers alike, the meetings attracted the attention of the media and government and therefore became important vehicles for the creation of "soldiers' opinion" and the spread of government propaganda.

The meetings attracted many prominent figures from Germany's military past. The lists of participants at the first four conferences at Bad Boll include Heinrich von Vietinghoff, Smilo Freiherr von Lüttwitz, Heinz Guderian, Gotthard Heinrici, Siegfried von Stülpnagel, and Erich von Manstein. Many figures at the meetings achieved fame only later, as members of the Blank Office and founders of the Bundeswehr. Wolf von Baudissin was a regular attendee at the meetings at Bad Boll, and his presence illustrated the growing government interest in controlling or evaluating the meetings' progress. In addition to Baudissin, Theodor Blank, Adenauer's future defense minister, and Fritz Erler, an SPD expert on defense, were among the speakers during the early 1950s.[10]

Heinrich Eberbach, an advocate of German rearmament in a European framework, organized the events at Bad Boll. Eberbach sought the government's participation and advice when planning the meetings. The former general corresponded frequently with the Blank Office, sending it his thoughts on how to gain former soldiers' support, as well as copies of the conference invitation lists, with likely candidates for a future officer corps highlighted.[11]

The meetings at Bad Boll and Hermannsburg (later Loccum) retained a certain religious flair by virtue of the sponsorship of the Evangelical Church. Numerous lecturers and discussion participants, both former soldiers and church officials, went to sometimes ungainly lengths to incorporate religion into their topics.[12] Some officers worried that Eberhard Müller, the leader of the academy, tried too hard to steer the discussions into religious topics, resulting in the soldiers' voices being drowned out by those of the theologians. A former soldier who attended a 1951 meeting at Bad Boll wrote to the academy and called the weekend fabulous insofar as it dealt with the military but added, "I don't quite know what to make of the theological hair-splitting."[13] But over time, the growing influence of Eberbach and increasing consultations with the Blank Office caused the discussions to stray far from their initial mission of bringing young soldiers and officers closer to the church. The meetings eventually became instruments for enlisting former officers in the Federal Republic's efforts to rearm. They also proved to be valuable tools for the molding of public opinion on the issues of European unification and rearmament.

Reflecting on the Past

One of the earliest meetings took place at the Evangelical Academy in Bad Boll in November 1950 and was called simply "Days of Reflection for Former Soldiers." In his invitation to prospective participants, the bishop of Württemberg expressed sympathy for former soldiers who suffered because of their service in the Wehrmacht while many leading proponents of Nazism went unpunished. The bishop rejected the argument that soldiers were by definition militarists and suggested that enough time had already passed to "subject past events to a sober examination." He urged his listeners "carefully [to] distinguish between the good, the superfluous, and the disastrous elements of the old soldierly tradition. We wish to try, in a comradely discussion, to tackle this problem in all openness."[14]

The event's organizers, Eberbach and Müller, wanted to provide a forum in which younger officers could reflect on their experiences during and after the war. They intended, as Eberbach wrote in a letter to other church officials in Württemberg, to bring the "war generation" closer to the church from which they had been alienated as Hitler Youth or SS officers.[15] The program therefore included lectures and panel discussions on topics such as "The 20th July—Oath and Responsibility," "The Former Career Soldier in the Struggle for Existence—Did His Education Stand the Test?," and "The Reservations of Former Officers toward Christianity and the Church."[16]

The main themes for the event, for which planning began prior to the Korean War, changed only slightly to reflect the renewed focus on German rearmament sparked by events in Asia. In his opening remarks, Eberbach departed from the concentration on the past implicit in the title "Days of Reflection" to emphasize the importance of such a meeting for the future of Germany and Europe. "The undigested wartime and postwar experiences must be cleared up," he stressed, "as an internal prerequisite for every further step" toward rearmament. Eberbach reminded his listeners that "we all stand here today with the same responsibility and search for a new path for Europe."[17]

The first discussions at Bad Boll also provided former officers with a platform from which they could publicly declare their stance on rearmament. Veterans' leaders quickly learned to exploit this opportunity. While men such as Hansen and Dethleffsen had the government's ear and made their misgivings known to those in responsible places, Bad Boll brought the stance of the soldiers to the public.[18] "The opinion of the former soldiers assembled at Bad Boll," the *Frankfurter Allgemeine Zeitung* reported, "was so unanimous and firm regarding rearmament that it can be summarized in one sentence, yelled excitedly by one of the younger officers in the hall: 'I cannot become a soldier in order to be the watchman at the prison door of Field Marshal von Manstein!'"[19] As described above, this was the position of every veterans' group and had been featured in every appeal, admonition, or outcry directed at the government by those organizations. The meeting at Bad Boll brought that stance to the public in a much more immediate form.

Nevertheless, the lectures and panel discussions, as well as the private and press reactions to the first convocation at Bad Boll, remained focused on the reflective elements of the topic. The American-sponsored *Neue Zeitung*'s headline called it a "discussion of the soldierly oath and responsibility," while the *Frankfurter Allgemeine Zeitung* and several letters from the participants to the organizers after the meeting similarly stressed the efforts to deal with the soldiers' oath to Hitler and to draw lessons from the past.[20]

Nationalism and German History

The themes of responsibility and "undigested wartime experiences" were inextricably linked to the soldiers' notions of nationalism and German history, and the discussions at Bad Boll mirrored former officers' private ruminations on the subject. Expressions of German nationalism were not popular in government circles or public forums after the collapse of the Third Reich. They were especially suspect when uttered by former soldiers. Terms such as "Fatherland" and "nationalism" were too closely linked to the memories of "living space" (*Lebensraum*) and National Socialism. Nevertheless, and in part owing to the "defamation" they suffered, former officers expressed love of their Fatherland and pride in having served Germany in one (and sometimes two) world wars.

The officers realized that "nationalism" was a negative term after 1945 and feared that it had lost its appeal among Germany's youth.[21] A healthy sense of nationalism, veterans' leaders argued, was necessary in order to meet the challenges they saw facing Germany, including the challenge of European unification. It was therefore their duty, as representatives of their people and carriers of the nationalist idea, to reinstill pride in their nation. The uniformity with which officers upheld the established benchmarks of nationalism, such as calling the German Democratic Republic "the Soviet zone" or even "Central Germany" (in reference to the lost territories in the east) or maintaining the plight of Berlin in the public consciousness, was remarkable.[22]

The former officers were not necessarily allied with other national-minded and anticommunist groups, however, particularly those on the extreme right. In fact, the groups striving most directly for a restoration of the Third Reich, such as the Socialist Reich Party (SRP), frequently promulgated a new variation of the notorious "stab in the back" myth. The new legend was critical of the *military* rather than the *political* leadership of the Third Reich. This new variant of the myth could cause the greatest mischief, according to the chairman of the Bavarian SPD, because it attempted to place the blame for defeat not on Hitler and his policies, but on the officers who sabotaged the war effort by (among other things) plotting to overthrow the Nazi regime in the famous coup attempt of 20 July 1944.[23] Nationalists they were, but former officers found few friends on the radical right.

To cultivate healthy nationalism, former soldiers advocated an honest appraisal of the Third Reich. In their memoirs, newsletters, and private correspondence, veterans' leaders incessantly called for Germans to confront their history in order to remove the burden of past crimes from the national conscience. Most often, "honesty" meant simply acknowledging the Wehrmacht's shortcomings, which had contributed to Germany's defeat, or being critical of certain traits in the German national character. This confrontation with the past sometimes devolved into histrionic episodes of self-flagellation. In a particularly striking example, Hans von Donat, in a manuscript entitled "A General Experiences Hitler and Nazism," launched into a tirade against the German people that included page after page of the German people's faults. "The Germans are . . . ," he began each page, followed by, "sickly vain and megalomaniac, ... gullible," brutal, jealous, and many other adjectives. Germans had poor childhoods, brutal mothers, and lacked civic courage, according to Donat.[24] Such observations were no doubt products of the resentment felt by many former officers at being let down by their own people. The officers could understand an enemy's hostility but not that of the Germans themselves, and they often responded bitterly.

More often, the officers presented what amounted to apologies for Germany's historical behavior. One popular excuse was the assertion that the Germans were not an aggressive and warlike nation as the Allies would have the world believe. In response to an article in a newspaper from the American zone that claimed that "Germans had been raised for more than 100 years only as aggressive warriors," former major general Friedrich von Mantey examined the wars between 1806 and 1914 and found the British, that paragon of democratic peoples, to have been the period's main combatants.[25] An historian from the United States lent this argument an air of respectability when he assembled a table of combatant nations over the preceding two centuries and placed Germany near the bottom of the list in terms of number of wars fought.[26]

These "honest" self-appraisals frequently concealed radical (if not always intentional) distortions of the truth. One prevalent interpretation of the meaning of the Third Reich and World War II was that both were part of a longer epic struggle between Europe and communism. Hermann Tholens believed that Hitler had "saved" Europe by staving off communist revolutions in several countries. Unemployment, agrarian debt, hopelessness, and the growth of the Communist Party made Germany ripe for Bolshevik revolution in 1933, according to Tholens. Only National Socialism saved the nation from disaster.[27] Tholens goes even further to credit National Socialism with the "salutary" effects of the defeat of communism in Spain and Léon Blum's overthrow in France. No doubt Hitler played a role in each of those two events, but to infer therefore that Hitler saved or stabilized Europe is utterly mistaken.[28]

Such interpretations indicate how willing many former officers were to believe that Hitler's regime had positive effects on Germany and Europe, and they consisted of two elements. Tholens mentioned the common assertion that Hitler solved the unemployment problem arising from the Great Depression. Among career soldiers, of course, the revival of military power that took place under National Socialism was extremely popular because it meant better career opportunities for them. That advancement within Hitler's army required officers at least outwardly to adopt a National Socialist frame of mind was a proviso that usually went unmentioned.

The second element of this interpretation was that German history, and in particular World War II, was the story of a cultural struggle between Europe and Asia. Such an interpretation has a long heritage. In 1914, the Kaiser and other elites cast World War I as the battle between Teutons and Slavs. The tendency to interpret history according to racial categories only increased during World War II, when Nazi anti-Semitism and Goebbels's propaganda machine encouraged soldiers to see the conflict as a watershed, a revolutionary battle for a new world order.[29] As a result, the former officers' interpretation of history was heavily tinged with racist and social Darwinist notions of the conflict of peoples and with barely camouflaged Nazi slogans. The former officers saw World War II and the impending Cold War as the continuing struggle of the "hard and unassuming" Asians against the "civilized" peoples of the West.[30]

Johannes Frießner, a major propagator of such historical myths, said, "We East Front soldiers knew exactly what it was all for, from the highest commander to the last man on the front. Each knew that he was obligated to protect his *Heimat*, house and home, in the end even freedom and culture."[31] According to Frießner the German soldier's mission during World War II had been a crusade against Bolshevism in defense of Europe. Soldiers fought with determination against the Soviet foe, not simply to prolong the war, Frießner argued, "but rather to prevent with every means—and when necessary—through the loss of our lives, the invasion of the Asians into the European cultural realm and therefore the extermination of our European essence."[32]

Frießner was not alone in depicting World War II as the battle of European culture versus Asiatic barbarism. One striking example appears in a letter from Helmar Langer to Frießner in which Langer ostentatiously declares his decision to join the newly formed VDS. "Through six unspeakable, difficult years of war," Langer wrote, "millions of German soldiers, and with them many other nations and peoples, stood shoulder to shoulder in the battle to preserve the occidental world. The outcome of this struggle is known." The VDS's appearance represented for Langer a battle cry, "the issuance of the last German reveille and as a consequence the last European–German act! In recognition of this . . . , as well as in the hope for the energetic fulfillment of the guidelines of the League of German Soldiers, I join it."[33] Langer concluded with a brief reference to his hopes for the fulfillment of the VDS's material demands as well, but the epilogue does not detract from the meaning of his ideals. Langer's sentiments certainly occupy one extreme of the spectrum of ideas held by VDS members, but many former officers shared Langer's feelings of living during a crucial period in world history, an epic culmination of thousands of years of historical evolution.

Years of Nazi propaganda affected the judgment of many former soldiers, who either consciously or unconsciously associated communism with the supposed "Jewish threat" that Hitler conjured. A member of the Christian Officers' Union who had been held prisoner in the Soviet Union recalled the "brutal faces" of the Russians and even told how an interpreter "of Jewish appearance" confiscated his copy of the New Testament as "propaganda."[34] Whether the interpreter was in fact Jewish is unclear and in any case immaterial for our purposes. The important point is that the officer suspected her of being Jewish, thus indicating his continued susceptibility to, and willingness to believe in, the Nazi propaganda linking Judaism and Bolshevism. One general even called the current struggle with the Soviet Union an extension of the "historical confrontation between German- and Slavdom" and called the Soviet occupation of Eastern Europe "the Asiatic–Bolshevist invasion," merely substituting the word "Asiatic" for "Judeo" in the litany so often intoned by Hitler and the Nazis.[35]

These memories, influenced by Goebbels's propaganda, of World War II as a European crusade against Bolshevism were a remarkably consistent leitmotif in the public pronouncements of former officers. Georg von Sodenstern even ventured that most Germans had seen the war as an "Atlantic" enterprise until the ill-advised demand for unconditional surrender by the United States and the other Allies opened Germany's eyes to its isolation in the fight against the Bolshevists.[36] It was a similarly grand feat of self-delusion to be able to state boldly and publicly, as did Frießner, that the entire course of World War II was a crusade against Bolshevism or to interpret, as did Langer, all six years of the war (including, of course, the campaigns against France and Britain) as "the battle to preserve the occidental world." Such historical gymnastics indicate that former officers hoped to make their nationalism more palatable by linking German national pride to its importance for the viability of Europe and European defense.

Another equally common argument linked German nationalism, and especially military prowess, to the survival of Europe. In postwar Germany, few contested such arguments. The Western Allies themselves clearly admired how well the Wehrmacht had fought against the Soviet Union and actively sought former officers' advice and assistance in defending Europe. The Americans hoped to tap into the wealth of German military experience when they set up such programs as the Operational History (German) Section in Allensdorf or the Naval Historical Team in Bremerhaven.[37] These groups consisted of former German officers who worked with the Americans in writing semiofficial histories of World War II from the German perspective. The projects were also meant to provide lessons for future conflicts. In his essay on the stance of former officers toward a defense commitment, Erich Dethleffsen highlighted the Allies' desire to preserve what they could of German military expertise when he concluded that "the Western world recognizes that because of our close contact with Bolshevism, we today have perhaps the strongest fighting spirit of the peoples of Europe and that our participation is the sine qua non for the defense of the Western world against a Russian attack on the continent."[38]

Former officers carried this notion back through history as well. The primary achievement of Germany, according to many of them, was its historic role as bulwark against the hordes of Asia. Hansen tried to emphasize the importance of a strong Germany in his English-language memorial sent to contacts in Great Britain and the British zone. Hansen recalled that since the foundation of the Holy Roman Empire, Germany had formed "the breastwork of the Occident and of Christianity against the onslaught of the assailing hords [sic] from the East, a bulwark that permitted the Western peoples of Europe to grow into nations and thereafter to take up their world-encompassing tasks centuries ago."[39]

Walter Görlitz, speaking to former soldiers at the Evangelical Academy at Loccum in 1954, offered a slightly more recent example of Germany's importance for Europe when he called Prussian field marshal Ludwig Yorck von Wartenburg (of Tauroggen fame), "the prophet of a unified Europe and the coming confrontation between continental power blocs."[40] Unfortunately, Görlitz left that comment and its contradictory implications largely unexplained. At a certain level, Yorck's era was merely analogous to the contemporary situation in Germany. In Yorck's time, two great continental powers (France and Russia) were vying for control of Europe, and the Prussian commander's choice in the winter of 1812–13 to join Russia and its allies represented a turning point in the history of Napoleon's domination of Europe. In the 1940s and 1950s, Germany was also the battleground between two opposing superpowers, and the Germans' "choice" for one side or the other could have been decisive. How Yorck's decision made him a "prophet of a unified Europe" is not so clear, however, or at least requires further explanation. Yorck also could be construed as one of history's most famous traitors, a fact that Görlitz left unmentioned. Yorck explicitly disobeyed his king's orders and turned his troops over to an invading army. The officers listening to Görlitz that day must have been aware of the parallels between Yorck's actions and, for example, those of Field Marshal von Paulus after the debacle at Stalingrad, yet no one mooted such a point in the discussions that followed Görlitz's lecture.

Wilhelm Ritter von Schramm, another frequent speaker at soldiers' gatherings, also tried to link German soldierdom to European unification by claiming that the men who staged the 20 July coup in 1944 were acting "in the sense of reconciliation, in the sense of a unified Europe, as one still hopes for today. These men were not traitors but pioneers of our times."[41] One problem with Schramm's thesis is that identifying "the" men of the July conspiracy is difficult, and attributing any single, clear idea to the group as a whole is even more problematic.[42] Adam von Trott zu Solz, an influential member of the Kreisau Circle (named for the aristocratic estate where the conspiratorial group met), did indeed propose a European federal system, but his plan can by no means be construed as expressing the other plotters' desires. The conspirators were simply too diverse in their backgrounds and beliefs for their thoughts to be categorized so neatly. From the conservative Carl Goerdeler to the idealistic and aristocratic Helmut James von Moltke, the leader of the Kreisau Circle, their ideas ran the gamut. In the end, many conspirators acted merely for the sake of action—out of a "sense of reconciliation," as Schramm suggested—and with little hope for success. However, too many of their ideas, like voting by family or restoring some sort of Bismarckian Mitteleuropa, were too anachronistic to consider them "pioneers of our times," as Schramm did.

Such statements about the meaning of Tauroggen or the 20 July conspiracy indicate the desire of German soldiers to prove that they were good Europeans. In trying to walk the fine line between enthusiasm for European unification and defense and their nationalist goals and desires to justify their own pasts, former soldiers encountered difficulties. Their manipulation of history to prove that World War II was a crusade against Bolshevism or that Yorck was a "prophet" carried with it the publicly unwelcome baggage that Hitler, who had started World War II, was also a good European and even a "prophet." The paradox inherent in publicly lionizing Moltke and Trott zu Solz while acknowledging the "insight" of Hitler, who had them both brutally executed, went unnoticed.

Germany was and had always been, the former officers believed, both the heartland of Europe and its defensive wall, both cultural center and frontier outpost of European civilization. Former officers truly believed in Europe as a philosophical construct, a "cultural zone," and as a political tool for resisting communism, but they found it difficult to abandon their belief in the central importance of Germany and the German Volk. At the back of all of these discussions of European unification was the adage cited by former bishop D. Theophil Wurm at the conclusion of his lecture at Bad Boll in 1950: "Respect every man's Fatherland, but love your own."[43]

Anticommunist Europe

Because of the public attention given to the first convention and the overwhelming interest of the participants, Eberbach and Müller gave later soldiers' conventions an even greater orientation toward the issues of rearmament and Europe. "The purpose of our first meeting ... was to aid the participants in reflecting and speaking out about the past," read the invitation to the 1951 conference. "Our second meeting looks ahead and will attempt to draw conclusions from the past and from the current circumstances." The Evangelical Academy was not the place to discuss the intricacies of military policy, insisted Eberbach, but it could effectively "deal with the question of which spirit, which tone, and which form a good armed forces ought to have." Since former soldiers were best qualified to clarify such questions, they had an obligation to do so.[44]

The second convention clearly reflected Müller and Eberbach's focus on the "new" issue of rearmament and the importance of a unified European front against communism. Lectures at the meeting in December 1951 carried titles such as "The Risk of a Defense Commitment," "The Ethos of a Defense Commitment," "To Safeguard or Create Tradition?," and "Leadership in the Military Units of the Future." As at the first convention, speakers were primarily soldiers and churchmen but included others as well, such as the editor of a French newspaper.[45]

According to the *Frankfurter Allgemeine Zeitung*, the idea of a unified Europe, and especially Franco-German cooperation, ran "like a red thread" through the discussions.[46] The discussions typically drifted toward the ideological and even the unreal.[47] The speakers at Bad Boll in 1951 stressed the ideological danger that the Soviet Union posed for Europe. In fact, this topic received almost as much attention as the more "practical" topics, such as the dangers and lessons to be learned from partisan warfare or the viability of past traditions for a new military. "The primary goal [of the Soviet Union]," Bundestag representative Robert Tillmanns reminded his listeners, "is the promulgation of world revolution." The military threat, he warned, was only one method, and by no means the most attractive, at the Soviets' disposal. Since the Soviet leaders believed that the triumph of communism was historically inevitable, they would be content to sit back and merely promote social and economic chaos in the West, hoping to speed the process of revolution. These were the motives, Tillmanns insisted, behind the recent Soviet diplomatic notes on the status of Germany: to break the unified European front that had emerged over the past few years in opposition to the communist powers.[48]

Following Tillmanns's speech was a lively discussion that illuminated the officers' concerns as well as their general approach to the threat of the Soviet Union. Surprisingly, many of those present accepted the relatively limited risk of an unprovoked Soviet attack on West Germany. Some participants expressed concerns that a strong European army might antagonize the Soviet Union and lead to a preventive war or that such an army might be used as a tool by the United States for a war of expansion. Tillmanns, in cooperation with Eberbach, quickly dismissed these arguments. Instead, arguments for an "ideological defense" against communist propaganda captured former officers' interest at Bad Boll. It is a pity, one participant lamented, "that we do not have anything to pit against the Russian chiliasm," citing the inadequacy of the current Western equivalents—democracy, rule of the masses, and the glorification of cinema values.[49]

Several participants expressed similar regrets that Europe had no motivating ideal similar to the Soviet Union's alleged faith in world revolution and social equality. "The West has a static idea. It wants to protect and defend what they call in America 'freedom and prosperity.' The East, however, has a dynamic idea. It has written world revolution and liberation on its flag."[50] Müller reminded the discussion participants that "in recent years Russia has conquered with cannons that do not fire."[51] Audience members frequently mentioned the possibility of a renewed military crusade to silence these "cannons," but this idea was always quickly rejected. None of the former soldiers or theologians wanted to live under communism, but neither did they have the stomach for another war.[52] War and communism could be resisted, many believed, only by a Europe well equipped with both armored divisions and defensible ideals.

Motivating European Soldiers

According to former officers, the viability of any proposed European army depended on the motivating ideology behind such a force rather than its practical organization.[53] Some officers had experience in motivating multinational forces. Johannes Frießner recalled commanding units in the Baltic along the Narwa River, which he called "the boundary between the Occident and Asia." On this remote front, "men of the Nordic peoples . . . fought for the European cultural idea on the soil of an allied, but foreign, country, Estonia." Yet despite the "idealism" of these "young, specially selected Nordic volunteers of the best racial stock," the soldiers still needed some motivation, some explanation to understand why they defended foreign soil.[54]

Frießner's thinly veiled reference to the Waffen-SS as the model for any future European army is shocking but not uncommon in postwar Germany. Understandably, the organizations of former Waffen-SS soldiers attempted to further the idea that the military wing of the SS was not only distinct from regular SS units, which were associated with the concentration camps, but was also "the first carrier of the European idea" in the fight against Bolshevism. The organization of former European soldiers of the Waffen-SS published an article in its newsletter, *Der Wiking-Ruf* (The Viking call), that claimed that Waffen-SS soldiers, drawn from many European nations, did not fight merely for Germany. While they viewed Germany "as the heartland of a united Europe and believed they saw in Germany the banner-carrier of a new social order, they fought *with* Germany, because there truly was no other way to protect Europe and therefore their homeland from the tidal wave of the Asian hordes." They fought against communism and for the European idea, they claimed.[55]

Former Wehrmacht officers were not always so anxious to propose the SS as the model for a European army, however. Even some who saw the East–West conflict in ideological terms were aware of the dangers of a resurgence of aggressive nationalism inherent in such a model. Erich Dethleffsen insisted that the notion of the SS as the precursor of a modern European army carried with it the vague notion of German leadership. Once the European nations created such an army, the growing power of Germany, which Dethleffsen felt was inevitable given its economic strength, would lead to an increased sense of self-worth among German soldiers and a concomitant breakdown in the spirit of cooperation necessary for the successful defense of Europe.[56] That there were problems other than German leadership associated with the Waffen-SS remained unmentioned. Nevertheless, former officers conceived of European unification and defense based on the experiences of German armed forces, whether Wehrmacht or Waffen-SS.[57]

The closest the participants at Bad Boll ever came to a consensus on a motivating ideology for a European army was a vague faith in "European culture" and Christianity. "We do not want 'killers' [as soldiers]," wrote W. Krelle following the 1951 meeting at Bad Boll, "but rather true carriers of European culture and the Christian traditions of the Occident."[58] Being a religious man, Eberhard Müller naturally focused on the potential of Christianity as a lowest common denominator, if not a unifying force. "It will be difficult to find a path through the diversity of ideas that impinge on us," he wrote in 1952, "if our ruminations are not anchored in the foundations of our faith, which has determined the last 2000 years of European history."[59]

The former officers, however, felt little real connection to the discussions of religion, even if their thoughts were sprinkled with such ideas. Future soldiers must be motivated by an appeal to the emotions, argued Hauck at one soldiers' convention. Such an appeal should include a consciousness of the duty to one's Volk and the cultural legacy of Europe. It would require a great awareness of history on the part of future officers, but it would be worth the effort, Hauck insisted.[60]

By referring to both Europe and Volk, Hauck illustrated the central element of the former officers' arguments. They saw Europe as a cultural entity and even supported some vague notion of unification in order to resist the threat of communism, but the big problem for former officers was reconciling their sense of nationalism with European unity. Their solution was unique: to express nationalism and national character *within* the idea of Europe. At the conclusion of the convention on "The Soldier and Public Opinion" at the Evangelical Academy in Hermannsburg, Baudissin summarized by proposing a list of tasks for the soldier in public, one of which was "to awaken a healthy national feeling because only a good German, Frenchman, etc. will be able to be a good European."[61]

Former soldiers expressed this sentiment elsewhere. The soldiers' organizations saw it as their duty to represent "the standpoint of a German patriotic sentiment based on an awareness of supranational European responsibility."[62] The parallel ideals of nationalism and a unified Europe came together in the statement of the VDS newsletter's goals, which included "engagement for the Volk and a unified Germany in the sense of the true, ethical, and traditional values of German soldierdom," as well as "the promotion of the necessary European community of fate and defense" and "a responsible declaration in favor of the Christian-occidental cultural realm."[63] Heinz Karst, a member of the Blank Office and later brigadier general of the Bundeswehr, concluded after speaking with former officers at a meeting of the former Fourth Panzer Division in Bamberg in 1953 that they were patriotic but truly open minded with regard to European unification.[64]

Despite occasional protestations to the effect that nationalism and the nation-state were outmoded forms of social organization, former officers could never bring themselves wholly to abandon "love of Fatherland" as a motivating ideology. Karl Koller, last chief of the Luftwaffe (air force) General Staff and VDS organizer in Bavaria, concluded his memoirs with a passage on Germany and Europe's future. "The Germans are a core people of Europe. According to their millennia-old tradition, their culture, and their spiritual and Christian world view, they belong to Europe and the West. Once again they will be important on this continent." Whatever the form of European unification, Germans would remain distinct and centrally important actors in the European arena.[65] Christianity, Europe, and Occidental culture were cornerstones of the soldiers' rhetoric, but Germany never ceased to be the focus of their attention.

Soviet Infiltration and European Values

The imaginatively titled "Third Soldiers' Convention" at Bad Boll in 1952 presented the same basic palette of issues as the previous meeting: European unity and the ethics of rearmament. Again Müller reminded participants that politics, treaties, and technical details were not within the Evangelical Academy's purview. "But reflections on the ethical foundations of a German Wehrmacht and the implementation of such thoughts will be our task."[66]

Müller laid out an agenda that included detailed discussion of the recently proposed EDC, but this lecture received practically no notice. Former soldiers' concerns for Soviet infiltration and a motivating ideology again dominated discussions. According to the official record of the proceedings, the majority of those present believed that it would mean cultural suicide merely to juxtapose a Western, Christian ideology to the Eastern ideology of Bolshevism.[67] Since the collapse of 1945, Baudissin added in a later lecture, Germans and especially the youth were suspicious of words and ideals, and they were therefore unwilling to accept the old arguments that made defending one's country a matter of course.[68]

Europe needed values, but many former soldiers were extremely wary of the idealistic language that flooded Europe from across the Atlantic. Freedom and democracy as defined by the United States would not inspire the loyalty and sacrifice necessary to defend Europe. According to Gerd-Peter Wunsch, who attended the Third Soldiers' Convention, the concept of freedom was a deceptive and useless slogan of ideological warfare and a dangerous ideology for the West to promulgate. "No state, no human society," Wunsch insisted, "can exist without coercion, and therefore it seems to me that the West possesses no more empty ... ideology [than] this word, [freedom], which it pits against the communist apparatus with an incomprehensible naïveté."[69] Wunsch's observation was not unique. Speakers at the 1956 gathering at the Evangelical Academy at Loccum likewise feared that the glorification of values like freedom caused them to become empty ideologies.[70] After twelve years of National Socialism, few Germans had much patience for anything labeled "ideology."

Many former officers declared all ideologies to be unsatisfactory. In 1950, former general Friedrich Hossbach described his impressions of the "World Conference for Moral Rearmament," held at Caux on Lake Geneva. Hossbach and several other former officers, young and old, who attended the conference were well received. The conference's appealing theme was that all current ideologies—communism, capitalism, and National Socialism—were inadequate to deal with the moral, economic, and military threats facing mankind. The leader of the conference advocated a return to Christianity and the Ten Commandments as the key to world peace and order. Even in this setting, however, Hossbach used the opportunity to link the ideological and the concrete. He appreciated the spirit of reconciliation that dominated the proceedings, but he nevertheless felt it necessary "as the senior German officer" to demand some promise from the Allies concerning German equality in the new European framework. Hossbach insisted upon the usual soldiers' prerequisites for participation: full sovereignty for Germany, the transfer of soldiers charged with war crimes to German jurisdiction, and the reestablishment of the soldiers' honor—"insofar as foreign nations are even justified or able to perform such a rehabilitation."[71]

This example, like many similar ones from the discussions at Bad Boll, illustrates former officers' willingness to engage in broad discussions of ideology and their concern for peace, but it also portrays their continuing preoccupation with honor and certain material demands. They were willing, in some cases, to make demands in exchange not only for their service in the Bundeswehr, but also for their participation in the "creation of ideology."

The paradox is, of course, that the system of beliefs held by former officers, who were so critical of the ideology of Western democracy, can only be seen as an ideology itself. Honor, loyalty, patriotism, the desire for a conflict-free society, the officers' self-perception as highly responsible and self-sacrificing individuals, and their pronounced anticommunism constitute a world view as powerful and ill-defined as "democracy." Soldiers masked their prejudices, as do most groups, by labeling them with the universalistic terms "values," "morals," or "virtues," but they were in their own way as ideological as the communists they so opposed.

Despite more concrete information over time concerning the details of German rearmament, meetings at Bad Boll in 1954 and 1955 also came back to the need for a motivating idea. "Infiltration and subversion are a greater danger for Europe than an attack out of the East," according to the summary of a discussion held in 1955. "The weakness of the West," the report continued, "is that it organizes discontent. Billions are spent every year for advertisements. Before a citizen learns for the first time that he must do something for democracy and the upbringing of his children, he learns a thousand times that a certain brand of cigarette is necessary for the enjoyment of his evenings."[72]

Such discussions of "democratic values" frequently expressed the usually better disguised hostility of many former officers toward the United States and other Western powers. Their captivity had done much to create resentment among former officers.[73] Many former soldiers voiced concerns about the sincerity of the Allies' goodwill toward Germany. References to the possibility that the United States would misuse a European army for its own purposes were fairly common, as were more explicit statements about the self-interest and rapacity of Germany's new-found partners. Hansen expressed his doubts concerning the good intentions of the British occupation authorities in his native Kiel. Most Britons wanted what was best for Europe and Germany, "but not . . . the ice-cold political calculators, who, under the guise of beautiful deeds and words further their (perhaps misguided) plans for the final elimination of

German competition in the coming world economic struggle."[74] Other officers blamed the United States and Great Britain for furthering the cause of the "demonic primeval entity," communism, and allowing it to penetrate Germany, the "Eastern Wall" of Europe.[75]

Former officers even went so far as to posit that American music and films were making Germany indefensible. While some Germans merely decried the contemporary "glorification of cinema values" portrayed in American movies, many soldiers saw "cowboy films and the hot jazz of the Americans" as a deliberate plot "to destroy our youth and make them unusable for a true soldierdom."[76] Editors in *Die Oase*, the DAK newsletter, wrote that because of jazz's corrupting influence, military music was especially necessary to correct the collapsing values of Germany's youth. "Military music is an important link between the population and the military." German youth, the veterans of Africa feared, "had lost every sense of true musical works" but could be "brought back again to the roots of music [through military music]."[77] The Americans had not only invaded Germany, but also sought to supplant the great achievements of German culture with their degenerate jazz.

Nevertheless, the vast majority of former officers living in the West decided that cooperation with the United States and loyalty to the Federal Republic were the only viable options. "Because we cannot join with the Bolshevists," one officer wrote, "because we also cannot—as long as we are divided and powerless—remain neutral between the two sides, there remains only a joining with the West, which naturally includes participation in defense."[78] These comments indicate both a strong anticommunism (siding with the Soviets was simply unthinkable) and a sober appraisal of the neutrality option.

One of the most important events of the late 1940s, the Berlin Blockade, goes a long way toward explaining the depth of many former officers' (and many Germans') commitment to West European integration. The isolation of Berlin by the Soviet Union for eleven months between June 1948 and May 1949 was a constant reminder of the communist threat and the protection offered by the United States. Soviet efforts to starve Berlin into submission and reverse American economic policy in Germany were deemed brutal by many in the Western zones, and the sight and sound of American planes roaring into Tempelhof Airport at the rate of two per minute did much to dispel some Germans' beliefs that the Americans would soon grow tired of European commitments as they had after World War I.

The uprising in Berlin in June 1953 was also significant in maintaining Germans' awareness of the reality of the Soviet system, as was the construction of the Berlin Wall in 1961. For the already strongly anticommunist former officers, Soviet tanks suppressing workers' protests in 1953 only underscored the servile nature of the German Democratic Republic's relationship with Moscow. No matter how critical the veterans were of American culture, American politics, and the Adenauer government's policies regarding pensions or rearmament, they were aware (if not always so appreciative) of the freedoms they enjoyed in contrast to their neighbors and relatives in the East.

The threat of the Soviet Union and the negative example of life in the German Democratic Republic provided strong incentives for the former officers to place their hopes for a German revival in Europe and the West. The former officers saw Europe and Germany under attack by a dynamic, highly motivated "primeval entity," against which Europe was unprepared to defend itself. Many believed, as did Langer (cited above), that the final round of the battle between East and West had begun and that the time for some cataclysmic "last European–German act" was at hand. Other more prominent military men joined Langer in his pessimism. Like Frießner, Sodenstern blamed the Allied powers of World War I and the Versailles Treaty for the current dangerous situation in Europe. The treaty meant, according to Sodenstern, "the decision of Europe voluntarily to renounce its active role in world history: insofar as it sacrificed large areas of its already limited living space to pan-Slavism, insofar as it weakened the appointed guardians of its eastern border." The meaning of history was nothing more than the triumph of the strong and the destruction of the weak, a condition he thought to be particularly evident in postwar Europe: "[I] believe," he wrote, "that in the course of events the demonic vision of Adolf Hitler will acquire no other meaning than as the last warning to a world that is gnawing away on its own corpse."[79]

These apocalyptic visions were products of a fear that Soviet propaganda would undermine the ability of the Federal Republic and Europe to defend themselves. Some concern existed among former officers and government officials in the Federal Republic over possible communist efforts to spread propaganda in the West and in particular to win over former officers to serve in the German Democratic Republic's KVP or the later National People's Army (Nationale Volksarmee—NVA). Rumors abounded in the late 1940s and early 1950s about efforts to recruit former soldiers for the KVP. Hans Korte wrote in December 1949, "I received the news from the rugged North that they are recruiting there fairly successfully for the 'Eastern army' under 'favorable terms,' especially for the air force, tank people, specialists, and submarine and torpedo-people. Other details not known. Three-year contract. 'Without me!' "[80] By closing with the rallying cry of those opposed to West German rearmament, which had already become an issue by December 1949, Korte wryly confirmed his loyalty to the Western "cause." He obviously believed, however, that some former comrades were taking advantage of the "good deal" offered by the communists.[81]

Fearing communist disruption of the 1953 elections, the VDS issued a warning to its regional branches to be alert for communist efforts to destroy polling places, voting booths, and ballots. In the warning sent to all the groups except those in Berlin (omitted for security reasons), the VDS suggested that veterans "place themselves at the disposal of the local police and electoral officials for the protection of the polling places." It admonished its membership to work quickly and inconspicuously in order not to create unrest in the public.[82] Former soldiers of the VDS could thereby prove their loyalty to the Federal Republic and practice their traditional role as defenders of the state even though a military career was not yet an option in the Federal Republic.

Other more fantastic stories circulated concerning Soviet efforts to sabotage plans for West German defense by infiltrating the officer corps. In a long letter to Konrad Adenauer, Hans Maislinger cited numerous examples of communist plots to win former career officers over to their cause. Maislinger told of now-communist former officers disguised as journalists attempting to sow dissension at VDS meetings, of young men being lured into the Eastern zone with promises of high pay, and—even more dangerous, given the defamation of the former career soldier—a new offer to former officers of the next highest rank, a commensurate salary, a free apartment, and other perquisites. "Where will all this lead?" Maislinger asked. "When we want to create a defensive army we will not be able to make dutiful soldiers out of fanatical or fanaticized

Communist Party members . . . , especially when these men come with instructions on how one makes the most powerful tank immobile with a handful of sand or a wrench!"[83]

The threat of infiltration, sabotage, or a mass exodus of former soldiers to the German Democratic Republic had a strategic as well as a factual component. One need only notice to whom most of these threats are addressed: to parliamentarians, especially foreign ones, and Western officials. By such threats, veterans' leaders hoped to scare concerned officials into supporting their demands for pensions and an end to the defamation of the German soldier. "One must understand the actions of every former officer who sees no other alternative than to apply to the Volkspolizei of the Eastern zone," Rudolf Veiel wrote in another such letter, this time to a member of the first Bundestag. He then asked the representative to examine the situation of Wehrmacht veterans in the East compared to the West. "*In the West*: Suffering and defamation. Apathy or complaints and slander in public. Work boycott by the factory councils and the unions. *In the East*: Wage of the earlier, when not of a higher, rank; respect and consideration as a human being and a soldier!"[84] Hansen used a similar strategy in his letter to Sir Brian Robertson, already mentioned in chapter 1, and so did many other former officers.[85] The veterans' leaders targeted their appeals for strategic effect. Hansen (in 1948), Veiel (in 1950), and Maislinger (in 1954) all meant to achieve an emotional effect and to lobby for increased benefits for former soldiers in the West, as well as to warn of the impending danger as they saw it.

This ominous vision of the future betrays something of the beliefs and prejudices common to the former officers who thought about such issues in the postwar period. Many felt that they were living at a crucial stage of history, in which the survival of cultures was at stake. They thought in social Darwinist terms of the struggle of races to determine mankind's destiny. An unsettling number of prominent former officers forgave the crimes of the Third Reich in an effort to justify their own service as a defense of European culture. The growing anticommunist sentiment in the West after World War II provided a convenient alibi for the former soldiers, who could then claim, even in the face of overwhelming evidence to the contrary, to have been visionaries fighting for the "European idea" against a Mongol invasion that, thanks to the soft-hearted diplomats of the United States and Great Britain, now had a foothold in the heartland of Europe.

Adopting the idea of European unification was not a purely tactical maneuver on the part of the officers or an effort to ingratiate themselves with the occupying powers. They certainly were aware of their importance for any proposed European defensive force and used that knowledge in their negotiations for their rights and honor. However, many former officers truly believed that they lived at a crucial moment in history and that European, not just German, culture was at stake. The destiny of the German soldier, they decided, lay in the West.

"Is there no such thing as a European Fatherland?" asked an historian at Bad Boll in 1951.[86] There was for former soldiers, if one measures the sheer amount of time they spent discussing the "Christian Occident" or the values of European civilization. However, the German Fatherland, to which they had devoted their lives, never ceased to be important.

The degree to which their ideas about Europe correspond to National Socialist doctrine is striking. The perception of the Bolshevist threat, the references to "Asiatic Bolshevism," the yearning for some ill-defined "organic" community, blaming the Western powers for the Soviet domination of Eastern Europe, and the language of an epic struggle for European culture all sprang from an ideological milieu created by, or shared with, National Socialism.

Like their attitudes toward politics, soldiers' ideas about European unification contained myriad paradoxes and a certain degree of hypocrisy. Former officers publicly blamed National Socialism for the dire straits in which Germany found itself in 1945 and for the destruction of their beloved army. Yet they were more willing than most to indicate the "benefits" that National Socialism had brought to Germany and Europe. They proposed plans based on National Socialist models for the rejuvenation of Europe and the defense of the "Occident," in both an ideological and a military sense, against the Soviet Union. That the Waffen-SS should provide the model for a European army or that geographically and racially defined "absolute" values should provide the motivation for Europe's defense against communism were ideas that ought to have fallen with the Thousand-Year Reich in May 1945. Such beliefs persisted in the minds of former Wehrmacht officers.

Like Hitler, former officers thought in terms of millennia and vague concepts such as "cultural areas" and "occidental values." As a result, the multitude of proposals, the endless speeches, and the innumerable essays that career soldiers wrote on the subject of European unification remained fantasies. Motivated by the need to exculpate themselves in the verdict of history and by a sincere desire to mold the future of Europe according to their own beliefs, their plans contained paradoxes and inconsistencies that not only made them unworkable, but also rendered them unacceptable to a government and a public with a different set of priorities. Therefore, just as in the political realm, the potential for radicalism, as well as any threat that those alternative ideas may have posed to the developing democracy in West Germany, remained confined to an increasingly impotent and politically insignificant military subculture within the veterans' organizations and their affiliated groups.

6

The Rift in Our Ranks: 20 July 1944

When North Korean soldiers crossed the border into South Korea in June 1950, West European leaders and their American allies were convinced that their Cold War enemies had developed a new tactic in their quest for world domination: war by proxy. The analogy for the European theater was clear. The East German KVP, covertly supported by Soviet forces, would overrun the newly created Federal Republic of Germany on its way to conquering the entire European peninsula. With this situation in mind and given the clear numerical superiority of Soviet and other communist forces in Europe, Western military planners saw the need for additional troops. They proposed what would have seemed unimaginable only three years before: to rearm the Germans.

The Germans called upon to plan for this new West German defense contingent quickly decided that one way to defuse the potentially explosive emotions surrounding rearmament was to link the new armed forces to the memory of those soldiers who had tried to kill Hitler on 20 July 1944. By claiming the legacy of the "good Germans" around Col. Claus von Stauffenberg, who had resisted Hitler, Konrad Adenauer and his security advisers (many of whom were linked to the conspiracy in some way) hoped to make the idea of a new German military more palatable to their domestic and foreign partners, who had suffered so much at the hands of the old one.[1]

Here the imperatives of rearmament and the rehabilitation, in some form, of German military traditions ran up against opposition from the organizations of former Wehrmacht officers, whose members of necessity would fill the ranks of the new army's leadership. In the late 1940s and early 1950s, the self-image of many former Wehrmacht officers depended on their being able to justify their service under the Third Reich in terms of their loyalty to the German Volk and the necessity of "doing their job" at the front. In so doing, however, those officers situated themselves ideologically in opposition to the conspirators of 20 July 1944. By dutifully fulfilling their military obligations, they supported the regime that Stauffenberg and the others tried to overthrow. Many former officers were therefore ambivalent about their government's fascination with 20 July and the efforts to rearm Germany under the aegis of the conspirators' legacy.

For the former officer corps, suffering from a strong identification with Hitler and the Third Reich, the adoption of Stauffenberg and the other plotters as models of military civic virtue in West Germany created a number of problems. Many officers identified with the conspirators because of the military background of men like Stauffenberg and because of some superficial similarities between the conspirators and themselves in terms of political and social vision. They were eager to use the example of the military conspirators to support their argument that the officer corps had been the element of society least corrupted by Nazi influence. Yet their attitude toward the coup attempt was overwhelmingly negative. Many veterans objected not only to the coup's timing and the means employed by the conspirators, but also to the plotters' willingness to assassinate the supreme commander of the Wehrmacht, to whom they had sworn an oath of allegiance. To these former officers, steeped in military tradition, "political murder" (as they called it) greatly offended their sense of honor and duty.

Because of this ambivalence, the discussions that took place among former officers indicate the difficulty with which many made the transition from the National Socialist dictatorship to the pluralistic, parliamentary democracy developing in the Federal Republic after 1949. The ways in which the honor-bound former officers negotiated the minefield of truth, myth, and public opinion that surrounded the 20 July coup attempt gives important clues to the structure of their political ideology, conception of their role in the Third Reich, and desire for acceptance in the Federal Republic.

Since this study seeks to understand the development of democracy in postwar Germany, situating it within the large historiography dealing with the details of the coup and the plotters' goals is difficult because, in fact, much of the discussion hinges precisely on the former officers' and the public's *mis*perceptions of the conspiracy. The work is not wholly irrelevant to the historiography of 20 July, of course. Recent literature has concerned itself with the legacy of the coup.[2] The discussion within the veterans' organizations shows how this legacy was instrumentalized. It also reveals one way in which 20 July contributes to postwar democracy, though not in the direct way the German government has often claimed.

20 July 1944 Coup Attempt

The details of the assassination attempt need only be outlined here.[3] On 20 July 1944, Stauffenberg flew from his station in Berlin to the Wolfschanze, Hitler's headquarters in East Prussia, carrying with him two bombs. Stauffenberg, as the "trigger man" for a conspiracy of military and civilian notables, intended to use the bombs to kill Hitler at a briefing scheduled for that afternoon.

Although Stauffenberg's bombs failed to kill Hitler, who suffered only an injury to his right arm, a perforated eardrum, and the loss of a new pair of pants, the effects of the attempted assassination and coup reverberated for the remaining nine months of the Third Reich. Several conspirators—Stauffenberg and a number of others captured at the Bendlerstrasse headquarters in Berlin—were summarily executed by Gen. Fritz Fromm. An estimated seven thousand arrests followed in the next few months, and at least 150 people committed suicide or were executed, many of them in the last weeks of the war at the Gestapo prison at Flossenbürg.[4] The attempt spelled the end of resistance efforts by the military, the group that had, until that moment, the most realistic chance of overthrowing Hitler.[5]

Though the plotters were extremely diverse, the most obvious institutional connection among them was the Wehrmacht. Stauffenberg was a colonel in the General Staff. The main group of conspirators in Berlin included two prestigious officers, Gen. Erwin von Witzleben, and former chief of the General Staff Col. Gen. Ludwig Beck, as well as many other high-ranking military men. Field Marshal Erwin Rommel was also indirectly linked to the coup and was allowed to commit suicide as a result, though his role in the conspiracy was far less active than is portrayed in the many films glorifying Rommel's life. Though sometimes portrayed as a strictly military coup (particularly by the Nazis themselves), the conspiracy also included many civilians, ranging from conservative parliamentarians and diplomats to Social Democrats to the aristocratic radicals in the Kreisau Circle.

20 July in Postwar Germany

Robert Weldon Whalen, in a recent work on the plot to kill Hitler, notes the incredible volume and variety of postwar commentary on the coup attempt. As of 1984, there had been over six thousand works published on the subject of resistance to Nazism. "Posterity has fretted over and gnawed at and broken its teeth on the conspiracy, and refused to let it go."[6] One reason the coup attempt refused to fade from memory was that it conveniently meshed with the ideological agendas of both new German states in the growing Cold War after 1949. As the division of Germany became more concrete, both the Federal Republic of Germany and the German Democratic Republic developed a pantheon of heroes that best suited the purposes of the separate regimes. While the occupation governments in both East and West quickly suppressed and disbanded many of the indigenous antifascist groups that emerged during the final months of the war, both camps were anxious to link their respective German clients to elements of the wartime resistance in order to legitimize their rule.[7]

Politicians, veterans, journalists, and historians on both sides of the Elbe River focused on the types of resisters and the elements of the resisters' ideas that best suited their Cold War agendas. Not surprisingly, historians and publicists in the Soviet zone and the leaders of the later German Democratic Republic identified "resistance" with the actions of socialist and communist elements of the working class to undermine the National Socialist regime. The "workers' state" needed worker-heroes.[8]

Because of its foundation in the Wehrmacht and among conservative circles around Carl Goerdeler and Ulrich von Hassell, the 20 July conspiracy did not achieve the prominence in the East that it enjoyed in West Germany. A number of public declarations and official publications praising the attempt on Hitler's life did nevertheless appear in the Soviet zone of occupation in 1945 and 1946. In 1947, former members of several resistance groups formed the Union of Those Persecuted by the Nazi Regime (Vereinigung der Verfolgten des Naziregimes—VVN) in order to encourage historical study and commemoration of all resistance movements throughout Germany. The VVN even attracted some fifty-five thousand visitors to an exhibit in Berlin in 1948 that honored 20 July and included communist and other resistance groups.[9]

By the end of the 1940s, however, the powers that be in East Germany were squeezing the conspiracy out of the public limelight, first by highlighting only the socialist elements within the plotters' group and their connections to the Communist Party, and then by dismissing the coup as a reactionary imperialist plot directed against the Soviet Union.[10] If they acknowledged worthwhile resistance within the military at all, East German sources focused primarily on the activities of the Soviet-sponsored NKFD and BdO, which existed within the prisoner of war camps. East German officialdom also recognized the military elements of the Soviet spy network known to the Gestapo as the Red Orchestra (Rote Kapelle).[11] East Germans considered these groups, as well as resisters in communist organizations or among the working classes, to be harbingers of the new Germany being created on the eastern side of the Elbe River.

In the West, however, resistance groups like the Red Orchestra or the NKFD were quite often seen as traitors who had not only caused the deaths of untold numbers of Germans by giving information to the enemy during wartime, but had also paved the way for another dictatorship—a Stalinist one—to achieve a foothold on German soil.

In the Federal Republic, resistance to Hitler quickly became identified with groups such as the Kreisau Circle, its allies among conservative politicians, and the conspirators within the Wehrmacht, all of whom were linked to the 20 July attempt. As a result, the conspiracy became an integral part of the nascent West German state's self-image. Of noble (or at least respectable) upbringing, espousing sometimes democratic and even Christian Socialist political ideas, and sharing in many cases a military connection, the conspirators served as valuable tools for a West German government run by Konrad Adenauer and the CDU that was attempting not only to establish its democratic credentials, but also to pursue a policy of rearmament in the face of stiff public opposition.[12] As Frank Stern points out, the conspirators helped conservative politicians "to dream of an untainted German conservatism, without Hitler."[13]

Though the conspirators' alleged democratic ideals had no direct effect on the Basic Law or the structure of the Federal Republic, countless pronouncements by Chancellor Adenauer, President Heuss, and other major West German political figures indicate that they intended the spirit of 20 July to be a major element in establishing the new regime's legitimacy.[14] The conspirators' actions and moral convictions created, some believed, "the moral preconditions" for the Federal Republic by proving that noble and ostensibly democratic sentiments had survived the "Twelve-Year Reich."[15] Pundits were also fond of claiming that the conspiracy contained representatives of every stratum of society, so that their example helped to blunt the charge of Germans' collective guilt for the war and atrocities committed under National Socialism.[16]

The picture that resulted from the government's efforts to extol the 20 July conspirators was somewhat distorted, however. Since the 1960s historians such as Hans Mommsen and Hermann Graml have shown that the conspirators' program was hardly as clear or as democratic as some in the 1950s suggested. The conspirators, while often from starkly different backgrounds, were hardly a representative slice of German society.[17] Nevertheless, many Germans in the decade following the war willingly overlooked the conspirators' often authoritarian proposals for Germany's future or their unrealistic appraisals of the chances of negotiating an end to the war. Witzleben, Stauffenberg, and the others became models for the conscience of Germany, proving that much that was good and noble had managed to survive despite the Third Reich.[18]

The government's effort to mythologize the coup attempt was made easier by the fact that little scholarly work had been done on the conspiracy apart from the seminal works of Hans Rothfels and Gerhard Ritter.[19] Reliable information about the conspiracy itself, let alone the intricate constitutional plans of groups like the Kreisau Circle, was not widely disseminated. Only the vaguest notions of the plotters' real plans permeated the public's consciousness, shaped strongly by both National Socialist slander and the almost equally distorting efforts of officials in the Federal Republic to enshrine the conspirators in the pantheon of good Germans.[20]

As a result, while the conspirators' actual social and political ideas have been a subject of great interest for historians in the past thirty years, they are not necessarily relevant to the public perceptions in the 1950s of the coup attempt.[21] Given the often distorted view promulgated by West German officialdom, the degree to which the coup's legacy was politicized, and the prejudices held by many Germans, understanding how the legacy of the coup, real or imagined, was used in the postwar period is more important for our purposes.[22]

The Federal Republic actively promoted the conspirators as models of civic courage in a number of ways. In 1951 and 1954 Adenauer himself gave prominent speeches praising the resistance; the Bundestag issued a statement in 1953 lauding the services for the German people by those who had resisted Hitler. President Heuss gave a highly publicized speech on the anniversary of the coup attempt in 1954 in the Bundestag, and countless other party, church, and educational leaders followed suit.[23]

Approval of 20 July became an acid test of officers' loyalty to the Federal Republic. In 1955, the Bundestag ordered the creation of the PGA. The PGA's guidelines tellingly included the following: "The future soldier must acknowledge the decision of conscience by the men of the Twentieth of July 1944. He should combine this [recognition] with respect for them and for the many other soldiers, who, with a feeling of duty, risked their lives to the very end [of the war]."[24] Although the PGA was technically independent of the government, many of its selection criteria, and particularly those relating to 20 July, were developed at a much earlier conference at Weinheim (near Heidelberg) and attended by Theodor Blank and other government officials.[25]

Especially after uprisings in East Berlin in June 1953, the resistance legacy became ammunition in the war of words waged with East Germany. Rothfels, in a lecture commemorating the tenth anniversary of the coup, called 20 July and 17 June "particularly linked dates" because both involved resistance against "foreign occupation."[26] Though Rothfels goes on to admit that the comparison is tendentious, politicians and pundits made the linkage quite frequently. Eight years later, Ernst Lemmer, the federal minister for "Greater German questions," tapped into the same logical vein when he lamented the fact that "Sixteen million of our countrymen are still living under an oppressive fate that the men and women of the Twentieth of July tried to cast off forever."[27]

A similar if less momentous example of the instrumental importance of 20 July occurred in 1952. Former colonel Adolf Dickfeld founded the Society of Carriers of the German Knight's Cross (Gemeinschaft Deutscher Ritterkreuzträger) and planned its first meeting for November. Theodor Blank accepted an invitation to speak, but the government soon discovered that Dickfeld may not have been a colonel and was wanted in Austria for alleged smuggling, using an assumed name, fraud, and currency violations. After much negotiation and fretting about the potential public impact of either forbidding the meeting or allowing it to take place, the government and the society were able to reach a compromise: the meeting could take place as planned, although without the presence of Blank and on the condition that the assembled soldiers issue a statement affirming their rejection of radicalism, their approval of the Federal Republic, and their admiration for the 20 July conspirators' courage. This statement assuaged the government's fears despite the fact that an observer at the meeting noted at least one society member giving the Hitler salute as he entered the hall.[28]

The government also used more overtly propagandistic methods to enforce a particular view of 20 July. The federal minister for refugees, Hans Lukaschek (himself a member of the Kreisau Circle), gave a speech in 1952 that the Press and Information Office of the Federal Republic reproduced under the simple headline "20th of July 1944 Shows Way for the German People."[29] When President Heuss commemorated the tenth anniversary of the coup attempt, all factions of the parliament voted to have the speech distributed free of charge to teachers and students in the Federal Republic.[30] Years later, the government continued its campaign to establish 20 July as a national legend by publishing a collection of documents and analyses through its Federal Office for Political Education.[31]

Although historians were later to fault the conspirators as opportunistic or authoritarian, initial writings on the coup in West Germany mimicked the government's pronouncements and were generally positive. In particular, writers such as Countess Marion Dönhoff emphasized the democratic and ethical nature of the revolution proposed by the conspirators, especially the Kreisau Circle.[32] Speaking in 1954, Wilhelm Ritter von Schramm claimed that the conspirators were "pioneers of our times" who acted "completely in the spirit of reconciliation, in the spirit of a unified Europe," and whose "clear political program" it was the duty of contemporary Europeans to fulfill.[33]

A spate of popular films in the mid-1950s also reinforced the conspirator-as-hero legend by emphasizing the event's drama, the conspirators' nobility, and the tragedy of their failure, while necessarily obfuscating the details of Stauffenberg's planned postwar order. *Es Geschah am 20. Juli* (It happened on the 20th of July) and *Der 20. Juli* (The 20th of July) both appeared in 1955. The *Frankfurter Allgemeine Zeitung* wrote the following about the conspirators in its review of the latter film: "Theirs was a moral revolution, not only against Hitler but against the deep-rooted conception that freed not only Hitler, but also all Germans from every moral law."[34]

As a result of these inputs from a variety of media, public attention coalesced around a short list of ideas attributed to "the men of 20 July," drawing largely from the concepts outlined above and centering on the ethical nature of the conspirators' resistance to National Socialism. The public associated the conspirators with individual responsibility and a return to Christianity, with both antifascism and anticommunism, and with a strong sense of respect for one's fellow man. Described as "good democrats," the plotters were also identified with a government based on free speech, free press, and free association.[35]

Yet despite the overwhelmingly positive spin placed on 20 July by the media and the government, public opinion remained noticeably divided. A June 1951 public opinion poll indicated that only 40 percent of respondents approved while 30 percent disapproved of the efforts of the conspirators (the remaining 30 percent either expressed no opinion or did not know of the event).[36] A slightly later poll by the Allensbach Institute for Demoscopy was more varied in its categorization of respondents and similarly found that among the general population, the ratio of positive to negative opinions was 40 percent to 30 percent. The later poll revealed more, as Table 1 indicates.

Men claimed far more knowledge about the coup than women (only 5 percent claiming no knowledge, as opposed to 15 percent of women). The table also clearly reveals how the interpretation of 20 July impacted the Federal Republic's political culture, with the mainstream parties of both right and left much more prominently endorsing the coup and the parties of the extreme right and special interest groups espousing more negative reactions. Members of the SRP were nearly unanimous in their opposition to the coup, with a remarkable 81 percent of its constituency judging negatively. This fact is not so surprising when one realizes that

Table 1. Answers to the question: "In your opinion, how should the men of 20 July be judged?"

Group	Positive	Negative	No Opinion	No Knowledge of 20 July
Men	43	38	14	5
Women	38	24	23	15
Total	40	30	19	11
Political Party				
CDU	47	21	19	13
SPD	47	29	17	7
FDP	56	33	9	2
Bavarian Party (BP)	35	26	17	22
German Party (DP)	33	49	11	7
BHE	37	46	6	11
SRP	15	81	4	–

Source: Noelle-Neumann and Neumann, *Jahrbruch*, 138; reproduced in Volkmann, "Die innenpolitische Dimension," 489.

the founder of the SRP was none other than former major Otto Remer, the man responsible for the rapid suppression of the coup in 1944.

Several factors account for the German public's ambivalence toward the conspiracy. The abuse heaped upon the plotters by the Nazis in the aftermath of the coup had some effect. Though postwar occupation officials anxious to stamp out militarism would be unwilling to acknowledge the fact, a rift had opened between the officer corps and the German people long before 1944, and the immediate response of many Germans to the coup had been to join with the Nazis in decrying the cowardice and treason of Stauffenberg and his fellow officers.[37]

The coup attempt was also an implicit refutation of the idea of a "Zero Hour" (*Stunde Null*). By proving that resistance had been possible, the conspirators pointed a silent, accusing finger at all Germans who had not acted to overthrow the Nazi regime.[38] The conspirators' moral stance and remarkable courage was bound to evoke shame among people whose actions did not measure up to that virtually unattainable standard. The government's too rosy picture of the conspirators and their ideas only compounded these problems.

Defensiveness therefore prevailed among the public when issues surrounding 20 July were raised. From uncensored testimony provided by visitors to the VVN's 1948 Berlin exhibit, we can understand how the confrontation with the conspirators' moral example clashed with individuals' memories of past complicity and present perceived suffering. One visitor noted that he had been impressed by the exhibit and was, as a Christian, opposed to the atrocities that the Nazis had committed. But "when will mankind improve? My uncle and two friends my age died in the current concentration camps [constructed by the Soviets]! When will people finally stop? How can I endorse the current political direction in light of these incidents?"[39]

Public discomfort with the glorification of the conspiracy meant that critics of 20 July achieved a certain prominence. Otto John's mysterious defection to East Germany in 1954 raised questions as to his wartime loyalties as well. John, a former conspirator and president of the Constitutional Court, added credence to the widely held presumption that the conspirators had committed an act of treason and not resistance. Otto Remer also achieved notoriety during his well-publicized trial in 1952, though the verdict against him in that trial did more to improve the conspirators' prestige than to diminish it.[40]

Hans Hagen, Remer's political officer in 1944, also survived the war and publicly lobbied against the coup as a model of civic responsibility, though in less extreme terms than Remer. At a soldiers' conference at the Evangelical Academy in Bad Boll in November 1950, Hagen gave a speech entitled "The 20th of July—Oath and Responsibility," in which he attributed the coup's failure to the power of the officer corps' oath to Hitler and the cowardice (though he never uses that word) of the conspirators. The coup failed, Hagen succinctly stated, because despite the detailed planning, no one was willing to sacrifice himself. "The single moment when the assassin left the bomb alone sufficed to allow the oath-bearer [Hitler] to remain alive, as though fate did not want to accept such an inconsistency."[41]

The conspirators wanted to build a new world, Hagen admitted, but no one was willing to be the sacrificial victim whose death would sanctify the new order. It was pointless, Hagen concluded, to glorify Stauffenberg and the other conspirators as heroes and prophets from the vantage point of 1950. Most postwar commentators credited the conspirators with a great sense of moral responsibility, but Hagen argued that the soldiers who did not act, or who acted to crush the coup in 1944, did so because they too felt a moral responsibility to the German Volk, which was engaged in a life or death struggle on two fronts. "That we did not present to the world a picture of a fortress garrison that tears itself to pieces before the enemy breaks in seems to me to be a conciliatory motif in this symphony of ruin."[42]

Figures with an even higher public profile reinforced these negative opinions, so that such criticism became part of the mainstream public dialogue concerning 20 July. Many of the earliest and most influential postwar pronouncements regarding the coup came from the Wehrmacht's senior ranks. While testifying at Nuremberg, both Col. Gen. Alfred Jodl and Field Marshal Gerd von Rundstedt condemned the coup as an act of cowardly treason. "How one can conduct an external war during which one's existence or nonexistence is at stake and at the same time make revolution . . . ? I have no idea," Jodl said. Rundstedt seconded Jodl's interpretation, calling the coup attempt "common, naked treason."[43]

Hasso von Manteuffel seems to have originated the charge against the conspirators—repeated ad nauseam by Hagen and others in the 1950s—that using a bomb was a dishonorable assassination method and accounts in large part for the coup's failure. Why had no officer found the courage, Manteuffel asked in 1949, simply to pull out a pistol and settle things with Hitler face to face? Of course, Manteuffel ignored the many obstacles to such action and probably was ignorant of the conspirators' desire to eliminate Himmler and Göring at the same time.[44] Nevertheless, his formulation gained currency because it resonated with the discomfort many Germans felt about resistance in general and about the timing and method of the assassination attempt in particular. The charges of treason (àla Jodl and Rundstedt) and cowardice (àla Manteuffel) would remain constant features of public discussions surrounding 20 July.

Former Career Soldiers and 20 July

If ambivalence and defensiveness prevailed among the general public, such attitudes were even more pronounced within the ranks of former career soldiers. Initial reactions to the coup in 1944 had been mixed at best. While there were countless examples of comradeship and courage as officers at various posts tried to shelter those under suspicion, most career soldiers met the news of the assassination attempt with shock and dismay. Many officers were, of course, too busy trying to hold together Germany's rapidly disintegrating fronts to have thought deeply about the coup. If they did, most evidenced little understanding for the attempt to kill the commander in chief, to whom all had sworn a personal oath.[45] Such emotions persisted long after the war and were only exacerbated by the situation in which officers found themselves after 1945. Given their heightened sensitivity to charges of complicity with the regime, their response to the glorification of the conspiracy was even more characterized by defensiveness than the general public's.

Attitudes toward 20 July among former career soldiers were complex because, for a number of reasons, they stood to gain from the glorification of the coup attempt. Men such as Remer and Hagen obviously had a vested interest in condemning the attempted coup, but other officers were only indirectly affected by it. Especially older officers of higher rank and longer service felt compelled to comment on the historical interpretation of the assassination plot since they believed that it fundamentally influenced the image of German soldierdom. These self-defined custodians of soldierly tradition were most ambivalent in their attitude toward the coup and the conspirators because of their simultaneous identification with the conspirators and disapproval of the conspirators' methods.

The most obvious connection the veterans felt was that many of the conspirators were themselves officers. What they had done reflected on the whole officer corps, for better or worse. This identification placed former career soldiers and especially their organizations in a difficult position. Career soldiers were twice as likely as the general population to disapprove of the coup attempt, according to the poll by the Institute for Demoscopy cited above. While a roughly similar percentage of officers approved of the coup (35 percent as compared to 40 percent of the general population), the number expressing no opinion or no recollection of the event fell drastically (to 4 and 2 percent respectively). Fifty-nine percent of former career soldiers judged the men of 20 July negatively—nearly twice as high a percentage as that of the general population.[46]

The fact that the percentage of officers who saw the coup's merits was roughly the same as the public's reveals that these traditionalists were not simply out of step with the postwar political scene, as was often the case regarding other issues. Rather, it indicates that some former officers, like their civilian counterparts, were participating in the efforts to grapple with (and rehabilitate) the recent German past. However, because 20 July impacted the Wehrmacht, emotions concerning it ran much higher among the former officer corps. The overwhelming majority of career soldiers condemned the coup attempt when it came down to a simple matter of judging the event as the poll asked them. This final judgment indicates that many former officers did not want to be associated with men that they deemed noble yet misguided, in the best case, or assassins and murderers, in the worst.

Hans-Erich Volkmann, in his article on the domestic–political aspects of German rearmament, cannot decide whether the "demonstratively negative judgment" of 20 July by former career soldiers is better understood as "an intense connection to National Socialism or as a consequence of their upbringing to a specific military ethos."[47] Certainly, the officers, like many Germans, imbibed the spirit of Nazism and continued to espouse ideas common in National Socialist propaganda. The papers of the veterans themselves, however, indicate that for most, the primary concern was the coup attempt's impact on the image and values of German soldierdom.

During the late 1940s, when the so-called defamation of the German soldier was at its height, many former officers blamed the conspirators for the low esteem in which soldiers were held by the general population. As noted above, of course, the public was not universally in favor of the conspiracy's glorification. Most Germans felt no more positively inclined toward the coup than did former officers, so soldiers were not really so isolated in this regard as they imagined. Because of their defensive attitude, however, the public ceremonies and the speeches by government officials rankled.

In part because 20 July was so mythologized by the government, opposition to the coup attempt became a way for former officers to express more general discontent with current West German politics. At a meeting of former soldiers near Celle in 1951, the motto, according to Hans Korte, was "Without us [an explicit reference to "Ohne mich"], against the advisers of the federal government (that is, Speidel and Heusinger), against the people of 20 July, who should not be allowed to show their face in the new Wehrmacht."[48]

There existed a great deal of concern among former career officers about the coup's implications for the honor of German soldierdom, as is made clear by the motto of the gathering mentioned above. Former colonel Ludwig Gümbel expressed that belief when, during a speech on 20 July, he acknowledged the conspirators' sacrifices for the German Volk but insisted that by planning such a coup, they were denouncing the "eternal values of soldierdom." The conspirators must "forego any effort to return to soldierdom because their return would mean endangering the soldierly spirit, without which any defense contribution is unthinkable."[49] Not everyone shared Gümbel's exact sentiment, but many were equally concerned with the potential impact of the coup attempt on the nature of the soldierly profession in the future.[50]

Many former officers, including Hansen, imagined a "court of honor" at which individual soldiers would be tried for their actions on 20 July to determine whether their behavior could be construed as treasonous or cowardly.[51] Other officers would well have understood the impulse behind such a proposal. A court of honor had already examined most conspirators' actions. In 1944, Hitler charged Heinz Guderian with the task of expelling from the Wehrmacht those soldiers guilty of treason as a result of the coup attempt. Guderian's comrades often credit him with doing his best to save as many soldiers as possible from the clutches of the Gestapo. Guderian nevertheless discharged his duties and crowned his achievements with an order, issued by Field Marshal Wilhelm Keitel, declaring the "disgraceful proceedings surrounding 20 July" officially terminated as far as the armed forces were concerned. Keitel also ordered, as many former officers would later wish were possible, that "every mention of the consequences of 20 July" was henceforth forbidden. The case was closed, and any further discussion of the matter would only carry with it the "seeds of destruction."[52]

In the spirit of Keitel and Guderian, Heinrich Behr wrote in 1951 that "today one must ask each of the men of 20 July *when* he was there and *how* he was there. One thing is certain now as then: desertion is now as then a crime worthy of death."⁵³ Even the lower ranks of soldiers insisted, according to Gert Spindler, that a distinction be made between the honorable and the dishonorable acts of resistance, that sentence be passed on the "recognized and convicted traitors," and that their "expulsion from the ranks of former soldiers" be made public.⁵⁴ The fact that Spindler, like the more radical Gümbel, even imagined that someone could be expelled from an army that no longer existed and that men like Hansen and Behr would propose courts of honor to determine a former officer's fitness for service in the Bundeswehr indicate how immersed in tradition many former officers were.

The discussion among former officers concerning the historical meaning of the 20 July coup attempt naturally centered on its potential impact on the structure of authority in any future German army. "The oath as an obligation to a person is doubtless discredited by the political events between 1933 and 1945," wrote former general Kurt Brennecke, the Bonn chairman of the GfW. "One cannot and may not ignore this question of '20 July.' This question will be posed to the leader of tomorrow by his soldiers."⁵⁵ The issues of loyalty and oath, some argued, would be especially crucial when one realized for what purposes a future *West* German army might be used.⁵⁶

As Donald Abenheim indicates in his book on the Bundeswehr's search for usable traditions, 20 July became strongly associated with the new army's notion of "Internal Leadership," the vague, controversial concept governing the way leadership and authority would be structured in the new armed forces.⁵⁷ The example of the conspirators was meant to provide, as Kielmansegg later phrased it, not prescriptions for action, but models of bearing.⁵⁸

Many former officers were concerned that because of the difficulty and divisiveness of 20 July, it could not possibly be incorporated into the new army's leadership and discipline guidelines. Soldiers, they feared, would remain unmotivated by the examples of Beck and Stauffenberg. "No new Wehrmacht can be created on a foundation of disloyalty, and that is exactly what is demanded, even if this 'decision of conscience' should be recognized," wrote Werner Fuchs in 1955.⁵⁹ Members of Großdeutschland were relieved to read in their newsletter, *Die Neue Feuerwehr*, that not everyone in the government shared the government's enthusiasm for glorifying the conspirators to the exclusion of other potentially positive role models. In an interview published in the September 1959 issue, Erich Mende, FDP delegate to the Bundestag and member of the defense committee, reassured the readers that he did not wish to glorify the conspirators at the expense of older traditions. Scharnhorst, Blücher, Gneisenau, and Yorck deserved their place in the heroes' pantheon. "Especially Scharnhorst is a good example for the democratization of the army," Mende suggested. "Also in the Second World War there were outstanding soldiers to whom army could form connections. I think of Rommel or Mölders, naturally not of Schörner."[60]

The wariness of former officers concerning the 20 July legacy was evident in nearly every discussion of the proposed German defense contribution during the early 1950s. At a conference at the Evangelical Academy at Bad Boll in 1951, the participants were unanimous in wanting to put an end to 20 July, to set it apart from the normal course of German military history. According to the *Frankfurter Allgemeine Zeitung*, former soldiers could be proud that their comrades had acted out of conscience to try to save Germany, but for a future German army, the conspirators' actions could represent only some vague moral example, not a model for action.[61]

While they criticized the glorification of the conspirators and worried about the attempted coup's impact on the soldierly profession, however, many career soldiers recognized the positive effects that its public portrayal had on the officer corps' prestige. After all, because of the actions of Stauffenberg, Beck, Rommel, and others, the officers could claim, not entirely incorrectly, to have been members of an organization that formed a bastion of resistance to Hitler's schemes. Beck counseled against the attacks on Poland and France. Rommel urged Hitler to negotiate with the Western Allies after the landings at Normandy in order to stabilize the decaying Eastern Front, and Stauffenberg, finally, came closest to eliminating Hitler. The military had been one of the last organizations to fall to the Nazi "coordination," they argued.

Some former officers were inclined, therefore, to try to use the publicity generated by 20 July to promote the cause of veterans. One soldiers' newspaper recognized in 1954 that 20 July was the key to overcoming international opposition to rearmament because "[it] has perhaps decisively contributed to the German name regaining the measure of respect and prestige that is granted to it by the world."[62] Similarly, when it became known that the Bundestag had voted to publish President Heuss's speech on 20 July, at least one associate of Hansen's regretted that the VDS had not taken a lead in the propaganda effort and published a similar brochure.[63]

Many soldiers also faced the dilemma of personally identifying with the plotters, despite any qualms about methods or loyalty or oaths. The military men among the conspirators, like other career officers, shared certain values and ideas as a function of their class background, training, and careers. The conspirators were personally brave, successful, and highly decorated. Men like Ludwig Beck and Erwin von Witzleben were seen as models of soldierly skill and demeanor. Stauffenberg was a highly decorated officer who had been severely wounded in North Africa, losing an eye, an arm, two fingers on his remaining hand, and suffering hearing loss. Yet during his convalescence, he steadfastly refused pain medication, relying instead on his powers of endurance, and he recovered in record time. Most former officers could only admire such a model of ascetic perseverance. Add to that Stauffenberg's impeccably noble upbringing and one realizes that Stauffenberg, even in the absence of the conspiracy, could easily have been a legend within the officer corps.

Even the conspiracy's nonmilitary members shared with former officers of the postwar period certain ideals, such as valuing responsibility, loyalty, and duty. In a style that had a distinctly soldierly ring and that would frequently be repeated by former officers after 1945, Helmut James von Moltke (the leader of the Kreisau Circle) wrote that "a feeling of responsibility requires both freedom and commitment. All actions that affect the community, that is, all imaginable actions, must be informed by this feeling of responsibility."[64] Just as the former officers prided themselves on their decisive nature and their willingness to take responsibility, Ger van Roon described Moltke as willing to volunteer for any operation, devoting his whole person to an action, "unconfused by social accident or class prejudice . . . . His whole being was dedicated to practical action."[65] Similarly, Roon describes the defining characteristics of Moltke's friend and fellow conspirator Peter Yorck von Wartenburg (a lieutenant in the reserves) as "loyalty, consciousness of duty, acknowledgement of responsibility to the community, [and] a patriotic attitude."[66] Such phrases had been part of the litany used by career officers to describe themselves and their worthy comrades for centuries and remained important after 1945.

There is no direct evidence that former officers tried to school themselves in the intricacies of the conspirators' ideas. Relying primarily on the public commemorations of the coup attempt and the little information that could be gleaned from other media, they believed that they understood what the conspiracy had been about. Interestingly, there are at least superficial similarities between the ideas for the future political structure of Germany as outlined in the few remaining papers of the military and civilian resistance and those expressed within officers' circles immediately following the war.[67] For example, officers shared the conspirators' hopes that the end of the war would bring Germany a chance for renewal. They spoke of living in a period of epochal and fundamental change, in which the best and most idealistic forces available in Germany needed to be mustered in order to avoid an apocalypse. Words like "Occident," "community," and "responsibility" litter the writings of both the conspirators and former career soldiers.[68]

Former major Karl Heinrich Helfer understood these similarities when he proposed that the "study of the ideas of Stauffenberg and his friends that dealt with the reconstruction of a German state [would be] more important and more fruitful for the future," even though he feared that the disagreements over the coup attempt itself might divide soldiers. Many young soldiers had realized by the end of the war that Germany needed to abandon dictatorship. Though they served loyally (because of the Allied demand for unconditional surrender), Helfer recalled their receiving the nickname "the young Turks." Though not entirely appropriate, Helfer insisted that the nickname indicated "that the essential desire of this stratum was to be seen in the effort [to create] a new and even a democratic state."[69] Helfer saw the conspirators' political ideas uniting former soldiers, even if the coup remained divisive.

Indeed, many former officers shared with the conspirators the notion of a conflict-free society and a suspicion of self-serving political parties.[70] The conspiracy's "apolitical," ethical character was a common feature of postwar commemorations and was proven by the "fact" that the plotters had come from all "estates, directions, and confessions," as Rothfels phrased it.[71] The former officers' desire to be apolitical or above politics coincided with the feeling of the members of the Kreisau Circle and the

Goerdeler group that parliamentary democracy had proven unworkable. Although the former officers vented these suspicions at the same time that they intoned their support for a pluralistic and democratic state, their attitude was not necessarily hypocritical or even contradictory. The resistance groups had sometimes expressed similar suspicions of the Weimar political parties and yet were deemed by the postwar pundits to have been champions of democracy.

Postwar West Germany identified one important specific idea with the conspirators: anticommunism. It has been the subject of historical debate to what degree Stauffenberg and the others cooperated with communists and how that cooperation would have been affected had the coup succeeded.[72] Though the Kreisau Circle had been willing to negotiate with the communists in preparing the coup attempt, most of the members shuddered at the thought of a communist—and especially a Bolshevist—domination of Germany. Even Julius Leber and Adolf Reichwein, the Social Democratic proponents of talks with the communists, were ambivalent about communism, and Stauffenberg, the other advocate of negotiations, had in 1941 or 1942 abandoned even the idea of overthrowing Hitler because of the ongoing war against the Soviet Union. "We must first win the war," he said to his cousin, Hans Christoph von Stauffenberg. "One does not do such a thing [overthrow Hitler] during a war, especially not during a war against the Bolshevists."[73] Though Stauffenberg eventually and obviously changed his mind on the subject, his attitude in the early 1940s indicates that he must have made the decision to negotiate with the communists only reluctantly. In any case, in the highly politicized Cold War context, the conspirators' anticommunism was taken for granted.

Former officers saw in the conspirators' alleged rejection of communism one of 20 July's few saving graces. By the early 1950s, nearly all former officers living in the Federal Republic agreed that Germany must be "rescued" from communism. Reinforced by the postwar spin placed on 20 July, veterans latched onto this element of the conspirators' ideology, turning Moltke and Goerdeler into Cold War prophets and attempting to justify their own continuation of the war as a crusade against communism. The fact that many officers who claimed to have been fighting the good fight against the communists had in fact done their best to defeat the Allied armies in France in 1944 did little to disturb the surety of their conviction that they, like the conspirators, had wanted to rescue Germany from the Bolsheviks.[74]

Some of the proposals for European federation promulgated by soldiers after 1945 are unmistakably similar to those of Adam von Trott zu Solz. The supposed "essential" strengths of the German people that Trott cited as the Germans' contribution to a unified Europe bore an overt similarity to those that the nationalistic officers expressed in statements, like Helfer's in 1951, that the former soldiers' duty was to represent "the standpoint of a German patriotic sensibility based on an awareness of supranational European responsibility."[75] Though the similarities may seem fairly superficial at first glance, they indicate, along with the other elements of the conspirators' lives and personalities, the grounds for a potential identification with the plotters by career officers both during and after the war. Nor was the admiration and identification strictly one way. Conservative conspirator Carl Goerdeler viewed the German officer corps as a model of an organic, self-reliant community.[76]

Former officers in the postwar period did not necessarily share the conspirators' political ideas (as broad as they were), nor did they even understand the proposals of Moltke, Stauffenberg, and Goerdeler for Germany's future. What is important is that within the vast ideological legacy of the coup attempt certain elements appealed to veteran officers. They selected from among the various elements of the conspirators' worldviews the ideas that meshed most comfortably with their own cosmology. They conveniently ignored Stauffenberg's eventual willingness to enlist the aid of communists in his struggle against Hitler or the prominence of both right- and left-wing Social Democrats within the conspiracy. They admired Ludwig Beck for his soldierly demeanor and expertise but neither acknowledged his exemplary behavior in defiance of Hitler nor heeded his prewar maxims that "there are limits to your obedience" and "exceptional times demand exceptional actions."[77]

So while former officers overwhelmingly disapproved of the coup attempt, they were often not without sympathy for the conspirators, and they were certainly more than willing to reap the occasional benefits, in the form of improved prestige and grudging respect, that accrued to the officer corps for the efforts of a few of its members against Hitler.

This ambivalence, however, created problems for organizations of former officers. Hans von Donat in particular hoped to limit the constituency and the tasks of the BvW strictly to officers, their pension issues, and the fight against the defamation of the former German soldier, so as to prevent the inevitable "passionate battles of opinion" over such issues as rearmament, politics, and 20 July.[78] Former colonel general Kurt Student similarly pleaded at the VDS's founding meeting in September 1951 that the organization's goals be strictly limited to fighting defamation and promoting comradeship.[79]

Many veterans felt that the public demanded some official response from soldiers regarding 20 July.[80] Individual soldiers and veterans' leaders struggled to balance their personal disapproval of the methods used on 20 July with a willingness to accept the pure motives behind the attempt to assassinate Hitler. The most spectacular of these struggles occurred at Frießner's 1951 press conference, already discussed in chapter 2. The *London Times* reported that Frießner explained the VDS's aims to the foreign press, "and in doing so he unconsciously combined a sense of mysticism, a touch of self-pity, soldierly German pride, and uncompromising demands for the rehabilitation of the German man of arms in a way that did not surprise, but did disturb, his audience."[81] Particularly disturbing were Frießner's comments on the coup attempt: "As a soldier and a Christian, I reject political murder, especially when at the front one is fighting for existence or nonexistence. The soldier cannot appreciate that the supreme commander is to be murdered behind his back." Frießner interjected that he understood the difficulty of the conspirators' decision and that many acted from noble motives of conscience and patriotism, but he insisted that the coup was ill conceived in timing and method. "One does not set a case under the desk of the victim, but rather draws one's pistol and shoots the man and then oneself dead," Frießner averred. "All of those who suddenly claim to have known that the state leadership was leading the entire nation into chaos should have acted sooner. I believe it to be absolutely essential for the future that a line be drawn and a reconciliation of the parties in the spirit of the common goal take place."[82] Like Manteuffel, Hagen, and the other more extreme critics of the plotters, Frießner objected to the cowardice of the method and insisted that had Stauffenberg stayed with the bomb and sacrificed himself, the coup would have been a success. Many other former officers shared this opinion, which was so clearly based in soldierly notions of honor.⁸³ As they saw it, attempting to flee the scene and survive was the tragic flaw (in a dramatic sense) in Stauffenberg's conspiracy.

In light of the many supportive letters Frießner received following the press conference, it is clear that his views on 20 July and other issues reflected those of some of his comrades. The letters betray former officers' bitterness and indicate the degree to which the coup's legacy was tied to their efforts at self-justification. By endorsing Frießner's views, career soldiers could express their ambivalence about the issues of timing and method, treason, and the loyaly oath, which were the main themes of postwar criticism of the coup. Former colonel general Kurt Zeitzler even congratulated Frießner on his election as president of the VDS and claimed that Frießner's words were spoken from his very soul.⁸⁴

Somewhat ironically, Frießner's statements about 20 July also reflected the views outlined in a declaration drafted by Hansen in March 1951 that received widespread notice and little criticism:

> The rift that has broken into our ranks because of 20 July must be bridged. Some of us stayed true to the oath; others, in further reaching recognition of all that was occurring, placed loyalty to the Volk above duty to the oath. No one should be reproached because of his attitude, as long as not self-interest but rather noble motives determined his action. From this recognition of motive it must follow that one must have understanding for the conduct of others!⁸⁵

Hansen first drafted this declaration as BvW chairman, before the foundation of the VDS and Frießner's interview, in order to find some common ground among former officers on this potentially divisive issue. It quickly became the model for "soldiers' opinion" on the issue, and many other groups adopted some version of it as their official stance toward the coup attempt.⁸⁶ Hansen's declaration was designed to promote mutual understanding by recognizing the perceived duties of both the conspirators and those who did nothing to resist Hitler, but Hansen was unable to escape the primary assumption he shared with almost all of his former comrades, which was that duty came above all else.

Even so, Hansen's statement bears a remarkable similarity to the official stances taken on the issue of resistance versus loyalty by Adenauer, military reformers, and even former conspirators like Kielmansegg. Speaking at a lecture series in 1984, Kielmansegg iterated that "those soldiers who did their duty in good faith and in good conscience should not permit any reproach or any attack on their moral character to concern them."[87] The future Bundeswehr general and adviser to Theodor Blank, Adolf Heusinger, expressed his understanding for those who remained loyal in 1944: "There was no fundamental decision for everyone, only tragic, irreconcilable conflicts of duties."[88] Though Hansen's and Heusinger's ideas and Frießner's comments differed in critical ways—such as calling the conspirators "murderers" and otherwise criticizing the assassination attempt—Hansen and Frießner, Kielmansegg and Adenauer all shared certain motives—namely, the desire to rehabilitate the soldiers who did *not* perpetrate the coup and to prevent the issue from being divisive within the ranks of former officers.

Despite the conciliatory tone of Hansen's statement and the fact that government officials and others echoed its sentiments, the military resistance to Hitler continued to divide former officers, creating a problem of membership that organization builders like Hansen and Frießner were anxious to address. Both men wanted to put and end to the event, to prevent its being discussed. In the aftermath of his press fiasco, Frießner even expressed the wish to make the "cursed conflict disappear from the face of the earth." "Therefore, the commandment of the hour is to speak of it as little as possible."[89] Frießner could have been quoting Keitel's 1944 order directly. Hansen's declaration did not please all former officers, however, and the issue periodically resurfaced for years to come.[90]

In one way, the former officers' preoccupation with honor and treason coincided with the public discomfort concerning the conspirators' actions and those of other resistance groups like the NKFD. Interestingly, the NKFD rarely appeared in the soldiers' papers in relation to 20 July, but soldiers' discussions of the prisoner of war issue betray the conviction that the NKFD and its officers-only counterpart, the BdO, crossed the boundary between loyalty and treason.[91] The case of Otto John, however, sparked animated discussions among former officers as to the wartime activities of John's fellow conspirators and whether they too were simply Soviet spies. The cases of Hans Oster and Wilhelm Canaris, known for their resistance activities within German military intelligence, also aroused criticism, both in the public and among former officers because their activities, which involved providing sensitive information to the Soviet Union, looked like "common" treason, which may have cost German soldiers their lives. Stauffenberg's "high" treason had been directed against the criminal government of the National Socialists.[92]

As one former officer noted, the conspirators of 20 July emerged as victors despite their coup's failure in 1944. Hitler was defeated, and several of the plotters who managed to escape the Gestapo were raised to positions of power in postwar Germany. Their memory was given a place of honor in the Federal Republic's historic iconography. The coup attempt came to represent both the tragedy of the Third Reich and the salvation of a Germany that (so the story went) had tried to resist, if only belatedly and unsuccessfully.[93]

Many former officers simply wanted to be done with the whole affair, as evidenced by their constant pleas to put an end to that discussion. Individuals and groups of officers continuously pleaded with their comrades that 20 July be declared off-limits as a topic of discussion. They called it divisive, destructive, and a danger point. But because 20 July affected soldiers so deeply and was so important to the Federal Republic's political mythology, former officers and their organizations had to confront the issue year after year.[94]

In 1952, Dönhoff recognized the problems that many former officers faced when dealing with 20 July. The first problem was that the event was too closely identified with the military and thus became an issue of disloyalty versus loyalty. Too often the public forgot that many of the conspirators and resistance leaders were civilians, ambassadors, and civil servants. Second, Dönhoff noted that the defensiveness of many former officers on the subject of resistance stemmed from an unfair measure of heroism established by the conspirators. "To demand heroism as the norm," she wrote, "is simply absurd." She regretted that instead of truly honoring those who had acted, most public debates ended up condemning those who had not acted. "No wonder those who, neither cowardly nor guilty, but who in the sense of 20 July were also not heroes, feel first indignation and then resentment toward those who unjustifiably were set up as the measure." Yet Dönhoff refused to let former officers lapse into complacency on the subject of their service and responsibilities in the Third Reich. Their notions of honor, duty, and loyalty were simply outdated in an era "in which the state, even the democratic state, exercises a power barely imaginable even a few decades ago. . . . The standards of the nineteenth century are no longer adequate."[95]

Some soldiers understood that 20 July was not simply about who did or did not break his oath and was instead a remarkable circumstance that never should have needed to occur in the first place. Heinrich Eberbach, who was himself involved in the coup, objected to arguments by Hans Hagen and others about the significance of the oath to Hitler and the "disastrous" effects of glorifying the conspirators. Eberbach disparaged Hagen's notion of the oath, elaborated at the conference at Bad Boll in 1950, as "romantic."[96] Herbert Selle also recognized the extraordinary demands placed on the consciences of officers in the Third Reich. There are circumstances that could lead a high-ranking officer to disobey the political leadership, Selle suggested. Though these circumstances were extremely rare in an orderly, constitutional state, the "immoral National Socialist state . . . challenged the men responsible for the leadership of the army several times within a very limited time frame to turn against [the state] out of the highest sense of moral responsibility."[97] Both Eberbach and Selle concluded that in a just and orderly political system, no coup would have been necessary. The fact "that many high military leaders of the German Wehrmacht in the Third Reich, just like large circles of the Volk, did not recognize that they no longer served an orderly *Rechtsstaat* [constitutional state] . . . was not only their fatal error, but their tragic guilt."[98]

That is the message of 20 July 1944. The coup was not about loyalty or treason or maintaining the values of eternal German soldierdom. The conspiracy involved a group of Germans, not just soldiers, realizing that they no longer lived in a state governed by law and that they served an immoral system. As Sodenstern noted in 1947, "The realities of soldiering posed career soldiers in the Third Reich more difficult problems than any other occupational group in the world has ever been confronted with."[99] This statement is true in both a military and a moral sense. The foreign policies of Hitler's Third Reich confronted the Wehrmacht with the impossible task of fighting a war on two fronts against overwhelming odds. Hitler's military, racial, and occupation policies confronted the officers with what was, for them, a choice between loyalty and humanity. Unfortunately, the vast majority of former officers were unable or unwilling to face the moral issue of service in the Third Reich as Stauffenberg, Beck, and others did. Fortunately, they were not able to solve their military dilemma either.

The former officers' attitude toward the canonization of the 20 July conspirators indicates the trouble that many members of this former elite had in adjusting to the political culture of the new German state. Feeling themselves defamed by the German public and the German (and Allied) governments, the officers were nevertheless dedicated to the reconstruction, both physical and moral, of Germany. As such, they were worried that the wrong message was being sent to future generations of Germans by a government and a public willing to glorify the actions of men the officers considered to be assassins. The majority of officers concerned with the coup attempt's implications wished simply to ignore the event and, echoing Keitel, to strike it somehow from the pages of history. Hansen's statement contains elements of this sentiment, as do the statements of many former officers in their private letters.

And yet officers' unwillingness to confront the past was without significant political or social consequences. They protested, wrote position papers, and sought to turn certain elements of the coup attempt to their benefit, but the veterans and their organizations were able to do little to change the government's policy regarding the coup or its role in the new army. After the shock waves emanating from Frießner's disastrous press conference subsided, most former officers quietly turned their attention to other matters. The 20 July conspiracy caused neither the massive splintering of the soldiers' organizations nor an undermining of the Bundeswehr's morale and discipline, as some had feared. The sound and fury that surrounded the discussions of the conspiracy among former officers signify, on the one hand, the officer corps' continuing isolation in a polity that still held it largely responsible for the horrors of World War II. Yet they also show ways in which former officers shared the concerns and ideals of both the German public and the government of the Federal Republic. As some public opinion data and the similarity of

Hansen's declaration to other statements on 20 July indicate, the views of former officers on the issue of service under the Third Reich were not fundamentally different from the mainstream. The officers, like the public, felt uncomfortable about the glorification of the coup attempt, and the officers, like the government, wanted to see a new German army at almost any cost.

Former officers felt isolated and betrayed; they railed against the government's glorification of "traitors"; they fretted about their beloved honor code and the German military's future. Ultimately, the fundamental coincidence of their interests with the public's and with the goals of those in power, in conjunction with similar circumstances in other areas of their lives, helped to ease the transition of the former officers into the democratic West German political culture.

Conclusion

Democracy in the Federal Republic of Germany has not shared the fate of its Weimar counterpart. Never in its history has the current German democracy experienced the radical, violent political culture that characterized the 1920s. Former officers played a crucial role in promoting that violence and destabilizing the republic during the Weimar era. Their quietism and acceptance of the current democratic state explains, at least in part, why it has survived for so long.

Career soldiers faced serious challenges in their effort to assimilate after World War II. Allied occupation regimes bent on eradicating National Socialism and militarism attacked their way of life and their value system. The Allied governments' decision to dissolve the Wehrmacht and (in most cases) to halt the payment of pensions to career soldiers swept away officers' careers and livelihoods. Many of their number were subject to investigation or prosecution for war crimes.

Even more dismaying to the officers was the German people's willingness to join with the occupation regimes in heaping vitriol on the Wehrmacht leadership. Numerous press articles condemned the "generals' clique" that conspired with Hitler to begin World War II. Privately, many Germans blamed the officer corps for losing the war that had begun so promisingly. Discrimination in schooling, in the workplace, and elsewhere left a burning sense of bitterness and betrayal in the hearts of many veterans.

Although most officers had not been Nazi Party members, there can be no denying the overtly National Socialist tone of their statements and ideas. Especially with regard to the causes and course of the war, 20 July, communism, and the role of a united Europe, the old soldiers shared much with the National Socialists. They dreamed of a unified society without political divisions, a Germany rearmed along the lines of the Wehrmacht, and a European political system in which Germany played its rightfully dominant role. While one cannot say that what they desired was Volksgemeinschaft, Lebensraum, and Festung Europa (Fortress Europe), these elements of the Nazi program still fascinated many former officers after 1945.

In what amounts to a disturbing parallel with the authoritarian traditions of Germany's past, former soldiers portrayed politics as a scandalous occupation, practiced by self-serving, prejudiced, and ignorant schemers who sought only to line their pockets by serving special interests at the German people's expense. The soldiers and their organizations therefore never quite trusted the government and its representatives. Former officers preferred fringe groups and "movements" rather than parties. They exhibited a dangerous willingness to lapse into bitter grumbling about the weakness of democracy and its adherents.

Despite these ominous signs, former officers chose not to resist the seemingly inexorable tide of events leading toward democracy, Western integration, and rearmament under the Blank Office's reformist ideas. Motivated by the need for personal vindication and the desire to rebuild their beloved Fatherland, these men joined the public debates on Germany's future. In the 1920s, the German military constantly meddled in politics, finally sending one of its own to serve briefly as chancellor. Paramilitary bands of former soldiers took to the streets to realize their vision of Germany based on the "community of the front." After 1945, former officers wished to be Germany's "soldierly conscience," but they strove for that goal as citizens, not as an army. Veterans' organizations became part of a "society of organizations . . . work[ing] together in the common interest of reconstruction."[1] Several fortuitous circumstances eased the transition from soldier to citizen.

The Allied policy of holding millions of German soldiers of all ranks captive for some period yielded several benefits, however unintended. Well-educated, patriotic officers rankled under camp life. While they sat idle or performed some menial task on foreign soil, Germany was being remade in their absence. They did not wish to be left out. Officers could not rely on the powerful myth of the "front experience" (as they had after 1918), but they did cling tenaciously to the myth of the military's traditional service to the Volk. Serving the people, rather than undermining the state, became the goal of career soldiers and their organizations, which is a marked contrast with the 1920s. Their self-sacrificing ideology also went a long way toward lessening the sting of rejection when their services were so often not welcome or required.

Nor could the former officer corps rely on its traditional esprit to allow it to survive in isolation from the rest of society. No longer were they the homogenous body that Seeckt and others had forged from "men of character." The Third Reich's ideological demands and the massive casualties of World War II created social, generational, and political divisions within the officer corps that were impossible to ignore. Allied controls disarmed them in more than just a military sense. Politics and the past created dissension within the veterans' organizations that made them unable to act as a "state within a state," as the army had in the 1920s.

The Cold War context proved to be decisive as well. The soldiers' loathing for communism, bolstered as it had been by education, war, and captivity, found a welcome echo in American propaganda and became a powerful integrative force. The desire to keep West Germany free of communism pending some eventual re-unification sparked the fire in many a soldier-activist's chest. Anticommunist and even antisocialist prejudices informed their political proposals; anticommunism fueled their interest in European unification; anticommunism dominated their thinking on rearmament issues. Even in their largely negative interpretation of the 20 July conspiracy, the former career soldiers were often guided by the principle that what Stauffenberg had done, regardless of the merits of his act, had benefited the Soviets and resulted in the occupation of much German soil. By bringing rearmament to the center of the German political arena, the Cold War elevated the officer corps, if not to its previous elite status, at least to a position of prominence and limited influence.

In its eagerness for sovereignty and legitimacy, the Federal Republic pursued policies that gave former officers a stake in the new democratic society. Adenauer intended to use rearmament as a wedge to pry German sovereignty from the grip of the Allied occupation regimes. To do so, he needed the support of the military elite and its organs, the veterans' associations. The Blank Office courted former officers; the political parties solicited their views on military policy. The government's efforts to establish its own legitimacy through generous social programs meant that the soldiers' pension demands were satisfied expeditiously, if not perfectly. The satisfaction of those pension demands alone goes a long way toward explaining the quietism of former career soldiers after 1945. As Diehl has pointed out, however, generous social programs do not ensure the survival of a state (witness Weimar). Diehl concludes that the competition that ensued among organizations of war victims to curry favor with the new state helped to ensure its eventual success.[2]

Equally important is the fact that in making their demands, the officers sought to coopt the language of democracy for themselves, to redefine it rather than destroy it. Instead of seeking to undermine an unpopular system, the former career soldiers attempted to work within the system to effect the desired changes. Democracy, even if ill defined, always remained the foundation of their plans and proposals. One can, in fact, adapt the Federal Republic's motto (Freedom, Right, Unity) almost exactly to fit the soldiers' desires and demands for the postwar era. "Freedom" meant the end of discrimination against soldiers in the workplace and releasing the war criminals. "Right" meant the restoration of their legal entitlement to pensions and an end to the alleged defamation of the German soldier. "Unity" of course meant a united Germany, not just in geographic but in political and social terms as well.

The former officers' potential for radicalism was not limited solely by their political isolation, the presence of occupation armies, or their fear of being left out of the rebuilding process. Despite their defensiveness on the surface, many underwent a real, if not always obvious, conversion either sometime during the war or shortly after it. One cannot ignore the extreme negative impact of the realization that they had served an ignoble and evil cause. Such a realization lessened even the most vocal former officers' enthusiasm for radical solutions and significantly reduced the size of any aggressive or radical party's likely following.

While former officers did not ultimately reject the postwar order, they did hope fundamentally to alter the course of developments by instilling the new democratic Germany with the values and traditions of eternal German soldierdom. First among those valuable traditions was character, the trait that had theoretically marked one for selection to the officer corps since time immemorial. Character encompassed all that was honorable in Germany's military past and excluded all that was embarrassing or negative. The Nazis' ideological requirements and the manpower demands of the war meant that character had been devalued during the Third Reich, to the detriment of Germany. But those losses could be made good in the future. Loyalty, bravery, honor, and a willingness to assume responsibility—all traits of a person of character—would lead Germany into a bright new age. Only a Germany united under these principles could ever, the officers believed, resist the powerful ideological pull of Soviet communism. The soldiers hoped to use their particular talents (character, patriotism, and anticommunism) to establish themselves as a soldierly conscience for the nation.

In terms of their beliefs and ideals, former officers benefited from a complex combination of isolation from and agreement with mainstream society. Like many Germans, they hoped to "draw a line under" the past in order to achieve a fresh start, free of guilt brought on by events prior to 1945.[3] In their rejection of both National Socialist and communist visions of the future, officers also found themselves in agreement with the mainstream. When their views did not coincide with those of the rest of German society, officers found themselves without allies. Their traditions and specialized concerns for honor and military values did not resonate with postwar society.

Certain inescapable paradoxes also limited the impact of the soldiers' ideas. The officers preached the joys of accepting responsibility but insisted that their conduct during the war had been unimpeachable because they had just been following Hitler's orders. They hated the term "politics," and they decried special interests. Yet they lobbied for their pensions and campaigned for their ideas all the same. They benefited from the notion that the army had mounted a meaningful resistance to Hitler, thanks to Stauffenberg's coup attempt, yet they simultaneously attacked the conspirators as traitors and murderers. The paradoxes contained within their arguments clearly indicate the importance of these political posturings for the officers' psychological defense mechanisms. The armed forces had been their life, and the military's fall from the pinnacle of social prestige and political power over the previous few decades, reaching its nadir between 1945 and 1950, evoked strong reactions among former career soldiers. Their efforts to salvage some of that prestige simply alienated them further from the majority of Germans.

A Social Democratic press release in September 1951 clearly encapsulated the former officers' situation, as well as some of the paradoxes inherent in their activities. "Up to this point," the writer of the article observed, "the generals who have shoved themselves into the foreground have shown only their tenacious devotion to the past, the spirit (or demons) of which they apparently wish to carry over into our own time." Many former officers may have been well intentioned but could not escape their upbringing. Commenting on the attitude of men like Frießner, the writer suggested that their behavior was "far less the result of a nationalistic or even National Socialist credo than the upshot of a life in which only tradition played a role, which neither could prevent the ruins of 1945 nor has a place in the world marred by those ruins. . . . A general in civilian clothes whom it pleases to have a colonel in civilian clothes speak to him in the third person will clearly not grasp that."[4]

After 1955, former officers faced much less pressing issues. The Federal Republic's social programs met their pension needs, if not always their demands. Even their idealistic demands for honor and a "new Germany" lost center stage to the serious political concerns of economic reconstruction, nuclear arms, and the Cold War. At later meetings of the Evangelical Academies, for example, old soldiers took a back seat to a younger group of Bundeswehr officers more in touch with the centers of power and the realities of the European scene. With the new army's fundamental elements in place, with the potential unification of Germany receding into the background, and with European unification proceeding at a pragmatic snail's pace, the fire slowly dissipated from the speeches and statements of the soldiers' organizations and their leaders.

The veterans' leaders turned instead to the problem of maintaining their organizations' membership when the influence of the VDS and other groups was tangibly declining. In the end, the organizations could do little more than plead for loyalty based on past deeds and the promise of continuing comradeship. The VDS expressed pride in its members who enlisted in the Bundeswehr and vowed never to forget them. Then came the pitch: "We may be allowed to expect the same loyalty from you toward your old organization, which was a support for you in the stormy times, which renewed and tightened the bond of comradeship, and which not least of all wanted to be your willing helper in the resolution of your pension affairs."[5]

In an effort to retain the members who joined the new armed forces, dues were even made voluntary for enlistees. The VDS has been unable, however, to attract many soldiers from the Bundeswehr. The Bundeswehr League became the group of choice among younger officers. The VDS remains largely the haven of former Wehrmacht veterans. As of 1993, the VDS had a mere twenty-five thousand members, of whom 85 percent were over the age of sixty-five.[6]

Rooted in their traditions and eager to contribute to Germany's renaissance, former officers played an active role in politics in the late 1940s and early 1950s, albeit often at the extreme margins. Through a combination of good fortune, tradition, and a lack of alternatives, the majority of former officers successfully adapted to the new democracy. Though they tried to redefine that democracy on their own terms, the representatives of German soldierdom were too isolated within society to alter the mainstream debate on Germany's future. Ultimately, they were forced either to join that mainstream or fade from significance. That they carried with them the intellectual baggage of their education, their association with Nazism, and a deep bitterness over their treatment during the postwar period only makes that successful transition more significant.

Notes

Abbreviations

In addition to the abbreviations used in the text, the following abbreviations are used in the notes.

BAMA Bundesarchiv-Militärarchiv—Federal Military Archive
BB   Archive of the Evangelical Academy, Bad Boll
FAZ   *Frankfurter Allgemeine Zeitung*
LOC   Archive of the Evangelical Academy, Loccum
MP   Member of British Parliament
MdB   Mitglied der Bundestag—Member of the Bundestag

Introduction

1. Buesch, *Military System and Social Life*, 50–65.
2. Joachim Wüst to Johannes Frießner, 23 September 1951, BAMA N528-55.
3. For a scathing account of the ways in which German officers enriched themselves, see Goda, "Black Marks," 413–52.
4. Craig, *Politics*, 375.
5. Kershaw, *Hitler Myth*.
6. Meyer, "Zur Situation," 579.
7. This discussion of former officers does not primarily deal with the very small number of officers who actually worked directly for the Federal Republic crafting the rearmament plans in the Chancellor's Office and the later Ministry of Defense. Reform-minded former officers such as Wolf Baudissin, Johann Adolf Kielmansegg, and Adolf Heusinger (who worked for Theodor Blank) had a much more direct impact on rearmament plans than did the leadership of the veterans' organizations, who tended to be older, more traditional, and therefore less willing to countenance the kinds of changes that were clearly necessary in order to accomplish the goals that the Bundeswehr (armed forces of the Federal Republic) was supposed to achieve. Since this work treats the development of German society and not rearmament per se, it largely ignores these reformers, who in many cases, because of their support for the "new look" German army, were practically ostracized from the "soldiers' community."

8. "Wohin, Alte Kameraden?," *Westdeutsche Allgemeine Zeitung*, 5 May 1954, BAMA BW9-757. Numbers are confirmed by an article in the VdH's *Der Heimkehrer* entitled "Soldat—Veteran—Tradition," *Der Heimkehrer*, October 1953, p. 5, BAMA MSg3-242/1. On the Wehrmacht's use of women (some 500,000 by 1945), see Kundrus, "Nur die halbe Geschichte."

9. "Wohin, Alte Kameraden?" *Westdeutsche Allgemeine Zeitung*, 5 May 1954, BAMA BW9-757.

10. Diehl, *Thanks*, represents the most thorough study of these organizations and places them accurately within the context of other similar organizations that existed during the earlier decades of the twentieth century.

11. Bars and restaurants all over Germany reserve at least one table, or *Stammtisch*, for regular patrons who come to enjoy conversation and a drink in the afternoon or evening.

12. "Wohin, Alte Kameraden?," *Westdeutsche Allgemeine Zeitung*, 5 May 1954, BAMA BW9-757.

13. I find Jeffrey Herf's notion of "multiple restorations" very useful in this regard (Herf, "Multiple Restorations").

1. "Pushed Aside, Persecuted, Prosecuted": Organizational Efforts, 1945–1951

1. H. Lauts, "An die Deutschen Soldaten!" 1951, BAMA N617-5. The flyer has no date, but was presumably written in 1951, based on the issues addressed in the text. The reference to "six years" of activity on the part of the "powers of the Federal Republic" must refer to the postwar activities of the political parties.

2. On the problems faced by former soldiers and officers returning from war, see Smith, *Heimkehr*.

3. Meyer, "Soldaten ohne Armee," 684.

4. Ruhm von Oppen, *Documents on Germany*, 68–69.

5. Ruhm von Oppen, *Documents on Germany*, 151–52.

6. Gottfried Hansen to Steltzer (Oberpräsident Schleswig-Holstein), 18 May 1946, BAMA N222-1.

7. Gottfried Hansen, Zum Thema "Burger II.Klasse," 9 February 1947, BAMA N222-3.

8. Pollock and Meisel, *Germany under Occupation*, 179–96.

9. Hansen to Dr. Weisser, 12 August 1946, BAMA N222-2.

10. Böckmann to Dr. Geiler (Min. Pres. Groß Hessen), 20 May 1946, BAMA N222-3.

11. Konteradmiral Schubert, "Ist der ehemalige Berufsoffizier für den Lehrerberuf geeignet?" August 1946, BAMA N222-2.

12. Indictment and Final Report to the President from Robert H. Jackson; in Pollock, *Germany under Occupation*, 29–33, 46–51.

13. Hansen, "Zur Protestkundgebung," 19 July 1948, BAMA N222-12.

14. Gert Spindler to Johannes Frießner, 11 September 1951, BAMA N222-108.

15. All statistics taken from Noelle-Neumann and Neumann, *Jahrbuch*, 379.

16. Ruhm von Oppen, *Documents on Germany*, 445–46.

17. Diehl, *Thanks*, 229–30.

18. On the economic situation of officers, see Diehl, *Thanks*, and Meyer, "Soldaten ohne Armee."

19. Hans von Donat, "Elendchronik," 1945–1951, BAMA N571-228.

20. Groppe, "Abschrift der Anl.4 einer Denkschrift des Generallts a.D. Groppe über die Pensionen der ehemaligen Wehrmachtsangehörigen," 27 January 1949, BAMA N222-22. The compiler was presumably Lt. Gen. Theodor Groppe, a well-known Catholic general.

21. In March 1948, the occupation regimes empowered the eleven states of the three Western zones to grant limited "subsistence allowances," but many failed to do so until much later. Hesse granted such support only in November 1949, five months before the new federal government assumed responsibility for the payments. VDS Groß-Frankfurt Mitteilungsblatt 1, June 1950, p. 2, BAMA MSg3-11/1.

22. Nordwest-deutschen Rundfunk announcement, 11 August 1946; cited in Hansen to Weisser, 12 August 1946, BAMA N222-2.

23. Oberstleutnant a.D. Max Lebius to Hansen, 16 January 1947, BAMA N222-3.

24. Diehl, *Thanks*, 141–42. On the situation of civil servants, see Garner, "Public Service Personnel."

25. Prewar and wartime benefits were determined by the WFVG/WEFVG (Wehrmachtsfürsorge- und Versorgungsgesetz/ Wehrmachtseinsatzfürsorge- und Versorgungsgesetz); Diehl, *Thanks*, 43–53.

26. That few believed any longer that the German civil service, especially under the Nazis, was an apolitical body had not yet dawned on many former officers. There is something of a paradox here, though, since many former officers seem to have acknowledged that the civil service was severely compromised by

National Socialism when they complained that former "party comrades" and even Nazi judges were receiving their pensions while career soldiers were not. When officers wished to emphasize their own traditions of service (see chapter 3), the civil servants were "apolitical," and when they wished to focus on the injustices of the pension regulations, the civil servants were "Nazis."

27. Bark and Gress, *History of West Germany*, 239. On compensation for war losses, see Hughes, " 'Through No Fault of Our Own.' "

28. Diehl, *Thanks*, 152–53. The issue of wartime promotions is an interesting one. Promotions came much faster during the war because of casualties but also depended in part on an officer's political behavior. Veterans' leaders spoke frequently of the disintegration of their once unified corps, brought on by careerism and conformity. In practical terms, however, the problem of ideological conformity among Wehrmacht officers surfaced only rarely. Qualms about the political taint of the Waffen-SS (armed forces of the Nazi Party elite guard) prompted many longer-serving officers to refuse Waffen-SS officers admission to their postwar organizations. By contrast, veterans' organizations eagerly courted younger Wehrmacht officers (more likely to have received dubious promotions).

29. Diehl, *Thanks*, 140.

30. Schmid in the *Verhandlungen des deutschen Bundestages*, 6 April 1950; cited in Diehl, *Thanks*, 161.

31. Diehl, *Thanks*, 161.

32. Hansen to Teichert, 1 August 1946, and Teichert's reply, 5 August 1946, BAMA N222-2.

33. Control Council Directive 38 in Ruhm von Oppen, *Documents on Germany*, 168–79.

34. Dr. Schmidt to Hansen, 15 October 1946, BAMA N222-2.

35. Blankenhorn to Schlafejew, 15 September 1950, BAMA BW9-3103; cited in Diehl, *Thanks*, 155–56.

36. See footnote 60, p. 289, in Diehl, *Thanks*.

37. Jungsozialisten pamphlet, no date (1955?), BAMA BW9-746. The pamphlet lists the decisive factors leading German youth to join the Foreign Legion (based on interviews of those arrested while trying to join or who subsequently escaped) as the following: homelessness (50 percent), unemployment (19 percent), unsettled familial relationships (20 percent), lust for adventure (8 percent), and fear of punishment for a crime (1 percent). The conclusion was that the government must provide work and housing as well as conduct an educational campaign on the evils of the Foreign Legion. I cite the date in the text as possibly 1955 because

of a reference to the number of German dead at Dien Bien Phu (c. 46,000) and because 1954–1955 were the years when the French Foreign Legion was making headlines in Germany.

38. Foreign Office to Blank Office, "Re: the statements of a Foreign Legionnaire on the conduct of German commanders in the Foreign Legion," 16 May 1955, BAMA BW9-746.

39. Bark and Gress, *History of West Germany*, vol. 1, 283.

40. On the PGA, see Georg Meyer: "Zu Fragen der personellen Auswahl," 351–65; "Zur inneren Entwicklung."

41. Meyer, "Soldaten ohne Armee," 750.

42. Some interesting data concerning the current occupations of former officers appear in the participant lists of the meetings of the Evangelical Academy at Bad Boll.

43. Waldenfels to Senator Vandenberg, 31 May 1948, BAMA N222-11.

44. Frau Anita Sievert in VDS Groß-Frankfurt Mitteilungsblatt 2, February 1951, p. 1, BAMA MSg3-11/1.

45. One of many is a letter dated 5 October 1946 (sender's name illegible), BAMA N222-2.

46. Landtag delegate Dr. Rief, speech, 4 May 1948, BAMA N222-11.

47. Echternkamp, "Wut auf die Wehrmacht?," examines the early coverage of the Wehrmacht in postwar newspapers. The author confirms that officers in particular suffered from a negative public image because of the exposure of the army's policy of plunder and murder in the war crimes trials and elsewhere.

48. Letter to the editor, *Echo der Woche*, 23 December 1949, BAMA N528-104. This letter's author earned the scorn of General Johannes Frießner, a former officer active in veterans' organizations, for being so cowardly as to sign only his initials.

49. Reben to Hansen, 25 February 1947, BAMA N222-3.

50. Letters to the editor, *Neue Zeitung*, 4 March 1950, BAMA N222-49.

51. Letter to the editor, "SZ" (*Süddeutsche Zeitung?*), 28/29 November 1951(?), BAMA N528-68. Date but no year listed. The letter presumably comes from 1951 or later since Stahlhelm officially reappeared in February 1951. It was originally a pre–Third Reich era veterans' organization.

52. Letter to the editor, *Die Freiheit*, 18 March 1949, BAMA N222-26.

53. Clasen to Frießner, 23 August 1951, BAMA N528-56.

54. *Grafischen Post*, June 1952; cited in VDS Nachrichtenblatt 4, 1952, BAMA MSg3-269/1.

55. *Vorwärts*, 18 November 1948, BAMA N528-68. The original reads: "Sie standen in Frankreich und Polen / Sie standen an Wolga und Don / Sie haben geraubt und gestohlen / Und wissen jetzt gar nichts davon."

56. "Die Jugend ist gegen Militarismus," *FAZ*, 12 May 1955, BAMA N222-156.

57. Frießner commented at a speech at the Evangelical Academy at Guntershausen: "Many may have reacted poorly to their military service; many may also have had the poor luck to have come across unqualified superiors—noncoms or officers. There are black and white sheep everywhere!—But army life never harmed anyone." Frießner, "Soldatentum oder Militarismus," 1 September 1950, p. 9, BAMA N528-22.

58. Georg Hanck to Hansen, 15 November 1954, BAMA N222-153A.

59. Noelle-Neumann and Neumann, *Jahrbuch*, 137.

60. Volkmann, "Die innenpolitische Dimension," 486–88.

61. An early and important work on the soldiers' organizations is Schenck zu Schweinsberg, "Die Soldatenverbände," 96.

62. Hansen to Rogalewsky, 22 November 1949, BAMA N222-37.

63. Admiral Hansen lived in Kiel.

64. Meyer, "Soldaten ohne Armee," 726. See the exchange between Hansen and Böckmann, circa 4 January 1947, BAMA N222-3 and, more significantly, the initial contacts between Hansen and Donat on 18 October 1948 in BAMA N571-124.

65. Adams to Mewis, 14 October 1948, BAMA N571-124.

66. Aktennotiz Bussche, 5 November 1951, BAMA BW9-3086. For more on the workings of the Blank Office, see Greiner, "Die Dienststelle Blank"; Foerster, "Innenpolitische Aspekte"; and Krüger, *Das Amt Blank*.

67. On bans of radical organizations see BvW Groß-Frankfurt, Mitteilungsblatt -1, c. June 1950, p. 1, BAMA MSg3-11/1. Meyer also mentions a few banned organizations in "Soldaten ohne Armee," 726.

68. These included Engelbert Frank's Hilfsverein für ehemalige berufsmässige Angehörige der Deutschen Wehrmacht und ihrer Hinterbliebenen, founded in July 1948. Raul Mewis founded BEWAH (Betreuung ehemalige Wehrmachtsangehöriger u. deren Hinterbliebene) in August 1948.

69. The creation of the VDS is covered in chapter 2.

70. Schubert, "Grundsätzliches für die Arbeit an dem Problem 'Berufssoldaten,'" no date (presumably late 1948), BAMA N222-13.

71. Mitteilungsblatt BvW Groß-Frankfurt, May or June 1950 (date unreadable), p. 1, BAMA MSg3-11/1.
72. Rundschreiben der Notgemeinschaft . . . für das Land Nordrhein-Westfalen, 29 March 1950, BAMA N222-49.
73. Hansen to Deyhle, 2 April 1950, BAMA N222-49.
74. H.D. von Conrady, "Gedanken über den VDS," c. November 1951, BAMA N222-107.
75. Diehl, *Thanks*, 175.
76. Primarily by Diehl, *Thanks*.

2. Creating Soldiers' Opinion: The Verband Deutscher Soldaten

1. In Körber, ed., *Soldat im Volk*, 151.
2. The Kyffhäuserbund was refounded by former general Wilhelm Reinhard on 26 July; Stahlhelm issued its official statement of purpose on 1 April; BAMA BW9-3086. There is even a mention of the refoundation of the socialist veterans' group Reichsbanner in a letter of 12 July 1951 from Trettner to Dethleffsen (BAMA N648-8), though it seems to have disappeared very quickly.
3. Frießner expressed these hopes in an infamous press conference on 22 September 1951, discussed in this chapter below and in chapter 6. AP report on Frießner speech, 22 September 1951, BAMA N222-107.
4. Programm des BdV (Bund der Versorgungsberechtigten), 15 November 1950, BAMA BW-9-3103.
5. Mitteilungsblatt VDS (at that time the BvW) Groß-Frankfurt, early 1950 (pre-June, but otherwise date is illegible), p. 2, BAMA MSg3-11/1.
6. *Das Eichenblatt* 17, June 1958, BAMA MSg3-238/1.
7. Stahlhelm declaration, 1 April 1951, BAMA BW9-3086. German prisoners worked for the Allied governments on construction or agricultural projects and even performed certain military duties, such as mine-clearing. At one point, as many as two thousand prisoners were killed or wounded per month in mine-clearing operations in North Africa. Smith, *Heimkehr*, 24–25.
8. *Die Oase* 2, February 1953, BAMA MSg3-144/1-2. "Afrikaner" refers here to the former members of the Africa Corps, not the Dutch settlers of South Africa. The members of the DAK called each other "Afrikaner" and called the members of the German colonial forces from World War I the "Alte Afrikaner."
9. *Die Oase* 8, August 1954, p. 5, BAMA MSg3-144/1.
10. *Die Oase* 4, April 1955, p. 7, BAMA MSg3-144/1-2.

11. "Der Mensch Rommel," *Die Oase* 2, February 1955, p. 4, BAMA MSg3-144/1–2.

12. Trettner to Hansen, 11 December 1954, BAMA N222-153.

13. "Mit Rommel bei Tobruk, *Die Oase* 5, May 1955, p. 6, BAMA MSg3-144/1–2.

14. "Hüter einer großen Tradition," *Die Oase* 10, October 1956, pp. 7–8, BAMA MSg3-144/1–2.

15. *Die Oase* 1, January 1954, p. 6, BAMA MSg3-144/1–2.

16. *Die Oase* 9, September 1956, p. 7, BAMA MSg3-144/1–2.

17. *Die Oase* 11, November 1954, p. 3, BAMA MSg3-144/1–2.

18. "Mehr Verständnis für Asiens Völker," *Die Oase* 9, August 1954, pp. 9–10, BAMA MSg3-144/1–2.

19. *Das Eichenblatt* 12, March 1957, pp. 1 and 21, BAMA MSg3-238/1.

20. *Die Neue Feuerwehr* 41, September 1955, p. 14, BAMA MSg3-176/1.

21. *Die Neue Feuerwehr* 41, September 1955, p. 14, BAMA MSg3-176/1.

22. The Federal Constitutional Court declared the KPD unconstitutional in 1956. The government applied for this ruling at the same time (1951) that it asked the court to declare unconstitutional the right-wing Socialist Reich Party (SRP), in which Maj. Otto Remer (of 20 July fame) was active. The court declared the SRP illegal in 1952 but deliberated on the issue of the KPD for nearly five years before making a ruling.

23. *Die Neue Feuerwehr* 41, September 1955, p. 13, BAMA MSg3-176/1.

24. "Traditions-Erlaß vom grünen Tisch?" *Die Neue Feuerwehr* 83, March 1959, p. 4, BAMA MSg3-176/1.

25. See "Gleiches Recht für 131er," *Die Neue Feuerwehr* 41, September 1955, p. 2, BAMA MSg3-176/1 (among others).

26. "Zieht einen Schlußstrich," *Die Neue Feuerwehr* 41, September 1956, p. 6, BAMA MSg3-176/1.

27. "Ein Wort zum 'Fall Manteuffel: Wie lange noch solche Prozesse?" *Die Neue Feuerwehr* 89, p. 3, September 1959, BAMA MSg3-176/1.

28. "Zwischen den Konferenzen: Der 17. Juni," *Die Neue Feuerwehr* 86, June 1959, p. 2, BAMA MSg3-176/1.

29. Two examples are issues 84 and 85 of *Die Neue Feuerwehr* (April and May 1959), which printed statistics about Berlin on pages 7 and 8 respectively. BAMA MSg3-176/1.

30. "Gleiches Recht für 131er," *Die Neue Feuerwehr* 41, September 1956, p. 2, BAMA MSg3-176/1. Significantly, Großdeutschland also nearly always

surrounded the initials of the country, DDR (Deutsche Demokratische Republik), with quotation marks to indicate its nonexistence in the minds of its members. See *Die Neue Feuerwehr* 86, June 1959, p. 8, BAMA MSg3-176/1.

31. "Furcht vor der Wiedervereinigung," *Die Neue Feuerwehr* 83, March 1959, p. 3, BAMA MSg3-176/1.

32. Diehl, *Thanks*, 93.

33. "Nullachtfuffzehn," *Frankenpost*, 20 March 1954, BAMA BW9-757.

34. Programm der 2. VdH Diskussionswoche, 10–18 May 1954, BAMA BW9-758.

35. "Die Frauen sind schlecht weggekommen," *Der Heimkehrer*, 5 November 1954, p. 3, BAMA MSg3-242/1.

36. That washing powder would have been advertised to women in 1950s Germany seems indisputable. The intended audience of the more neutral ads (such as for books) was often made clear by a picture of a woman in the ad itself. See *Der Heimkehrer*, 5 November 1954, BAMA MSg3-242/1.

37. By the late 1950s, some of the newsletters were including photographs, charts, and maps to entertain their readers, but the earlier circulars, especially those of the VDS, were remarkably bland.

38. "Soldatentum ohne Fanfaren," *Der Heimkehrer*, June 1953, p. 5, lists the goals of a committee of soldiers' groups, of which the VdH was a member. "Grundsatzdebatte im Verband der Heimkehrer," *Der Heimkehrer*, 5 September 1954, p. 3, discusses new goals. Both in BAMA MSg3-242/1.

39. "Entwurf für die Proklamation," no date, presumably c. July 1951, BAMA N648-7. This statement closely echoes the Nazi slogan "Gemeinnutz vor Eigennutz" (the common good above the individual good).

40. Frießner, "Zweck und Aufgaben des 'Verbandes Deutscher Soldaten,'" late 1951–early 1952, BAMA N528-70. There is no date on the document, but it is apparently a speech that Frießner gave shortly after the press conference of September 1951 (discussed below) and several more times in the course of that year. It appears to have been printed and circulated in January 1952.

41. Axel v.d.Bussche to Günther, 1 August 1951, BAMA BW9-3085.

42. Erich Dethleffsen, "Aktennotiz über meine Besprechung im Bonn am 31.8.1952, 1 September 1951, BAMA N648-7.

43. Dethleffsen headed an organization called the Economic-Political Society of 1947 (Die Wirtschafts-politische Gesellschaft von 1947), which, though Dethleffsen often denied it, received funds from the federal government and took a very pro-U.S. stance on rearmament.

44. There were numerous proposals regarding the composition of the board, but the final list included the following: Assmann, Blum, Crüwell, Gille (Waffen-SS), Guderian, Gümbel, Haenschke, Hansen, Hausser (Waffen-SS), Herr, Krakau, Manteuffel, Mohr, Mosbach, Potthoff, Ramcke, Reinhard, Ringeling, Röhlke, Seideman, Steinhoff, Student, Stumpff, Velten, and Vollbracht; 17 September 1951, Protokoll der Tagung am 9. September 1951 in Bonn, p. 10, BAMA N648-7.

45. According to a UP press release, Frießner met Schumacher on 19 September and shortly thereafter planned to meet the leaders of the unions. BAMA N528-39.

46. Frießner, "Das Auslands-Presse—Interview," late 1951, BAMA N528-37.

47. Frießner to Manteuffel, 15 September 1951, BAMA N528-48.

48. Frießner, "Wechmar," no date, BAMA N528-37. Frießner's position on the 20 July coup attempt will be discussed in chapter 6.

49. Frießner, "Wechmar," no date, BAMA N528-37.

50. Peter von Zahn, "Von Nah und Fern," 25 September 1951, pp. 1–2, transcript in BAMA N648-7.

51. "Von Tag zu Tag," 24 September 1951, BAMA N528-39.

52. Schoettle to Veiel, 4 October 1951, and Mayer to Veiel, 5 October 1951, BAMA N528-39.

53. Bundespresseamt, "Mitteilung an die Presse," 2 October 1951, BAMA N528-39.

54. "Beschluss der ausserordentlichen Vertretersammlung des Landesverband Würt-Baden," 31 December 1951, BAMA N571-378.

55. Colonel Bonatz to Hansen, 4 November 1951, BAMA N222-107. Bonatz led the Bamberg group of the BvW (second largest behind Munich and made up of two-thirds noncommissioned officers).

56. Frießner, "Das Auslands-Presse—Interview," typed version, late 1951, BAMA N528-37.

57. General a.D. von Vormann to Trettner, 2 November 1951, BAMA N528-53, and VDS, "Zur Information für die Presse," 10 December 1951, BAMA N648-7.

58. Dethleffsen, "Stellungnahme zur Einladung des 'Goslarer Arbeitsausschusses,'" c. February 1952, BAMA N648-7.

59. Keilig, "Protokoll" (Bonn), 22 February 1952, BAMA N222-120.

60. Nachrichtenblatt VDS/BVW Landesverband Südweststaat 7, pp. 1–3, November 1952, BAMA MSg3-269/1. Nearly all former officers referred to those

convicted as either "so-called war criminals", "war criminals" in quotation marks, or "war-convicted" to indicate their disapproval of the verdicts. In fact, it was the official policy of the VDS to do so. See the minutes of the meeting of the board of directors and the central committee of the VDS, October 1954, BAMA N222-153.

61. The composition of the VDS can be estimated based on the statistics from one of the south German branches in 1954: 75 percent career soldiers (almost equally divided between officers and noncommissioned officers), 8 percent army bureaucrats, and 17 percent widows. Officers' widows outnumbered the widows of noncommissioned officers more than two to one. Another interesting statistic is that almost one-third of the former officers in the VDS had entered the army as soldiers and risen through the ranks; thus nearly 50 percent of the members had at one time been noncommissioned officers. Nachrichtenblatt des VDS/BVW Landesverband Südweststaat 20, July–August 1954, BAMA MSg3-269/1.

62. F. Burghardt to Frießner, 13 January 1952, BAMA N528-56. Frießner underlined this passage and scribbled "Ja" in the margin to indicate his agreement.

63. Hansen to Steltzer (Oberpräsident Schleswig-Holstein), 18 May 1946, BAMA N222-1; Hansen, "Zur Frage der Fürsorge für die Berufsunteroffiziere der ehemaliger Kriegsmarine," September 1946, BAMA N222-2; Hansen, "Zum Thema Burger II. Klasse," 9 February 1947, BAMA N222-3; and Hansen to Theodor Heuss, 15 September 1949, BAMA N222-37 are a few of the many letters and essays, spanning a period of three years, dealing with the subject of militarism and the political neutrality of soldiers.

64. See chapter 3 for more on the origins and importance of this service notion.

65. Adenauer speech, 3 December 1952, before the Bundestag upon the second reading of the Deutschland and EVG treaties; reprinted in Nachrichtenblatt des VDS/BVW Landesverband Südweststaat 8, 1952, p. 2, BAMA MSg3-269/1.

66. Nachrichtenblatt des VDS/BVW Landesverband Südweststaat 12 and 13, April and May 1953, BAMA MSg3-269/1.

67. Hansen to Blank, 14 February 1953, BAMA N222-221.

68. Blank to Hansen, 19 February 1953, BAMA N222-221.

69. Besprechung Hansen/Blank, 16 March 1953, BAMA N222-221.

70. Dethleffsen to Crüwell, 4 November 1952, BAMA N648-2.

71. Crüwell to Dethleffsen, 11 November 1952, BAMA N648-2.

72. As late as 1956, Großdeutschland printed an article in *Die Neue Feuerwehr*, entitled "The Cold Coordination of the Soldiers' Unions," condemning

the tactics of the VDS in trying to unify the veterans' organizations. Cited in Mosbach to Landesverband chairmen, 25 July 1956, BAMA N222-162.

73. The words *Verantwortungsgefühl* (responsibility), *Tapferkeit* (bravery), *Pflichterfüllung* (duty), *Kameradschaft* (loyalty), and *Gehorsam* (discipline) form a litany intoned by all veterans' organizations.

74. For example, Meyer, "Zur Situation," 674. Diehl fleetingly refers to a military subculture in *Thanks*, 178.

75. See any of the examples in BAMA MSg3-269/1.

76. VDS Groß-Frankfurt, Mitteilungsblatt 1, 14 January 1953, p. 2, BAMA MSg3-11/1.

77. "Das Rommel-Sozialwerk," *Die Oase*, October 1956, p. 8, BAMA MSg3-144/1.

78. VDS Groß-Frankfurt, Mitteilungsblatt 8, 7 August 1951, p. 4, BAMA MSg3-11/1. Former officers apparently abused these networks at times. One regional group's newsletter warned members about former master sergeant Alfred Kretschmer, who had a letter of recommendation from the Württemberg/Baden branch of the VDS and was swindling money from other members. Kretschmer would claim to be getting work at any moment and then ask for a short-term loan so that he could survive until his first paycheck.

79. Information gleaned from the newsletters of the VDS Frankfurt branch between March 1950 and July 1955 (BAMA MSg3-11/1). A total of sixty-three separate job offers was listed in the newsletter, sometimes for multiple positions (up to eighty in one case).

80. Mitteilungsblatt VDS/BvW Landesverband Südweststaat, January 1953, p. 8, BAMA MSg3-269/1.

81. Mitteilungsblatt VDS/BvW Landesverband Südweststaat, August–September 1953, p. 31, BAMA MSg3-269/1.

82. *Die Oase* 8, August 1954, p. 5, BAMA MSg3-144/1.

83. VDS Groß-Frankfurt, Mitteilungsblatt 11, 7 November 1951, p. 3, BAMA MSg3-11/1.

84. Donat to Putzer, 6 October 1949, BAMA N222-36. Of course, the ad rhymes in German: "Was ich als Leutnant lernte in frohem beisammensein, trägt heute neue Ernte: ich kenne den besten Wein!"

85. On the problem of missing German soldiers, see Smith, *Die "vermißte Million,"* and Böhme, *Bilanz*. James Bacque, a Canadian, generated a controversy in 1989 when he suggested that over one million of the missing had been exterminated in U.S. POW camps (Bacque, *Other Losses*). Smith systematically

refutes Bacque's claim, as do Bischof and Ambrose, *Eisenhower and the German POWs*.

86. Nachrichtenblatt des VDS/BVW Landesverband Südweststaat, issues 1 (April 1952) through 20 (July/August 1954), BAMA MSg3-269/1.

87. The executive board of the GfW elected in 1954 consisted entirely of prominent former officers who, though not necessarily friendly with the VDS (men such as former general Wilhelm Reinhard had frequent run-ins with Hansen), shared many of the opinions expressed by the VDS and the other veterans' organizations. So while the GfW was more similar to a modern "think tank" than a veterans' organization, in most cases its aims and ideas were identical to those of the VDS, DAK, and others. Names of the executive board are found in the Nachrichtenblatt VDS/BVW Landesverband Südweststaat 20, 1954, p. 22, BAMA MSg3-269/1.

88. Cappele, Notizen zu dem Vortrag von Oberstlt. a.D. v. Zydowitz: "Wehrmacht—Ja oder Nein?," 1 March 1955, BAMA BW9-768. Emphasis in original.

89. Cappele, Notizen.

90. Linde to Blank Office, 5 December 1952, BAMA BW9-3089.

91. The program of a DAK meeting in Hanover is printed in *Die Oase* 9, September 1953, BAMA MSg3-144/1-2. Other examples, all nearly identical, can be found in *Die Oase* 6, June 1955, BAMA MSg3-144/1-2, and *Das Eichenblatt* 17, June 1958, BAMA MSg3-238/1.

92. Aktennotiz H. Karst, "Bericht über Treffen der Angehörigen der ehemaligen 4. Panzerdivision in Bamberg 20.–22.6.1953," 26 June 1953, BAMA BW9-3090. General Eberbach coordinated the soldiers' conferences at Bad Boll (see chapter 5 below).

93. *Die Oase* 9, September 1953, p. 2, BAMA MSg3-144/1-2. The 1953 game resulted in a 2-2 tie. A later game, played in 1956, saw the British emerge victorious in a 7-0 rout. The German veterans blamed age for the disastrous result since the British team was made up of active members of the Eighth Army rather than veterans of the African campaign.

94. "Mitteilungen des VdS-Bonn Nr. 7," Mitteilungsblatt 20 VDS/BvW Landesverband Südweststaat, 15 July 1954, p. 13, BAMA MSg3-269/1.

95. *Die Oase* 8, August 1956, BAMA MSg3-144/1-2.

96. Vermerk über Gründungsversammlung DAK (29.7), 30 July 1951, BAMA BW9-3086.

97. Vermerk über Gründungsversammlung DAK.

98. Indeed when alcohol was absent from a meeting, the absence garnered

special mention, as did the good behavior of the participants "in spite of" (or perhaps due to!) the lack of drink.

99. *Die Oase* 6, June 1955, BAMA MSg3-144/1-2.

100. Aktennotiz Linde, 18 November 1952, BAMA N222-147.

101. Programm der 3. Bundestreffen in Hanover (DAK), 12–13 September 1953, BAMA N222-147.

102. Messerschmidt, "The Wehrmacht and the Volksgemeinschaft," 730.

3. Service to the Volk: Traditions and the Lessons of Captivity

1. Hürten, "Das Offizierkorps," 239. The literature on the education and training of German officers is enormous. A number of other essays in Hofmann, ed., *Das deutsche Offizierkorps*, are indispensable, as are any of the many works of Detlef Bald, such as the following: *Der deutsche Generalstab; Der deutsche Offizier; Sozialgeschichte; Vom Kaiserheer zur Bundeswehr;* and Bald, Bald-Gerlich, and Ambros, eds., *Tradition und Reform*. Also very useful are Kitchen, *The German Officer Corps;* Meier-Welcker, "Der Weg zum Offizier"; and Messerschmidt, "German Staff Officers' Education." See also Ostertag, *Ausbildung;* Spires, *Image and Reality;* Thompson and Peltier, "Education of Military Officers."

2. Manteuffel made such a comment in his memoirs; cited in Breit, *Die Staats- und Gesellschaftsbild*, 121.

3. Breit, *Die Staats- und Gesellschaftsbild*, 141–45.

4. Hürten, "Das Offizierkorps," 240–41.

5. Breit, *Die Staats- und Gesellschaftsbild*, 145–46.

6. Seeckt, "An alle Generalstabsoffiziere," 18 October 1919; Document 35 in Bald et al., eds., *Tradition und Reform*, 156.

7. Seeckt in Bald et al., eds., *Tradition und Reform*, 154.

8. Seeckt, cited in Breit, *Die Staats- und Gesellschaftsbild*, 146.

9. Meier-Welcker, "Der Weg zum Offizier," 163, n. 101.

10. Bald, *Der deutsche Offizier*, 43.

11. Cited in Bald, *Der deutsche Offizier*, 113.

12. Bald, *Der deutsche Offizier*, 114.

13. "Richtlinien für die Ausbildung der als Führergehilfen in Aussicht genommenen Offiziere"; in Bald et al., eds., *Tradition und Reform*, 160.

14. Gordon Craig, cited in Messerschmidt, "German Staff Officers' Education," 12.

15. Contemporaries and historians alike have used the term Vernunftsrepub-

likaner (rational republicans) to describe many Germans' tenuous allegiance to the Weimar Republic.

16. Seeckt, cited in Craig, *Politics*, 377.

17. Not all officers were so cowardly in their response to the coup attempt. Gen. Walter Reinhardt, chief of army command in 1919–1920, and Gen. Walter von Bergmann, commanding troops in Stuttgart, both declared their support for the republic. Craig, *Politics*, 376–79.

18. Cited in Craig, *Politics*, 479.

19. From Hitler's Reichstag Speech, 13 July, 1934; cited in Breit, *Die Staats- und Gesellschaftsbild*, 165.

20. A great deal of work has been done since the mid-1980s on the subject of the ideological and moral commitment of the Wehrmacht to the principles of National Socialism. The classic works on the subject are by Messerschmidt and Müller. See Messerschmidt: *Die Wehrmacht im NS-Staat*; "Die Wehrmacht im NS-Staat"; "The Wehrmacht and the Volksgemeinschaft." See also Müller, *The Army, Politics, and Society*, and Berghahn, "NSDAP." Several more recent historians have moved beyond the work of Messerschmidt and Müller to assert that the common soldier and all levels of the officer corps were deeply affected by the ideological penetration of the Wehrmacht, not just the upper echelons—for example, Bartov: *The Eastern Front* and *Hitler's Army*. Others include Schulte, *The German Army*, and Streit, *Keine Kameraden*. Though he devotes more attention to the experience of the common soldier, see also Fritz, *Frontsoldaten*.

21. Active duty soldiers were not allowed to vote in Germany until the establishment of the *Bundeswehr* in 1955.

22. "Politische Erziehung und Unterricht der Wehrmacht," 30 January 1936; cited in Bald, Bald-Gerlich, and Ambros, eds., *Tradition und Reform*, 177.

23. Oberbefehlshaber des Heeres, Erziehung des Offizierkorps," 18 December 1938; cited in Bald, Bald-Gerlich, and Ambros, eds., *Tradition und Reform*, 182.

24. Bald, Bald-Gerlich, and Ambros, eds., *Tradition und Reform*, 181.

25. Absolon, "Das Offizierkorps," 251.

26. "Oberbefehlshaber des Heeres"; cited in Bald, Bald-Gerlich, and Ambros, eds., *Tradition und Reform*, 181.

27. "Kriegsakademie, Allgemeines," 17 June 1935; cited in Bald, Bald-Gerlich, and Ambros, eds., *Tradition und Reform*, 174.

28. "Oberbefehlshaber des Heeres"; cited in Bald, Bald-Gerlich, and Ambros, eds., *Tradition und Reform*, 181.

29. Any of the works by Bald cited in note 1 above provide excellent descriptions of the social recruitment policies of the Prusso-German army.

30. Seeckt, cited in Breit, *Die Staats- und Gesellschaftsbild*, 146.

31. It is beyond the scope of this work to comment on the continuities that exist between the educational principles followed during the Weimar and National Socialist years and those that guided officer training in the Bundeswehr after 1955. Suffice it to say that character and notions of service retained their prewar significance. Much of the work of Detlef Bald has been on this subject of continuity. The endpoint of many of his studies of the Weimar and Third Reich policies is to compare them to the policies adopted by the Bundeswehr. Martin Kutz has indicted the Bundeswehr for retaining character as a selection criterion in order to preserve traditional, conservative values in the military. Kutz: *Realitätsflucht* and *Reform*.

32. In 1957, the West German government created the Scientific Commission for the History of the German Prisoners of War, headed by Erich Maschke. The commission produced twenty-two volumes on the subject over the next sixteen years. For more on the Maschke commission, see the brief essay by Steininger, "Some Reflections on the Maschke Commission." The numbers provided by the Maschke commission, though dated, seem to still be the standard. The numerical estimates are provided in Böhme, *Bilanz*, pp. 45–46, 110, 142. Interestingly, a more recent work using Soviet archives has largely corroborated the story told by the Maschke Commission and testifies to its thoroughness and exactness even in the face of astounding difficulties with documentation. See Karner, *Im Archipel GUPVI*. Recently available Soviet documents seem only to confuse the story, making clear that the Soviets themselves were unsure how many German POWs were in the USSR at any one time. See V.B. Konasov, "K voprosu." Thanks to David Kerans for finding and translating the article for me. A new work, Borchard, *Die deutschen Kriegsgefangenen*, appeared too late to be consulted.

33. Cartellieri, *Lagergesellschaft*, 252.

34. Cartellieri, *Lagergesellschaft*, 251.

35. Cartellieri, *Lagergesellschaft*, 255.

36. Cartellieri, *Lagergesellschaft*, 251.

37. Cartellieri, *Lagergesellschaft*, 253.

38. Cartellieri, *Lagergesellschaft*, 255.

39. Cartellieri, *Lagergesellschaft*, 61–63.

40. Böhme, *Bilanz*, 97. The importance of this small number was complicated, however, by the fact that more than 1.2 million German soldiers were still

missing in action. Many people in the West suspected that the Soviets were holding far more than the number provided by Soviet officials.

41. Cartellieri, *Lagergesellschaft*, 327.

42. "Antifascist" is fairly obviously a code word in most cases, simply meaning procommunist. Much of the following is based on Robel, *Antifa*. Robel spent eight years as a POW himself, and his hostility toward the Soviet Union seeps through at various points. He is very anxious, for example, to refute the Soviet claim that the horror stories told by returning prisoners were merely "anticommunist propaganda." A much needed survey of Soviet reeducation efforts is in Smith, *War for the German Mind*.

43. The folly of heeding such calls to desert is indicated by the estimates that some thirteen to fifteen thousand Wehrmacht soldiers were executed (many for attempted desertion or self-inflicted wounds) and by estimates that (should a soldier succeed in deserting) somewhere between 90 and 95 percent of German soldiers taken in 1941 and 1942 died in Soviet captivity. See Bartov, *Hitler's Army*, 96, and Böhme, *Bilanz*, 110.

44. Robel, *Antifa*, 38–39.

45. Robel, *Antifa*, 44.

46. Robel, *Antifa*, 44–47.

47. The Reichswehr very clearly swore a personal oath to Adolf Hitler in 1934 (see above). But once in captivity, and especially after the war, it was very common for officers to reinterpret that oath as one to the Volk (in the person of its leader) rather than an oath to Hitler himself. The Soviets did not mind "helping" the officers to that conclusion.

48. Robel, *Antifa*, 52–56.

49. Robel, *Antifa*, 44–45.

50. Robel lists "Walther von Seydlitz-Kurzbach, Alexander Edler von Daniels, Dr. Otto Korfes, Martin Lattmann" as the few generals who joined the BdO upon its foundation. Robel, *Antifa*, 80–81.

51. Returnee interviews cited in Robel, *Antifa*, 93. One of the problems with Robel's citation of these interviews is that he often omits the interviewee's rank. Whether this practice is an oversight or a function of anonymity of the documents themselves, I do not know.

52. Robel, *Antifa*, 21, n. 48.

53. Cartellieri, *Lagergesellschaft*, 7.

54. The Allies agreed on the principal of political reeducation at Potsdam in 1945. Though the Potsdam agreement did not specifically address the issue of

educating POWs, both the Soviets and the Western Allies took advantage of the opportunities presented by a captive audience.

55. "Nachrichten für die deutschen Kriegsgefangenen in der Sowjetunion," no. 2, 3 January 1946; cited in Robel, *Antifa*, 98.

56. Robel, *Antifa*, 312.

57. The Western Allies held roughly twice as many prisoners as the Eastern bloc in 1945: 7.75 million compared to 3.3 million. Smith, *Heimkehr*, 11.

58. Böhme, *Geist und Kultur*, 15–18.

59. An exhaustive account of the British effort was written by the man in charge of the operation, Henry Faulk, *Re-education*. A more recent work on reeducation programs of all the Allies is Smith, *War for the German Mind*.

60. From *History of the Provost Marshal General: Prisoner of War Operations*, 582. Cited in Böhme, *Geist und Kultur*, 3.

61. Cited in Böhme, *Geist und Kultur*, 3.

62. Faulk, *Re-education*, 99 and 117.

63. The following quotes are taken from the report of this British reeducation official. Cited in Faulk, *Re-education*, 92–93. The presumably English-language original is located in the documents of the British Prisoner of War Division, but Faulk gives an incomplete citation. The following passages therefore rely on Faulk's translation.

64. Cited in Faulk, *Re-education*, 92–93.

65. Cited in Faulk, *Re-education*, 92–93.

66. Cited in Faulk, *Re-education*, 92–93.

67. Address of Provost Marshal General Lerch; cited in Böhme, *Geist und Kultur*, 11–12.

68. Declaration of the prisoners in Camp Ellis, Illinois, in *Der Ruf* 11, 15 August 1945; cited in Böhme, *Geist und Kultur*, 12–13. *Der Ruf* became famous after the war when a group of reeducation program graduates refounded the paper on German soil. Several of those involved in the new, short-lived *Der Ruf* went on to establish the influential literary movement Group 47. For details, see Smith, *War for the German Mind*, 165–69.

69. *Der Ruf* 2, 1 April 1945; cited in Böhme, *Geist und Kultur*, 30.

70. Cited in Cartellieri, *Lagergesellschaft*, 368.

71. Frießner, "10 Gebote für den P.W.," 6 May 1946, BAMA N528-69.

72. The following section relies heavily on documents from the Evangelical Academy. In the 1950s and 1960s, the various Evangelical Academies sponsored forums and workshops at which former soldiers (usually officers), politicians,

church leaders, youth leaders, and union officials (among others) discussed topics of mutual interest. Two of the academies, at Hermannsburg (which later relocated to Loccum, near Hanover) and Bad Boll (near Göppingen) were especially active. With titles like "Days of Reflection for Former Soldiers," "The Soldier and Public Opinion," and "Our Mission as Returnees," these workshops provide excellent material for the study of the postwar attitudes and experiences of former officers. The speeches and discussions often dealt with the problems of the prisoners of war, especially those still being held in the Soviet Union as late as 1955. Discussions of the particular difficulties of late returnees from the Soviet Union, such as their social readjustment, family relations, and career placement, dominated the conferences.

73. See the opening words of Gerd Heinz-Mohr and the lecture entitled "Gesamtschuld und Einzelschicksal als Problems des Gefangenen," by H. Ingensand, in the minutes of the workshop "Unser Auftrag als Heimkehrer," 29 July–1 August 1955, p. 35, LOC 1955.

74. Minutes of the workshop "Unser Auftrag als Heimkehrer," 29 July–1 August 1955, p. 35, LOC 1955.

75. Frießner, "Soldatentum oder Militarismus," 1 September 1950, BAMA N528-22.

76. Diester, "Meine Erlebnisse im amerikanischen Internierungslager Moosburg [Bavaria] 1945/1946," p. 105, BAMA N571-402.

77. Noack to Spindler, 23 November 1951, BAMA BW9-3086.

78. Donat, "Ein General erlebt Hitler und den Nazismus"; unpublished manuscript, BAMA N571-227, pp. 241b–241g. Another general held by the Soviets similarly felt that nicotine addiction revealed an inner weakness. He believed that smokers were more likely to be spies. Cited in Cartellieri, *Lagergesellschaft*, 122.

79. Frießner, "Soldatentum oder Militarismus," 1 September 1950, BAMA N528-22.

80. Cartellieri, *Lagergesellschaft*, 370.

81. Cited in Cartellieri, *Lagergesellschaft*, 172.

82. Cited in Cartellieri, *Lagergesellschaft*, 358.

83. Cartellieri, *Lagergesellschaft*, 370.

84. Diester, "Meine Erlebnisse," p. 9, BAMA N571-402.

85. Lempp, "Das innere Erleben in 9 Jahren russischer Gefangenschaft," 15–18 October 1953, BB-14 (1953).

86. Robel, *Antifa*, 44.

87. Cartellieri, *Lagergesellschaft*, 170.

88. Arnim declaration printed in *Der Ruf* 10, 1 August 1945. Cited in Böhme, *Geist und Kultur*, 53.

89. *Der Ruf* 10, 1 August 1945. Cited in Böhme, *Geist und Kultur*, 53–54.

90. Interviews in Cartellieri, *Lagergesellschaft*, 368–69.

91. H. Ingensand, "Gesamtschuld und Einzelschuld als Problems des Gefangenen," in minutes of the workshop "Unser Auftrag als Heimkehrer," 29 July–1 August 1955, p. 21, LOC 1955. Ingensand commits the unfortunately common fallacy of comparing the conditions in the POW camps to those in the German concentration camps.

92. H.D. von Conrady, "Gedanken über den VDS," c. November 1951, BAMA N222-107.

4. Unpolitical Soldiers: Veterans, Politicians, and Military Reform

1. Koshar, *Social Life*.

2. H. D. von Conrady, "Gedanken über den VDS," c. November 1951, BAMA N222-107.

3. Smilo Freiherr von Lüttwitz, "Die tragende Kraft des deutschen Heeres in den Krisenjahren des 2. Weltkrieges," December 1951, BAMA N10-15.

4. In the mid-1950s Johannes Frießner even suggested that a personnel committee of the sort that was set up to judge the fitness of former officers for commands in the new Bundeswehr (the Personnel Screening Committee) be established to screen politicians as well. Frießner, "Wirbel um den Personalgutachter-Ausschuß," no date, BAMA N528-70.

5. A letter from Hasso von Manteuffel to Erich Dethleffsen in July 1951 makes this realization explicit: "The foundation of a soldiers' group may never have a party-political aspect at its base but will have in every case political consequences domestically and abroad." Manteuffel to Dethleffsen, 17 July 1951, BAMA N648-6.

6. Ostau earned a reputation for publishing such manifestos and founding parties and organizations that, according to Meyer, often failed to survive their first meeting. Meyer, "Zur Situation," 723.

7. Ostau, "Offene Antwort an die *Neue Zeitung* in Munich," 10 July 1948, BAMA N222-13.

8. Spindler to Frießner, 11 September 1951, BAMA N222-108.

9. Program of the Tatgemeinschaft freier Deutscher, 10 July 1949, BAMA N528-67.

10. Program of the Tatgemeinschaft, 10 July 1949, BAMA N528-67.

11. Political pamphlet, "Was will die Deutsche Union?," c. March 1949, BAMA N222-26. It is interesting to note the frequent use of the word *abendländisch*, or occidental, rather than *europäisch*, or European.

12. The Deutsche Gemeinschaft was another of Ostau's creations. I assume that Donat was a member of the Deutsche Gemeinschaft because he consistently underlines the parts of its correspondence concerning deadlines and membership dues.

13. Korrespondenz der Deutschen Gemeinschaft, 27 February 1951, BAMA N571-141.

14. Protocol of the board meeting of the Arbeitskreis für Wehrforschung, 9–10 December 1957, BAMA N648-12.

15. The phrase comes from the World Conference for Moral Rearmament, held at Caux on Lake Geneva in October 1950. Hossbach to Frießner, 11 October 1950, BAMA N528-20.

16. Herr, cited in a letter from Spindler to Frießner, 19 November 1951, BAMA N528-51.

17. "Zweck und Aufgaben des 'Verbandes Deutscher Soldaten,'" January 1952, BAMA N528-70.

18. Frießner, "Soldatentum oder Militarismus," 1 September 1950, p. 9, BAMA N528-22.

19. Peter von Zahn, "Von Nah und Fern," 25 September 1951, transcript in BAMA N648-7.

20. Hansen to Adenauer, 21 July 1948, BAMA N222-12.

21. Just as the veterans' organizations hoped to influence public opinion in favor of rearmament, so too did participants of the meetings at Bad Boll wish to make their voices heard and thereby increase the "defensive will" of the German people. Hermann Foertsch proposed to Eberbach immediately following the first meeting at Bad Boll that another conference be held, to be entitled "The Soldier and Public Opinion," in order to discuss the various methods of influencing not only the press and parliament, but also the man in the street. H. Foertsch, "Gedanken für eine weitere Tagung der Evangelischen Akademie Bad Boll," c. December 1950, BB-11 (1950).

22. Hansen to Robertson, 1 May 1948, BAMA N222-10. Original in English.

23. Hansen to W.M.F. Vane, MP, 26 May 1948, BAMA N222-11.

24. Newspaper clipping, "Wer verteidigt die Demokratie?" No name or date, BAMA N222-11.

25. Hansen to Heuss, 15 September 1949, BAMA N222-37.

26. CDU to Hansen, 2 August 1946, BAMA N222-2.

27. Parteivorstand der SPD to Hansen, 5 August 1946, BAMA N222-2.

28. Letter from the Kommunalpolitischer Ausschuß of the local SPD; cited in Hansen to Steltzer, 27 June 1946, BAMA N222-1.

29. Manteuffel and Admiral Heinrich Heye later became representatives of the FDP.

30. "Was will die Deutsche Union?," no date, BAMA N222-26, and Donat to Heinzelmann (Deutsche Gemeinschaft), 24 November 1950, BAMA N571-141, provide examples.

31. Hansen to Kleikamp, 25 July 1948, BAMA N222-12.

32. Veiel, "Besprechungsgrundlage für die sofort zu führenden Verhandlungen mit den Württ. Bad. Bundestagsabgeordneten.," 24 May 1950, BAMA N571-124.

33. See an exchange of letters between Hansen and Spindler in late September 1951, BAMA N222-108.

34. Diehl, *Thanks*, 174.

35. Large, *Germans to the Front*, is a much needed general history of German rearmament after 1945, and it deals very comprehensively with the debates about the form the new army would take. For a concise discussion of the proposals for German rearmament before 1950, see Schubert, *Wiederbewaffnung und Westintegration*, 17–21. Other good sources on German rearmament during the period before 1955 are Militärgeschichtliches Forschungsamt, ed., *Aspekte der deutschen Wiederbewaffnung*; Fischer, *Wiederbewaffnung*; and Foerster, ed., *Von der Kapitulation*.

36. The KVP was ostensibly set up as police force, but its equipment and training gave it a military and offensive capability.

37. Mosen, *Bundeswehr*, 239 (n. 18), and Schubert, *Wiederbewaffnung und Westintegration*, 20–21.

38. "Die Jugend ist gegen Militarismus," *FAZ*, 12 May 1955, BAMA N222-156.

39. Luck, *Panzer Commander*, 329. Either Luck remembered the incident incorrectly or the officer with whom he was speaking did not understand the workings of the PGA, which screened former officers reapplying for the rank of colonel or above. The PGA was an independent committee, commissioned by the Bundestag, yet composed entirely of private individuals with (usually) strong anti-Nazi credentials, not party representatives.

40. "Führung der Verhandlung mit der Alliierten Hohen Kommission über die Unterbringung zusätzlicher alliierter Truppen und der Bearbeitung der allgemeinen Fragen der Sicherheit der Bundesrepublik." In Militärgeschichtliches Forschungsamt, ed., *Aspekte der deutschen Wiederbewaffnung*, 171.

41. Beauftragter des Bundeskanzlers für die mit der Vermehrung der alliierten Truppen in Deutschland zusammenhängenden Fragen. Noted in Nelson, *Germany Rearmed*, 32.

42. Militärgeschichtliches Forschungsamt, ed. *Aspekte der deutschen Wiederbewaffnung*, 198.

43. Bauer, *Deutsche Verteidigungspolitik*, 20. The unions lodged their disapproval of rearmament on 16 January 1955, as did a council of theologians meeting at St. Paul's Church on 29 January 1955.

44. Craig, *NATO and the New German Army*, 5; his source is unclear.

45. Dethleffsen, "Gedanken über die Haltung der Deutschen Generale für einen Fall von den Westmächten wiederverlangter deutscher Aufrüstung," 22 November 1949, BAMA N528-67.

46. *Der Spiegel* 39, 27 September 1950, BAMA N222-79.

47. *Der Spiegel* 39, 27 September 1950, BAMA N222-79.

48. "Marriage of convenience" (*Vernunftehe*) was an unfortunate choice of words since many soldiers and other Germans in the 1920s (as noted above) had been known as Vernunftsrepublikaner (rational republicans) and were later unwilling to defend the Weimar Republic against the attacks of the Nazis once the relationship was no longer so convenient.

49. Korte to Frießner, 15 August 1950, BAMA N528-20.

50. "Die Bilanz des Soldaten," *Stuttgarter Zeitung*, 27 November 1950, BB-11 (1950).

51. Claes and Müller-Brandenburg, "Ruf und Recht des deutschen ehem. Berufsoffiziers," 7 December 1950, BAMA N222-80.

52. H. Lauts, "An die Deutschen Soldaten!" c. 1950, BAMA N617-5. See also Reinhardt to Frießner, January 1951, BAMA N528-21.

53. One colleague wrote to Hansen in 1952 that threats of radicalization were causing great worries among Bundestag representatives and other government officials. Putzer to Hansen, 2 April 1952, BAMA N222-120.

54. Putzer to Hansen, 2 April 1952, BAMA N222-120.

55. Hansen to Sonja Donner, 12 December 1950, BAMA N222-80.

56. "Auszüge aus Briefen von ... an ... vom Juli 51," BAMA N222-119.

57. Meyer has written extensively about the attitude of veterans toward rearmament in "Zur Situation."

58. Hansen to Adenauer, 30 May 1955, BAMA N222-156, and Hansen to Mosbach, 12 July 1955, BAMA N222-156.

59. "Ehemalige Soldaten erörtern ethische Fragen," *Neue Zeitung*, December 1951, BB-12 (1951). The article maintains that the question of whether or not rearmament should occur was hardly even debated at the meeting in Bad Boll in 1951.

60. See Dethleffsen, "Gedanken über Ausbildung während des Krieges," written shortly after the war and then excerpted and sent on 15 April 1952 to Oberst a.D. Golling in the Blank Office; BAMA N648-2. Golling sent Dethleffsen his "Richtlinien für Bearbeitung von Dienstvorschriften" in March 1952 for approval and suggestions.

61. Dethleffsen to Emmerich, 19 December 1951, BAMA N648-2. Werl, Landsberg, and Wittlich were military prisons used to house convicted war criminals.

62. Müller to former soldiers in Württemberg, November 1951, BB-12 (1951). The organizer of a soldiers' conference at the Evangelical Academy in Bad Boll (discussed in more detail in chapter 5) insisted that such a conference was necessary because former soldiers were "especially called upon" to clarify the issues surrounding rearmament.

63. Satzung der GfW, 14 November 1955, BAMA N648-13.

64. "Der Bundesverteidigungsminister beim Kriesverband Flensburg des VdS," 12 July 1956, BAMA N222-162.

65. Albrecht to U.S. President, 11 December 1950, BAMA N222-80.

66. "Ohne uns oder mit uns?, der alte Soldat vor der Frage nach Krieg oder Frieden!," 6–8 December, BB-11 (1950).

67. Dethleffsen, "Die gegenwärtige geistige und soziale Situation der ehemaligen Offiziere und Unteroffiziere," September–October 1953, BAMA N648-17. Dethleffsen gave this lecture at the conferences on soldierly education. Baudissin convened one of the conferences, "Grundsätze für die Erziehung in den zukünftigen Streitkräften—1. Sachverständingentagung, at the Akademischen Bundesfinanzschule Siegburg on 25–26 June 1953. Brandstaedter to Dethleffsen, 27 August 1953, BAMA N648-2.

68. "Auszüge aus Briefen von . . . an . . . vom Juli 51," BAMA N222-119.

69. "Dear Mr. Sefton Delmer!," *Die Oase* 8, August 1954, p. 5, BAMA MSg3-144/1.

70. Trettner to Hansen, "Bundestreffen Afrikakorps," 11 December 1954, BAMA N222-153.

71. Aktennotiz Mosbach, 1 October 1956, BAMA N222-162. It is somewhat surprising that government officials were still belaboring the "without me" issue in 1956 since that mood had largely subsided, at least among the general population, even before the foundation of the Bundeswehr.

72. Rundschreiben Linde, 5 March 1954, BAMA N222-221. This notice may even have come at the insistence of the government, which had already denied the VDS's right to participate in the PGA in 1953. See Hansen to Blank, 14 February 1953, BAMA N222-221.

73. Conrady, "Gedanken über den V.d.S.," c. 10 November 1951, BAMA N222-107.

74. Keilig, "Gedanken zur Wehrgestzkommentierung," 16 June 1954, BAMA N222-156.

75. Rundschreiben (Entwurf) Hansen, late 1952?, BAMA N222-221.

76. Reischle to Donat, 21 December 1951, BAMA N571-161. Application procedures for the BGS were rigorous. Applications had to include a short biography and two recommendations, and they obligated applicants to serve if approved (unlike later Bundeswehr applications). Werbe-Merkblatt für das Schutz- und Begleitkommando der Bundesrepublik, October 1950, BAMA N571-161.

77. C.H. Lungershausen, "Bericht über die Tagung des Ausschusses ehem. Berufssoldaten . . . in der CDU . . . ," 21 June 1955, BAMA N222-156. Krafft Freiherr Schenck zu Schweinsberg, in his early work on veterans' associations, suggests that Hansen also overestimated the number of officers needed by the Bundeswehr. I saw no evidence of such a mistake, as government and veterans' officials seemed to be using the same numbers. Still, Hansen's position was weak, given the large number of applicants, whatever the number of positions. Schenck zu Schweinsberg, "Die Soldatenverbände," 137–38.

78. "Ein Wort für die Soldaten," *FAZ*, 10 November 1954, BAMA N222-153.

79. Bielefelder Soldatenring, "Protesterklärung des V.d.S. gegen . . . ," 28 July 1955, BAMA N222-156.

80. For an account of Blank's speech, see *New York Times*, 13 November 1955, p. 1. On the Bundeswehr's uniforms, see Nelson, *Germany Rearmed*, 155.

81. Frießner, "Zum Geburtstag der neuen deutschen Wehr," 22 November 1955, BAMA N528-70.

82. Critics often dubbed the plan "Inneres Gewürge" which means "internal strangulation."

83. It is telling that even a dictionary devoted to the subject offers only a provisional definition of Innere Führung. Zoll, Lippert, and Rössler, eds., *Bundeswehr und Gesellschaft*, 125. See also Germany, Bundesministerium der Verteidigung, *Handbuch Innere Fuhrung*. On the concept in general, see Militärgeschichtliches Forschungsamt, *Aspekte der deutschen Wiederbewaffnung*, 219; Blank, *Vom Künftigen Deutschen Soldaten*, 19 and 31; and Baudissin, "The New German Army," 3. The Defense Ministry tried to define the concept for its soldiers in a periodical called *Information für die Truppe*, published by the Bundesministerium der Verteidigung. See, for example issue 10, 1957, p. 28. See also Large, *Germans to the Front*, for a complete discussion of the reform movements that defined the new army.

84. *Information für die Truppe* 1, 1956, p. 32.

85. "Keine Diskriminierung!" *Stuttgarter Zeitung*, 3 August 1951, summarized in Presse- und Informationsamt der Bundesregierung, *Informationsdienst*, 8 August 1951, BAMA BW9-3085.

86. VDS Kreisverband Detmold, "Beurteilung der Lage des V.d.S.," 6 August 1956, BAMA N222-162.

87. Koshar, *Social Life*, xiii.

88. Koshar, *Social Life*, 166.

89. Koshar, *Social Life*, 286.

90. Hauck, "Ansprache des Gefühls in der Soldatenerziehung," 9–12 October 1952, BB-13 (1952). Reinhart Koselleck argues that the imagery of a heroic death is rare in postwar Europe. Two industrial world wars made death in war seem senseless, if not accidental. Hauck's remarks therefore indicate the uniqueness of the soldiers' milieu. Koselleck, "Der Einfluß."

91. "Die Bilanz des Soldaten," *Stuttgarter Zeitung*, 27 November 1950, BB-11 (1950).

92. Conference at the Evangelical Academy Bad Boll, "Gewerkschafter und Soldaten," 23–25 February 1959, program in BAMA MSg2-1890. Remarkably, the tone and content of the meetings changed relatively little from the days when Hauck spoke on topics such as "Tradition—To Create or Protect?" (as he did in 1951). The Bundeswehr officers (who in most cases had been Wehrmacht officers too) continued to apologize for the Wehrmacht, to deny charges of militarism and antidemocratic sentiments within the old army, to make the hostility between workers and soldiers during Weimar and the empire sound like a misunderstanding, and to cite the resistance movement within the Wehrmacht's General

Staff as evidence of the sound foundations upon which the Wehrmacht had rested. See the speeches by Riggert and Hinkelbein entitled "Gewerkschaft und Landesverteidigung" and "Soldatentum und Militarismus" (respectively) in the program cited above.

5. A European Fatherland? Anticommunism and European Defense

1. The Nazis continued until the very end of the war to voice the opinion that the Western Allies were "fighting for the wrong side" and to hope that the United States and Britain would "see the light" and join with Germany in a common "European front." Rumors to the effect that such an action was impending or had actually occurred circulated among the Wehrmacht, even after the war had ended. Meyer cites an example of a rumor of an impending British–German "crusade" as late as August 1946. Meyer, "Zur Situation," 600.

2. Most of the information on early ideas about European unification comes from the thorough account in Lipgens, *A History of European Integration*.

3. Lipgens, *A History of European Integration*, v–vi.

4. Lipgens, *A History of European Integration*, 81.

5. The Europäische Föderalistische Union (Cologne), the Europäische Gemeinschaft (Munster), the Paneuropa-Union (Hamburg), and the Union-Europa-Liga (Munich). Lipgens, *A History of European Integration*, 385.

6. Lipgens, *A History of European Integration*, 386.

7. Lipgens, *A History of European Integration*, 386–87.

8. A concise summary of these events is presented in Laqueur, *Europe since Hitler*, 129–39.

9. Johanna Vogel, *Kirche und Wiederbewaffnung*; Rausch and Walther, eds., *Evangelische Kirche in Deutschland*.

10. Both Blank and Erler spoke at a meeting in Bad Boll in 1954, "Friedenswille und Verteidigungsbereitschaft als erzieherische Ziele," BB-16 (1954), and Erler appeared again at a 1955 meeting, "Gespräch zwischen Politikern und Soldaten," BB-19 (1955).

11. Records of the "3. Soldatentagung," 1952, BB-13 (1952).

12. Almost as an afterthought, for example, former general Hauck included the importance of religion in addressing a soldier's emotion in his 1952 lecture on that topic. Hauck, "Ansprache des Gefühls in der Soldatenerziehung," pp. 10–11, BB-13 (1952).

13. "Auszüge aus Briefen zur Soldatentagung," pp. 2–3, BB-12 (1951).

14. Landesbischof Harig to former soldiers in Württemberg, October 1950, BB-11 (1950).

15. Eberbach an die Dekanatämter in Württemberg, October 1950, BB-11 (1950).

16. From the program for "Tage der Besinnung...," 18–22 November 1950, BB-11 (1950)

17. From Eberbach's "Pünkte für Eröffnung," written before the meeting, BB-11 (1950).

18. The participants at Bad Boll and at similar discussions elsewhere were in many cases the same people involved in the creation of the veterans' organizations and frequently shared ideas or consulted with Hansen, Dethleffsen, and the other major figures discussed in this work. In fact, the first meeting at Bad Boll was attended by Hans von Donat, Heinz Guderian, Smilo Freiherr von Lüttwitz, and Otto Flies, an associate and friend of Hansen. While these men had already petitioned the government on behalf of former soldiers, the meetings at Bad Boll represented a much more significant opportunity to reach the public and a wider circle of former soldiers than any of their other efforts.

19. "Steht der Eid über allem?," *FAZ*, clipping date merely "1950" in BB-11 (1950). Probably around 29 November, when another article on the Bad Boll meeting was published.

20. "Diskussion um Soldateneid und Verantwortung," *Neue Zeitung*, 30 November 1950, as well as other articles and letters in BB-11 (1950)

21. Former officers constantly reiterated the point that nationalism had no appeal to German youth. For two examples among many, see the minutes of the meeting "Internationale Soldatengespräche," 18–23 February 1956, p. 3, LOC-1956, and "Heimkehrer und Jugend: ein Diskussionsbeitrag," 6 June 1954, p. 4, BAMA BW9-758.

22. Großdeutschland was most attentive to such conventions; see its newsletters in BAMA MSg3-176/1, esp. nos. 41 (September 1955) and 84 (April 1959).

23. Engelbert Frank to Hansen, 18 March 1950, BAMA N222-49. The letter cites a discussion with the chairman of the Bavarian SPD.

24. Donat, "Ein General erlebt Hitler und den Nazismus," p. 273ff., BAMA N571-227.

25. Mantey to Hansen, no date (c. September 1946), BAMA N222-2.

26. *Deutsche Soldaten-Zeitung* 12, December 1953, p. 10. A similar article in the newsletter of one regional branch of the VDS/BvW cited the fact that between

1815 and 1914, Germany participated in only three wars while "democratic" Great Britain participated in ten. Nachrichtenblatt 18 VDS/BvW Landesverband Südweststaat, February–April 1954, p. 26, BAMA MSg3-269/1.

27. Tholens to Hansen, 18 October 1954, BAMA N222-153B.

28. Meyer has written an interesting analysis of two similar essays in "Zur Situation," 671–74. He outlines the various standard theses concerning the history of the Third Reich and World War II formulated by former officers: soldiers could not vote and therefore were not to blame that Hitler came to power; soldiers were party-neutral during the Weimar Republic; no one liked the Nazis' anti-Semitism very much; the events of 30 June 1934 surprised the Wehrmacht; the military maintained its comradely duties with respect to its "non-Aryan" members. And the list goes on.

29. For excellent examples of common Wehrmacht soldiers spouting Goebbels's propaganda slogans, see Fritz, " 'We Are Trying,' " 705–8.

30. Frießner, "Verbrannte Erde," no date, BAMA N528-70.

31. "Rede zu Gefallenengedenktag des Kameradschaftsverbandes Ungarischer Frontkämpfer im Münchner Rathaus," 25 May 1952, BAMA N528-70.

32. Frießner, "Soldatentum oder Militarismus," 1 September 1950, BAMA N528-22.

33. Langer to Frießner, 26 September 1951, BAMA N528-57.

34. Christliche Offizier-Vereinigung, "Letzte Tage—Bericht Kreiner," BAMA MP-108.

35. Georg von Sodenstern, "Entscheidung für Europa," *Deutsche Soldatenzeitung*, 29 November 1951, BAMA N594-11, and Leonhardt Cuno (a.k.a. Georg von Sodenstern), "Schuld im Spiegel der Geschichte," c. Spring 1947, p. 156, BAMA N594-10.

36. Sodenstern, "Der 'bedingungslose Kapitulation,' " 1947, BAMA N594-11.

37. Meyer, "Zur Situation," 678–84, 727.

38. Dethleffsen, "Gedanken über die Haltung der Deutschen Generale für einen Fall von den Westmächten wiederverlangter deutscher Aufrüstung," 22 November 1949, BAMA N528-67.

39. Hansen, "Memorial Concerning the Political Significance of the Defamation of the German ex-Wehrmacht Personnel," 1 December 1948, BAMA N222-18. Sodenstern makes the same point in "Schuld im Spiegel der Geschichte," pp. 162–63, BAMA N594-10.

40. Görlitz, "Die geistigen Grundlagen des Soldatentums," 8–12 May 1954, LOC-1954. As Napoleon retreated from Russia in December 1812, Yorck defied

his king's will by signing a neutrality agreement with the Russian tsar in the Lithuanian town of Tauroggen and later joined the pursuit of Napoleon back to France. (Prussia was technically a French ally at that point.)

41. Schramm lecture covered in *Karlstädter Zeitung*, 13 January 1954. Copy in BAMA BW9-768.

42. See chapter 6 for more on the ideas of the conspirators and on the officers' interpretation of the 20 July coup.

43. Wurm, "Nationalismus als Problem der neueren deutschen Geschichte," 18 November 1951, BAMA MSg2-1858.

44. E. Müller, invitation to the second conference at Bad Boll, November 1951, BB-12 (1951).

45. According to the record of Albert Finet's speech, the French editor mentioned the possibility of a European army defending itself against the United States, unlikely as that may seem. Someone later crossed these remarks out of the minutes, perhaps wishing to keep these unseemly comments off of the official record.

46. "Bekenntnis zur europäischen Armee," *FAZ*, 13 December 1951. BB-12 (1951).

47. In describing the many similar essays and discussions that he studied, Meyer judged that they "bespeak disconcertion as well as an ignorance of the developments in the world. They are peculiar, sometimes confused drafts and attempts, in light of the growing division of Germany and the world, to ruminate on conceivable future tasks in the military realm." Meyer, "Zur Situation," 687. While some participants at the discussions at Bad Boll (such as Baudissin and Kielmansegg) were not so clueless, Meyer's description fits many former officers and their ideas very well.

48. Tillmanns, "Das Wagnis eines Verteidigungsbeitrages," BB-12 (1951).

49. From the "Bericht über die Tagung...," p. 8, BB-12 (1951). It is unclear whether the reference of the participant (Waldburg-Zeil) to the lack of European chiliasm is a veiled expression of regret that Hitler's Thousand-Year Reich was no longer viable. The specific use of the word *Chiliasmus*, meaning the doctrine of Christ's thousand-year reign on Earth, makes such a conclusion tempting, but invitations to the Evangelical Academy were usually scarce, radicals were not welcome, and, after all, it is explicitly a reference to Christ, something not uncommon at these meetings. Also, given that Finet's "unfortunate" comments about a war against the United States were deleted from the official record and

Waldburg's were not, it seems unlikely that anyone at the academy noticed the parallel, if any was intended.

50. "Auch wenn das Vaterland im Schmutz liegt...," *FAZ*, c. 13 December 1951, BB-12 (1951).

51. Müller in notes on discussion of Tillmanns's lecture, Bericht über die Tagung..., p. 14, BB-12 (1951).

52. See Bericht über die Tagung..., pp. 14–16, BB-12 (1951).

53. The importance of strengthening a soldier's "defensive willpower" (*Wehrwillen*) was a centerpiece of National Socialist thinking about the people's community as Messerschmidt indicates in "The Wehrmacht and the Volksgemeinschaft," 722.

54. Frießner, "Ein Interview," 1948, BAMA N528-70. Frießner related this story using a fictional device, though why he did so remains a mystery. It indicates something of the fantasies so common among former officers in the postwar period. Not that the interview itself was so far-fetched. Such interviews (some would say interrogations) were commonplace, but they usually took place in prisoner of war camps or under the auspices of the Operational History (German) Section or some similar organization. It is unclear therefore whether Frießner was fictionalizing an experience he actually had or whether his desire to contribute his thoughts to the ongoing debate concerning rearmament was so great that he concocted a story about being sought out by the now slightly obsequious Allies, who belatedly recognized the value of his experience. This same passage appears almost verbatim without the frame of the fictitious interview in an article by Frießner entitled "Krieg des armen Mannes," *Münchner Allgemeine Zeitung*, 13 April 1951.

55. "Vom Bergfried aus gegen den Bolschewismus: Die ersten Träger des europäischen Gedankens," *Wiking-Ruf* 1, November 1951, p. 14, BAMA BW9-3086.

56. Dethleffsen, "Die gegenwärtige geistige und soziale Situation der ehemaligen Offiziere und Unteroffiziere," September–October 1953, p. 17, BAMA N648-17.

57. Many Wehrmacht commanders, Frießner included, had at various times during the war commanded Waffen-SS units. There was a strange tension among Wehrmacht veterans concerning the Waffen-SS, however. Former officers often recognized that the Waffen-SS units were highly motivated and effective in combat, yet they often resented the privileges of the Waffen-SS in terms of equipment and reinforcements. They rarely if ever reflected on what exactly

motivated the Waffen-SS. There was certainly no love lost between the two groups of veterans, and many Wehrmacht veterans refused to include Waffen-SS soldiers in their organizations. One unfortunate exception to that rule was the support given by many prominent Wehrmacht officers, including Guderian, to those prosecuted at the Malmédy trial in 1946.

58. "Auszüge aus Briefen zur Soldatentagung," p. 1, BB-12 (1951).

59. Müller to the former soldiers in Württemberg, September 1952, BB-13 (1952).

60. Hauck, "Ansprache des Gefühls in der Soldatenerziehung," p. 9, BB-13 (1952).

61. Baudissin, "Was verlangt der Soldat von dem die öffentliche Meinung gestaltenden Menschen?," 13–15 March 1952, protocol p. 12, LOC-1952.

62. Major i.G. a.D. K.H. Helfer to Dethleffsen, 8 August 1951, BAMA N648-9.

63. VDS Arbeitsausschuß, "Ziele der *Deutschen Soldatenzeitung*," 28 November 1951, BAMA N648-7.

64. Karst, "Bericht über Treffen der Angehörigen der ehemaligen 4. Panzerdivision in Bamberg 20–22.6.1953," BAMA BW9-3090.

65. Koller, *Der Letzte Monat*, 188.

66. Müller an die ehemaligen Soldaten in Württemberg, September 1952, BB-13 (1952).

67. 3. Soldatentagung (Protokoll), p. 4, BB-13 (1952).

68. 3. Soldatentagung (Protokoll), p. 5, BB-13 (1952).

69. Wunsch to Eberbach, 5 November 1952, BB-13 (1952).

70. Minutes of "Internationale Soldatengespräche," 18–23 February 1956, p. 4, LOC-1956.

71. Hossbach to Frießner, 11 October 1950, BAMA N528-20.

72. From the discussion of a lecture by General a. D. Günther Blumentritt, "Politiker und Soldaten" (Protokoll), pp. 3–4, BB-19 (1955).

73. Dethleffsen acknowledged this resentment and its impact on the former officers' "decision for the West" in "Die gegenwärtige geistige und soziale Situation der ehemaligen Offiziere und Unteroffiziere," p. 17, September–October 1953, BAMA N648-17.

74. Hansen to Praetorius, 17 July 1946, BAMA N222-1.

75. Frießner, "Christentum," BAMA N528-69.

76. "Erfahrungsbericht über 11 Veranstaltungen mit dem Film 'Wehrhaft und frei' . . . ," January 1954, BAMA BW9-756.

77. *Die Oase* 11, November 1956, p. 7, BAMA MSg3-144/1–2.

78. "Auszüge aus Briefen von . . . an . . . vom Juli 51," BAMA N222-108.

79. Cuno a.k.a. Sodenstern, "Schuld im Spiegel der Geschichte," c. Spring 1947, BAMA N594-10. Quotes taken from page 3 and page 156, respectively.

80. Korte to Frießner, 9 December 1949, BAMA N528-20.

81. No reliable information exists concerning how many former officers "defected" to the DDR nor of course what reasons each individual had for taking such action—whether out of conviction or need, for example. See Meyer, "Zur Situation," 686.

82. BvW Landesverband Wü/Ba to Mitgliedsgruppen, 1 September 1953, BAMA N571-141.

83. Maislinger to Adenauer, 28 August 1950, BAMA N222-80.

84. Veiel to Karl-Georg Pfleiderer, MdB, 17 November 1950, BAMA N222-81.

85. See Waldenfels to Gomme-Duncan, MP, 10 April 1948, BAMA N222-10, or Hansen to W.M.F. Vane, MP, 26 May 1948, BAMA N222-11.

86. "Auch wenn das Vaterland im Schmutz liegt . . . ," *FAZ*, c. 13 December 1951, BB-12 (1951).

6. The Rift in Our Ranks: 20 July 1944

1. On the search for acceptable traditions within the Bundeswehr, see the following: Abenheim, *Reforging the Iron Cross*; Groote, "Bundeswehr und 20. Juli"; Meyer, "Auswirkungen des 20. Juli 1944"; Wiggershaus, "Zur Bedeutung"; Buck, "Die Rezeption des 20. Juli 1944 in der Bundeswehr"; and Donate, "Deutscher Widerstand."

2. On the postwar legacy of the coup, see Whalen, *Assassinating Hitler*; the contributions by Mommsen and Large in Large, ed., *Contending with Hitler*; Steinbach, "Widerstand im Dritten Reich"; Holler, *20. Juli 1944*; and Neuss, "Wem gehört der deutsche Widerstand?" The *Zeitschrift für Geschichtswissenschaft* 42, no. 7, devoted an entire issue to the subject in 1994 that contains a number of thought-provoking articles, especially on the coup's impact on postwar East Germany.

3. Countless historians have described in great detail the events of the now legendary 20 July 1944. Hoffmann, *History of the German Resistance*, is the standard. For the sheer variety of topics explored and opinions expressed, I recommend Schmädeke and Steinbach, eds., *Der Widerstand gegen Nationalsozialismus*. Other works include Graml, Mommsen, Reichhardt, and Wolf, eds., *German Resistance*, and Ehlers, *Technik und Moral*.

4. The number of around 150 comes from Germany, Bundeszentrale für politische Bildung, ed., *20. Juli 1944*, 230. One VDS newsletter in 1954 cited an official source as giving the number of deaths at an extraordinary 4,980 men and women. VDS/BvW Landesverband Südweststaat Nachrichtenblatt 20, July/August 1954, BAMA MSg3-269/1.

5. A number of historians have insisted that the participation of the armed forces was absolutely essential to the success of any attempted coup—for example, Hoffmann, "Colonel Claus von Stauffenberg."

6. Whalen, *Assassinating Hitler*, 38.

7. Mary Fulbrook, *Divided Nation*, 135–36. Frevert has published a concise analysis of the legacy of 20 July in both Germanies in Assmann and Frevert, *Geschichtsvergessenheit*, 198.

8. A great deal of work has been done in recent years on the communist resistance to Hitler and its importance in legitimizing the German Democratic Republic. Merson, *Communist Resistance*, though not uniformly praised, represents a valuable single-volume treatment of the subject, and most of the recent works cited in notes 2 and 3 above contain contributions on the communist resistance.

9. Danyel, "Bilder vom 'anderen Deutschland,'" 618.

10. Reich and Finker, "Der 20. Juli 1944," 537–40. See also Rosenhaft, "Uses of Remembrance," and Reich, "Die Tradierung."

11. Research into these areas has increased in the West in recent years. Steinbach has written a number of articles on the subject, including "'Widerstand hinter Stacheldraht.'" See also Fischer, "Die Bewegung 'Freies Deutschland.'" See also Scheurig, *Verräter oder Patrioten*. An older narrative on the Red Orchestra is Perrault, *The Red Orchestra*. The history of the Red Orchestra has undergone a revision in the light of documents available since 1989. The group's activities are now much better understood thanks to Tarrant, *The Red Orchestra*, and Tuchel, "Das Ende der Legenden." Tuchel defends the Red Orchestra against the long-held Western assumptions that it was composed of Soviet spies, rather than resisters. It is interesting that in the post-1989 era, most politicians (and many historians) seem concerned somehow to unify all the various resistance groups or at least commemorate them equally. A unified Germany can apparently use a unified resistance, just as the two divided German states used two separate resistances: the ethical/military and the political/communist.

12. Several postwar political party leaders were involved in the conspiracy as well. Theodor Steltzer, founder of the CDU in Schleswig-Holstein, was associ-

ated with the conspiracy, and a number of Adenauer's ministers and advisers in the Chancellor's Office were also linked to the plot (Otto Lenz, Hans Lukaschek, Ernst Wirmer).

13. Stern, "Wolfschanze versus Auschwitz," 650.

14. Wiggershaus, Mommsen, and Large all make this point concerning the lack of direct constitutional influence. Wiggershaus, "Zur Bedeutung"; Mommsen, "Der Widerstand gegen Hitler"; Large, "Uses of the Past."

15. Steinbach, "Widerstand im Dritten Reich," 79. Dönhoff also claims the coup as the "moral foundation" of the Federal Republic: "I think Peter Yorck today would be a conservative in his relationship to the state . . . a liberal vis-à-vis his fellow citizens, and vis-à-vis society . . . a social democrat." Dönhoff, *Um der Ehre willen*; cited in Neuss, "Wem gehört der deutsche Widerstand."

16. Mommsen, "Der Widerstand gegen Hitler," 81.

17. For an early statement of the general critique, see Graml, et al., *German Resistance*. Müller has written in a similar vein, most recently in the introduction (coauthored with Mommsen) to *Der Deutsche Widerstand*. Mommsen debunks the idea that the participants in the coup came from all walks of life, as was often claimed by officials of the Federal Republic during commemorations of the event. He insists that the conspirators were almost exclusively "outsiders" from the upper middle and upper classes, which gave the coup an elite character. Mommsen, "Der Widerstand gegen Hitler," 89. Nevertheless, given the state of historical research and public knowledge about the coup in the early 1950s, the pronouncements by the government had a profound effect in shaping the public debate about the coup attempt.

18. For at least one example, see Friedländer, "Zuviel Gehorsam." The article vilifies the majority of the former officer corps, and particularly the generals, for not having acted in the face of injustice. Witzleben's contribution is mentioned as an indication of the correct and possible response to Hitler's "unconstitutional state."

19. Rothfels, *Deutsche Opposition*; Ritter, *Carl Goerdeler*. Other influential works, such as Schlabrendorff, *Offiziere gegen Hitler*, did appear, but research on the conspiracy remained in its infancy.

20. Much of the information regarding the conspiracy came, and still comes, from Gestapo records in the aftermath of the coup. Compounding that problem is the fact that much of the positive information about the coup derived from the postwar testimony of survivors and relatives of the conspirators whose politics and personal motives have sometimes colored their statements.

21. See Graml, et al., *German Resistance*; Roon, *Neuordnung im Widerstand*; Childers, "The Kreisau Circle"; Mommsen, "Der Kreisauer Kreis." On Stauffenberg, see Hoffmann, "Colonel Claus von Stauffenberg." Klemens von Klemperer has published a number of works on the foreign–political goals and connections of the conspirators, among them *German Resistance*.

22. It is interesting that confronted with a similar problem of reconciling reality and perception, Steinbach quoted Marc Bloch: "In a word, the question is no longer whether Jesus was first crucified and then resurrected, but how it came to pass that so many fellow humans today believe in the Crucifixion and Resurrection." From Bloch's *Apologie pour l'histoire*; cited in Steinbach, "Widerstand im Dritten Reich," 81. Translation taken from Marc Bloch, *The Historian's Craft* (Manchester: Manchester University Press, 1954), 32.

23. All of these speeches and more are cited in Wiggershaus, "Zur Bedeutung," 208–10.

24. Guidelines of the PGA; cited in Abenheim, *Reforging the Iron Cross*, 144. See also Meyer, "Auswirkungen des 20. Juli 1944," 467.

25. Abenheim, *Reforging the Iron Cross*, 140–41.

26. Hans Rothfels, "Das politische Vermächtnis," 329. Gerhard Ritter and Eugen Gerstenmaier also forged the link between the two events as early as 1955. Assmann and Frevert, *Geschichtsvergessenheit*, 198, mention the connections made by Ritter and Gerstenmaier.

27. Both the identification of Lemmer and the quote are taken from Emrich and Nötzold, "Der 20. Juli," 5–6. Cited in Large, "Uses of the Past," 174. Of course, the East Germans fought back using the same weapons, charging that the conspirators were imperialists and even going so far as to make films about the lives of some of the conspirators (such as Hans Speidel), linking them to treasonous acts and cowardly motives.

28. The Dickfeld affair is mentioned in the papers of the Blank Office, BAMA BW9-3088, especially in a letter from Rolf Johannesson to Hellmuth Heye, a copy of which finds its way to Drews in the Blank Office. No mention is ever made of what eventually happened to Dickfeld, a.k.a. Albert Winter, or whether he was sent back to Austria.

29. Presse und Informationsamt, *Bulletin* 95, 22 July 1952. BAMA N222-198B. Lukaschek was the federal minister for refugees from 1949 to 1953. He was the cofounder of the CDU in Berlin.

30. Zimmerman to Hansen, 16 October 1954, BAMA N222-153.

31. Germany. Bundeszentrale für politische Bildung, ed., *20. Juli 1944*.

32. Dönhoff is cited in Whalen, *Assassinating Hitler*, 40–41. Even later historians were guilty of this exaggeration of the democratic elements of the conspirators' vision. A mere four pages before Roon cites the authoritarian and aristocratic impulses of the Kreisau Circle's program, he somewhat incongruously calls the group's conception a "declaration for the pluralistic democratic state and for the free development of individuals and groups as the sovereign elements [of society]." Roon, *Neuordnung im Widerstand*, 385.

33. Schramm lecture covered in *Karlstädter Zeitung*, 13 January 1954. Copy in BAMA BW9-768. Schramm often commented on soldiers' issues and expressed opinions very similar to those of former officers. For example, his statement on 20 July closely mirrors one drafted by Hansen in 1951 that became the official stance of the VDS (see below). Schramm continued: "Those . . . who gave their blood on the battlefield did not fall in vain. Their death was a sacrament; they atoned for that sinfulness with which their peoples burdened themselves."

34. *FAZ*, "Gescheitert?," 20 July 1955, BAMA N222-199. Wiggershaus also mentions plays and novels, such as Theodor Plievier's *Stalingrad* and Carl Zuckmayer's *Des Teufels General*, as contributing to the general glorification of resistance. Wiggershaus, "Zur Bedeutung," 211.

35. Scholars of the coup itself will no doubt recognize that in a general way, this list of values is fairly accurate, though it homogenizes the groups involved in the plot and avoids many of the tendentious political issues raised by the ideas of Carl Goerdeler, the Kreisau Circle, or the other resistance organizations.

36. Whalen, *Assassinating Hitler*, 41. Whalen cites Tauber, *Beyond Eagle and Swastika*, 1127, for his table.

37. Meyer, "Auswirkungen des 20. Juli 1944," 477–78.

38. As seems often to be the case, Dönhoff provides an early and clear formulation of this principle. Dönhoff is cited in Steinbach, "Teufel Hitler-Beelzebub Stalin?," 651–52. Steinbach does not provide a reference for the quote, however.

39. Danyel, "Bilder vom 'anderen Deutschland,'" 618.

40. On Remer, see Steinbach, "Teufel Hitler-Beelzebub Stalin?," 652. On John's involvement in the conspiracy, see Hoffmann, "Colonel Claus von Stauffenberg," 638–39. On John's postwar activities, see Large, "Uses of the Past," 170–71, and a brief discussion in the introduction to Ueberschär, ed., *Der 20. Juli 1944*, which also mentions the Remer trial.

41. Hagen, "Der 20. Juli—Der Eid und die Verantwortung," 12 November 1950, p. 14, BB-11 (1950).

42. Hagen, "Der 20. Juli," 15.

43. This discussion of the influence of Jodl, Manteuffel, and others is taken from Meyer, "Auswirkungen des 20. Juli 1944," 488–89. Unfortunately, it is not clear from Meyer's footnotes exactly whence the Manteuffel citation comes; hence the unspecified date.

44. Hoffmann, "Warum misslang?"

45. Meyer, "Auswirkungen des 20. Juli 1944," contains an extensive discussion of the wartime impact of the coup on the armed forces. He also makes the worthwhile point that the attitude toward the coup varied drastically by branch of service.

46. Cited in Volkmann, "Die innenpolitische Dimension," 489.

47. Volkmann, "Die innenpolitische Dimension," 489.

48. Korte to Frießner, 31 May 1951, BAMA N528-20. The meeting near Celle was apparently called by a former Waffen-SS officer, but there is no indication that the meeting was solely for former Waffen-SS personnel. In any case, Frießner often insisted on treating the members of the Waffen-SS just as he would other comrades and dealt with the attitudes of the two groups interchangeably. See his letter to Korte, 25 May 1951, BAMA N528-20.

49. Gümbel, cited in Mosbach to Frießner, 2 October 1951, BAMA N528-50.

50. The leaders of the VDS and the former officers who worked more closely with the government viewed Gümbel as too radical. Erich Dethleffsen called Gümbel's suggestions laughable. Dethleffsen, "Schuld am Friessner'schen Versagen," late September 1951, BAMA N648-7. Gümbel was the chairman of the Bavarian branch of the BDS, a group whose potential radicalism worried the officials of the Blank Office. Gümbel himself had been awarded the Nazi Party's Order of the Blood and was being investigated in early 1951 for alleged anti-Semitic and neo-Nazi sentiments. See "Die Lage der BDS," *Der Informationsdienst*, 24 March 1951, BAMA BW9-3085.

51. Hansen, cited in Spindler to Frießner, "Stellungnahme zu den Aufgaben des Verbandes deutscher Soldaten aus den Kreisen ehemaliger Wehrmachtsoffiziere," 19 November 1951, pp. 4–5. BAMA N528-51.

52. A photocopy of Keitel's order is included in Militärgeschichtliches Forschungsamt, ed., *Aufstand des Gewissens*, 499.

53. Behr, cited in Spindler to Frießner, "Stellungnahme zu den Aufgaben des Verbandes deutscher Soldaten aus den Kreisen ehemaliger Wehrmachtsoffiziere," 19 November 1951, p. 5, BAMA N528-51.

54. Spindler to Frießner, "Stellungnahme zu den Aufgaben des Verbandes deutscher Soldaten aus den Kreisen ehemaliger Wehrmachtsoffiziere," 19 No-

ember 1951, p. 7, BAMA N528-51. Spindler's remark begs the question: How do you prevent someone from being a "former" soldier?

55. Brennecke in a personal comment attached to an official GfW position paper entitled "Oath," 22 June 1954, BAMA BW9-766.

56. Unknown to "Ade" [Eberhard Müller's son to Müller?], 15 July 1950, BB-11 (1950), makes an obvious if implicit reference to the use of West German troops to "liberate" the Eastern zone.

57. Abenheim, *Reforging the Iron Cross*, 147. The Bundeswehr devoted a whole chapter of its *Handbuch Innere Führung* to 20 July. Germany, Bundesministerium der Verteidigung, *Handbuch Innere Führung*.

58. Kielmansegg, "Gedanken eines Soldaten zum Widerstand," 217.

59. Fuchs to Hansen, 15 December 1955, BAMA N222-201.

60. "Ein bemerkenswertes Interview," *Die Neue Feuerwehr* 89, September 1959, p. 7, BAMA MSg3-176/1. Field Marshal Schörner was apparently a favorite of Hitler's and was named the new commander in chief of the Wehrmacht after Hitler's suicide. Mende's remark overstates the Blank Office's position by assuming that it would exclude the older heroes of the soldiers' pantheon, such as Scharnhorst or Gneisenau, in favor of the conspirators.

61. "Fortschritt heißt: in Form bleiben," *FAZ*, dated only 1951, BB-12 (1951).

62. "10 Jahre: 20. Juli 1944," *Deutsche Soldaten-Zeitung*, July 1954, p. 1.

63. Major a.D. Rudolf Zimmerman to Hansen, 16 October 1954, BAMA N222-153.

64. Cited in Roon, *Neuordnung im Widerstand*, 55 and 510.

65. Roon, *Neuordnung im Widerstand*, 55.

66. Roon, *Neuordnung im Widerstand*, 76.

67. Many of the ideas in common can be traced to the existence of a "national-conservative opposition," identified by K.-J. Müller: "Die deutsche Militäropposition," and "Die national-konservative Opposition."

68. Mommsen examines the sense of the linguistic and the ideological commonalties between the two groups in "Der Kreisauer Kreis." In reviewing Whalen, *Assassinating Hitler*, in *History* 80, no. 258 (1995): 171–72, Ian Kershaw succinctly catalogued the conspirators' "common traits" as "the tradition of self-sacrifice for public service, combined with an extreme sense of loyalty and moral responsibility in both private and public matters . . . the acute sense of honour . . . the Christian dimension of the resisters' ethical motivation." These are all characteristics strongly valued (if not always exhibited) by the former officers that I studied.

69. Helfer, cited in Weinstein, *Armee ohne Pathos*, 68.

70. Mommsen, "Social Views," 143–44.

71. Rothfels, "Das politische Vermächtnis," 541.

72. Virtually every account of 20 July deals with this issue in some way, but see in particular Hoffmann, "Colonel Claus von Stauffenberg."

73. Cited in Roon, *Neuordnung im Widerstand*, 286. Of course, the fact that Hans Christoph von Stauffenberg related this story during a speech in 1963 begs the question whether or not he emphasized Claus von Stauffenberg's anticommunism for Cold War purposes. Nevertheless, the traditional anticommunism of the German officer corps, the course of the war in 1941–1942, and the reluctance of even the socialist members of the Kreisau Circle to meet with communists lends credence to Freiherr von Stauffenberg's claim.

74. Many of the officers who later became very involved in veterans' affairs and in the creation of the VDS served in 1944 in the staffs of the armies on the Western Front. Blumentritt, Paul Hausser, Speidel, and Friedrich-August von der Heydte are just a few of the names that appear in the annals of both the High Command–West (Oberkommando West) and the VDS.

75. Helfer to Dethleffsen, 8 August 1951, BAMA N648-9.

76. Mommsen, "Social Views," 93.

77. Beck, cited in Bernard, "The German Resistance," 20–21.

78. "Stellungnahme des Landesverband Wü/Ba zu den neuen Absichten des 1. Vors. des BvW vom 26.6.1951," 27 June 1951, BAMA N571-378.

79. Student, cited in "Verband Deutscher Soldaten—Protokoll der Tagung am 9. September 1951 in Bonn," 17 September 1951, p. 10, BAMA N648-7.

80. At the annual meeting of the chairmen and the central committee of the VDS in 1954, the issue of an official response came up again, as it had in 1951 and 1953. Minutes of VDS meeting, 15–16 October 1954, BAMA N222-153.

81. "Ex-Soldiers of Germany—Former General's Call for Justice," *London Times*, 22 September 1951.

82. Frießner, "Auszug aus den Erklärungen des Gen. Oberst a.D. Frießner vor der ausländischen Presse in Bad Godesberg," 22 September 1951, BAMA N528-37.

83. There are countless examples among the letters of former officers on the subject. Apart from Frießner and Hagen, former general Traugott Herr expressed the same sentiment in a letter to Vize-Admiral a.D. Gustav Kleikamp, 22 June 1951, BAMA N222-198B, as did Werner Fuchs in a letter to Hansen, 15 December 1955, BAMA N222-201. One loyal former Nazi, August Cordes, was even willing

to grant that those committing high treason maintained their honor but only up to the point at which they became "dishonorable assassins and tried to slink away after planting the bomb!" Cordes to Rollmann, 15 May 1951, BAMA N222-198B.

84. Zeitzler to Frießner, 25 September 1951, BAMA N528-57.

85. "20. Juli 1944," VDS Landesverband Südweststaat, Nachrichtenblatt 20, July/August 1954, BAMA MSg3-269/1 (among other places). The Hansen declaration became a standard among soldiers, especially after the Frießner debacle, and even found its way into the Bundeszentrale für politische Bildung's collection. Germany, Bundeszentrale für politische Bildung, *20. Juli 1944*, 305. For more on Hansen's declaration see Meyer, "Auswirkungen des 20. Juli 1944," 490, and Wiggershaus, "Zur Bedeutung," 211.

86. The GfW in Bonn, for example, issued a statement in 1954, the language of which is almost identical to the Hansen declaration.

87. Kielmansegg, "Gedanken eines Soldaten zum Widerstand," 24.

88. Heusinger, *Befehl im Widerstreit*; cited in "10 Jahre: 20. Juli 1944," *Deutsche Soldaten-Zeitung*, July 1954, p. 1.

89. Frießner to Otto Mosbach, 6.10.1951, BAMA N528-50. Wiggershaus reminds us that Günther Blumentritt, who was also very active in postwar veterans' organizations, refused to even mention the coup or its implications in his *Deutsches Soldatentum*; cited in Wiggershaus, "Zur Bedeutung," 215.

90. At least three entire volumes (198–200) of Hansen's papers at the Federal Military Archive are devoted to his correspondence with comrades concerning 20 July and related issues, such as the soldier's oath.

91. The prisoner of war issue remained current in Germany throughout the early 1950s thanks to the fact that the Soviets continued to hold thousands of German soldiers captive until 1955. The captive soldiers and the experience of many former officers in Soviet captivity were central elements in ensuring the soldiers' anticommunism. See chapter 3 above.

92. The same volume of Hansen's papers that contains his correspondence with Boehm also includes a number of newspaper clippings regarding the John case.

93. Rollman to Kleikamp, 17 June 1951, BAMA N222-198B.

94. Major a.D. Neder to Frießner, 9 October 1951, BAMA N528-57.

95. Marion Gräfin Dönhoff, "Auflehnung gegen den Helden," *Die Zeit*, 17 July 1952, BAMA N222-198B.

96. Eberbach, cited in the minutes of the conference, p. 16, BB-11 (1950).

97. H. Selle, "Über die Grenzen des soldatischen Gehorsam," no date, p. 3,

BAMA N222-26. I believe this is Herbert Selle, though it is attributed only to "H." Herbert Selle was an officer in the Wehrmacht who fought (among other places) at Stalingrad. A Herr Zollenkopf introduced Herbert Selle to Hansen. Zollenkopf to Hansen, 25 April 1949, BAMA N222-26.

98. Selle, "Über die Grenzen," p. 2. Eberbach reached a similar conclusion. The U.S.–sponsored *Neue Zeitung* referred to Eberbach as the only former general present at Bad Boll in 1950 who spoke humanely because he maintained that a constitutional state was the precondition for a soldier's oath. "Diskussion um Soldateneid und Verantwortung," *Neue Zeitung*, 30 November 1950, BB-11 (1950).

99. Sodenstern, "Der Fahneneid des deutschen Soldaten," 1947, BAMA N594-11.

Conclusion

1. Bark and Gress, *History of West Germany*, vol. 2, xlviii.

2. Diehl, *Thanks*, 18 and 233.

3. The phrase comes from the German *"einen Schlußstrich zeihen."* The prevalence of such hopes to escape the moral consequences of the Third Reich is analyzed in Assmann and Frevert, *Geschichtsvergessenheit*.

4. SPD-Pressedienst, 28 September 1951, BAMA N571-141.

5. VDS Groß-Frankfurt, Mitteilungsblatt 11, 9 November 1955, p. 2, BAMA MSg3-11/1.

6. Author's conversation with Jürgen Schreiber, president of the VDS, 30 June 1993. The VDS had eighty thousand "corporate" members in 1993. This figure includes the membership of tradition societies and other soldiers' groups affiliated with the VDS. According to Schenck zu Schweinsberg, approximately eleven thousand VDS members (less than 10 percent of the membership at the time) received commissions in the Bundeswehr when it was formed. Schenck zu Schweinsberg, "Die Soldatenverbände," p. 137–38.

Glossary

Abitur—Final examination allowing graduation from secondary school.
Afrikaner—Literally "African." Here meaning a veteran of the North African campaign.
Antifa—Soviet-sponsored antifascist groups.
Bundestag—Federal parliament after 1949.
Bundeswehr—Armed forces of the Federal Republic of Germany.
Festung Europa—Fortress Europe. Nazi term referring to the security of German-occupied Europe during World War II.
Führer—Leader. Specifically, Adolf Hitler.
Gleichschaltung—Coordination. Specifically, the National Socialist penetration and control of nearly all state and social entities during 1933 and 1934.
Großdeutschland—Greater Germany. Also the name of an elite unit of the Wehrmacht.
Grundgesetz—Basic Law. The de facto constitution of the Federal Republic.
Heimat—Homeland
Hochverrat—High treason. Actions taken to overthrow the state or ruler.
Innere Führung or *Inneres Gefüge*—Internal Leadership or Internal Guidance. New leadership concept of the Bundeswehr.
Kyffhäuserbund—An imperial-era veterans' organization.
Landesverrat—Treason. Betrayal of one's allegiance, violation of oath.
Landtag—State parliament.
Lebensraum—Living space. Nazi term referring to Germany's need for conquered territory.
Luftwaffe—Air force.
Mitteleuropa—Central Europe. Usually connotes German domination.
"*Ohne mich*"—"Without me." Rallying cry of opponents of West German rearmament.
Rechtsstaat—Well-ordered, constitutional state with protections for the rights of the individual.
Reichswehr—German army of the Weimar period.

Rote Kapelle—Red Orchestra. Soviet spy ring operating in Nazi-occupied Europe and Berlin.

Soldatenstand—Soldier's estate.

Stahlhelm—Veterans' organization founded after World War I.

Stammtisch—Table in a bar or restaurant reserved for locals only.

Stand—Estate. The rough (and archaic) equivalent of "class."

Vernünftsrepublikaner—Rational republican. Someone who tolerated the Weimar Republic but felt no true allegiance.

Volksgemeinschaft—People's community. Nazi term referring to a unified National Socialist Germany.

Volkstrauertag—German holiday, roughly Memorial Day.

Waffen-SS—Armed forces of Nazi Party elite guard..

Wehrmacht—Armed forces of Nazi Germany.

Wehrmachthelferinnen—Women conscripted during World War II, often serving in antiaircraft batteries.

Wolfschanze—Wolf's Lair. Hitler's command center in East Prussia during World War II.

Bibliography

Archives

Bundesarchiv-Militärarchiv, Freiburg im Breisgau
   BW9: Deutsche Dienststellen zur Vorbereitung der Europäischen Verteidigungsgemeinschaft
   MP8: Christliche Offizier-Vereinigung
   MSg2: Soldatentagungen der Evangelische Akademie, Bad Boll, 1950–1965
   MSg3: Mitteilungsblätter Soldatenverbände
   N10: Nachlaß Smilo Freiherr von Lüttwitz
   N222: Nachlaß Gottfried Hansen
   N528: Nachlaß Johannes Frießner
   N571: Nachlaß Hans von Donat
   N594: Nachlaß Georg von Sodenstern
   N617: Nachlaß Hasso von Manteuffel
   N648: Nachlaß Erich Dethleffsen

Evangelical Academy, Bad Boll (Abteilung für Soldatenfragen)
   11: "Tage der Besinnung für ehemalige Soldaten," 18–22 November 1950
   12: "Tagung für ehemalige Soldaten in Württemberg," 6–9 December 1951
   13: "3. Soldatentagung," 9–12 October 1952
   14: "4. Soldatentagung," 15–18 October 1953
   15: "Soldatentagung für das württembergische Oberland," 5–6 December 1953
   16: "Friedenswille und Verteidigungsbereitschaft als erzieherische Ziele," 22–25 October 1954
   19: "Gespräch zwischen Politikern und Soldaten," 25–27 November 1955

Evangelical Academy, Loccum
   1952: "Soldat und öffentliche Meinung," 13–15 March 1952
   1954: "Geist und Technik im soldatischen Bereich," 8–12 April 1954
   1955: "Unser Auftrag als Heimkehrer," 29 July–1 August 1955
   1956: "Internationale Soldatengespräche," 18–23 February 1956

Newspapers and Periodicals

Cleveland Plain Dealer
Echo der Woche
Das Eichenblatt
Der Fortschritt
Frankfurter Allgemeine Zeitung
Grafischen Post
Der Heimkehrer
Information für die Truppe
Kieler Nachrichten
London Times
Manchester Guardian
Nationalzeitung—West
Die Neue Feuerwehr
Neue Zeitung
Die Oase
Rote Fahne
Der Ruf
Suddeutsche Zeitung
Der Wiking-Ruf
Vorwärts
Die Welt

Secondary Works

Abenheim, Donald. *Reforging the Iron Cross: The Search for Tradition in the West German Armed Forces*. Princeton: Princeton University Press, 1990.

Absolon, Rudolf. "Das Offizierkorps des deutschen Heeres 1935–1945." In Hofmann, ed., *Das deutsche Offizierkorps*, 247–68.

Assmann, Aleida, and Ute Frevert. *Geschichtsvergessenheit, Geschichtsversessenheit: Vom Ungang mit deutschen Vergangenheiten nach 1945*. Stuttgart: Deutsche Verlags-Anstalt, 1999.

Bacque, James. *Other Losses: An Investigation into the Mass Deaths of German Prisoners at the hands of the French and Americans after World War II*. Toronto: Stoddart, 1989.

Bald, Detlef. *Der deutsche Generalstab 1859–1939: Reform und Restauration in

Ausbildung und Bildung. Bonn and Munich: Bundesministerium der Verteidigung, Führungsstab der Streitkräfte, 1977.

———. *Der deutsche Offizier: Sozial- und Bildungsgeschichte des deutschen Offizier im 20. Jahrhundert.* Munich: Bernard & Graefe, 1982.

———. *Sozialgeschichte der Rekrutierung des deutschen Offizierkorps von Reichsgrundung bis zur Gegenwart.* Vol. 29 of *Schriftenreihe Innere Führung. Reihe Ausbildung und Bildung.* Bonn and Munich: Bundesministerium der Verteidigung, Führungsstab der Streitkräfte, and Sozialwissenschaftliche Institut der Bundeswehr, 1977.

———. *Vom Kaiserheer zur Bundeswehr. Sozialstruktur des Militärs: Politik der Rekrutierung vom Offizieren und Unteroffizieren, Europäische Hochschulschriften.* Frankfurt/Main: Verlag Peter D. Lang, 1981.

Bald, Detlef, Gerhild Bald-Gerlich, and Eduard Ambros, eds. *Tradition und Reform im militärischen Bildungswesen ... eine Dokumentation.* Baden-Baden: Nomos Verlagsgesellschaft, 1985.

Bark, Dennis L., and David R. Gress. *A History of West Germany: From Shadow to Substance, 1945–1963,* 2d ed. Cambridge MA: Blackwell, 1993.

Bartov, Omer. *The Eastern Front, 1941–45: German Troops and the Barbarisation of Warfare.* New York: St. Martin's Press, 1986.

———. *Hitler's Army: Soldiers, Nazis, and War in the Third Reich.* Oxford: Oxford University Press, 1992.

Baudissin, Wolf von. "The New German Army." *Foreign Affairs* 34, no. 1 (1955): 1–13.

Bauer, Karl. *Deutsche Verteidigungspolitik, 1945–1963. Dokumente,* 3d ed. Boppard am Rhein: Boldt, 1964.

Berghahn, Volker R. "NSDAP und geistige Führung der Wehrmacht, 1939–1943." *Vierteljahrshefte für Zeitgeschichte* 17 (1969): 17–71.

Bernard, Henri. "The German Resistance against Hitler." In *July 20, 1944: The German Opposition to Hitler as Viewed by Foreign Historians,* edited by Hans-Adolf Jacobsen, 13–42. Bonn: Press and Information Office of the Federal Government of Germany, 1969.

Bischof, Günter, and Stephen Ambrose. *Eisenhower and the German POWs: Facts against Falsehood.* Baton Rouge: Louisiana State University Press, 1992.

Blank, Theodor. *Vom Künftigen Deutschen Soldaten: Gedanken und Planungen der Dienstelle Blank.* Bonn: Verlag Westunion, 1955.

Blumentritt, Günther. *Deutsches Soldatentum im europäischen Rahmen.* Giessen: Westunion, 1952.

Böhme, Kurt. *Die deutschen Kriegsgefangenen in sowjetischer Hand: Eine Bilanz.* Vol. 7 of Maschke, ed., *Zur Geschichte.*

———. *Geist und Kultur der deutschen Kriegsgefangenen im Westen.* Vol. 14 of Maschke, ed., *Zur Geschichte.*

Borchard, Michael. *Die deutschen Kriegsgefangenen in der Sowjetunion: zur politischen Bedeutung der Kriegsgefangenenfrage 1949-1955; Forschungen und Quellen zur Zeitgeschichte,* vol. 35. Dusseldorf: Droste, 2000.

Breit, Gotthard. *Die Staats- und Gesellschaftsbild deutscher Generale beider Weltkriege im Speigel ihrer Memoiren.* Boppard am Rhein: Boldt, 1972.

Broszat, Martin, Klaus-Dietmar Henke, and Hans Woller, eds. *Von Stalingrad zur Währungsreform: zur Sozialgeschichte des Umbruchs in Deutschland.* 2. Aufl.; *Quellen und Darstellungen zur Zeitgeschichte,* vol. 26. Munich: R. Oldenbourg, 1989.

Buck, Robert. "Die Rezeption des 20. Juli 1944 in der Bundeswehr: Anmerkungen zu deren Traditionsverständnis." In *Der 20. Juli 1944: Bewertung und Rezeption des deutschen Widerstandes gegen das NS-Regime,* edited by Gerd R. Ueberschär, 214-34. Cologne: Bund-Verlag, 1994.

Büsch, Otto. *Military System and Social Life in Old Regime Prussia, 1713-1807: The Beginnings of the Social Militarization of Prusso-German Society.* Translated by John Gagliardo. Atlantic Highlands NJ: Humanities Press, 1997.

Cartellieri, Diether. *Die deutschen Kriegsgefangenen in der Sowjetunion. Die Lagergesellschaft: eine Untersuchung der zwischenmenschlichen Beziehungen in den Kriegsgefangenenlagern.* vol. 2 of Maschke, ed., *Zur Geschichte.*

Childers, Thomas. "The Kreisau Circle and the Twentieth of July." In *Contending with Hitler: Varieties of German Resistance in the Third Reich,* edited by David Clay Large, 99-118. Washington DC and Cambridge: German Historical Institute; Cambridge University Press, 1991.

Craig, Gordon. *The Politics of the Prussian Army, 1640-1945.* Oxford: Oxford University Press, 1955.

———. *NATO and the New German Army.* Princeton: Center of International Studies, Princeton University, 1955. *Memorandum no. 8.*

Danyel, Jürgen. "Bilder vom 'anderen Deutschland': Frühe Widerstandsrezeption nach 1945." *Zeitschrift für Geschichtswissenschaft* 42, no. 7 (1994): 611-22.

Diehl, James. *The Thanks of the Fatherland.* Chapel Hill: University of North Carolina Press, 1993.

Donate, Claus. "Deutscher Widerstand gegen den Nationalsozialismus aus der Sicht der Bundeswehr." Ph. D. diss., University of Bamberg, 1976.

Dönhoff, Marion Gräfin. *Um der Ehre willen: Erinnerungen an die Freunde vom 20. Juli*, 1st ed. Berlin: Siedler, 1994.
Echternkamp, Jörg. "Wut auf die Wehrmacht? Vom Bild der deutschen Soldaten in der unmittelbaren Nachkriegszeit." In *Die Wehrmacht: Mythos und Realität*, edited by Rolf-Dieter Müller and Hans-Erich Volkmann, 1058–80. Munich: Oldenbourg, 1999.
Ehlers, Dieter. *Technik und Moral einer Verschwörung: der Aufstand am 20. Juli 1944; Schriftenreihe der Bundeszentrale für politische Bildung*, Heft 62. Bonn: Bundeszentrale für politische Bildung, 1964.
Emrich, Ulrike, and Jürgen Nötzold. "Der 20. Juli in der öffentliche Gedenkreden der Bundesrepublik und in der Darstellung der DDR." *Aus Politik und Zeitgeschichte* 26 (1984): 3–12.
Faulk, Henry. *Die deutschen Kriegsgefangenen in Großbritannien: Re-education*. Vol. 11, part 2, of Maschke, ed., *Zur Geschichte*.
Fischer, Alexander. "Die Bewegung 'Freies Deutschland' in der Sowjetunion: Widerstand hinter Stacheldraht?" In *Aufstand des Gewissens: der militarische Widerstand gegen Hitler und das NS-Regime, 1933–1945: im Auftrag des Bundesministeriums der Verteidigung zur Wanderausstellung*, edited by Militärgeschichtliches Forschungsamt, 439–64. Herford: E. S. Mittler, 1984.
———. *Wiederbewaffnung in Deutschland nach 1945; Schriftenreihe der Gesellschaft für Deutschlandforschung*, vol. 12. Berlin: Duncker & Humblot, 1986.
Foerster, Roland. "Innenpolitische Aspekte der Sicherheit Westdeutschlands, 1947–1950." In Foerster, ed., *Von der Kapitulation*, 403–576. Munich: Oldenbourg, 1982.
———, ed. *Von der Kapitulation bis zum Pleven-Plan*, 4 vols. Edited by Militärgeschichtlichen Forschungsamt. Vol. 1, *Anfänge westdeutscher Sicherheitspolitik, 1945–1956*. Munich: Oldenbourg, 1982.
Friedländer, Ernst. "Zuviel Gehorsam." *Die Zeit*, 27 May 1948, 1.
Fritz, Stephen. *Frontsoldaten: The German Soldier in World War II*. Lexington: University of Kentucky Press, 1995.
———. "'We Are Trying...to Change the Face of the World'—Ideology and Motivation in the Wehrmacht on the Eastern Front: The View from Below." *Journal of Military History* 60, no. 4 (1996): 683–710.
Fulbrook, Mary. *The Divided Nation: A History of Germany, 1918–1990*. Oxford: Oxford University Press, 1992.
Garner, Curt. "Public Service Personnel in West Germany in the 1950s: Controversial Policy Decisions and Their Effects on Social Composition, Gender

Structure, and the Role of Former Nazis." In *West Germany under Construction: Politics, Society, and Culture in the Adenauer Era*, edited by Robert G. Moeller, 135–98. Ann Arbor: University of Michigan Press, 1997.

Germany. Bundesministerium der Verteidigung. *Handbuch Innere Führung; Hilfen zur Klärung der Begriffe; Schriftenreihe Innere Führung*. Bonn: Bundesministerium der Verteidigung, 1957.

———. Bundeszentrale für politische Bildung, ed. *20. Juli 1944*. 5th ed. edited by Erich Zimmermann and Hans-Adolf Jacobsen. Bonn: Presse- und Informationsamt der Bundesregierung, 1964.

Goda, Norman J. W. "Black Marks: Hitler's Bribery of His Senior Officers during World War II." *Journal of Modern History* 72, no. 2 (2000): 413–52.

Graml, Hermann, Hans Mommsen, H.-J. Reichhardt, and E. Wolf, eds. *The German Resistance to Hitler*. Berkeley: University of California Press, 1970.

Greiner, Christian. "Die Dienststelle Blank: Regierungspraxis bei der Vorbereitung des deutschen Verteidigungsbeitrages von 1950–1955." *Militärgeschichtlichen Mitteilungen* 1 (1975): 99–124.

Groote, Wolfgang von. "Bundeswehr und 20. Juli." *Vierteljahrshefte für Zeitgeschichte* 12, no. 1 (1964): 285–99.

Heer, Hannes, and Klaus Naumann, eds. *Vernichtungskrieg: Verbrechen der Wehrmacht 1941–1944*. Hamburg: Hamburger Edition, 1995.

Herf, Jeffrey. "Multiple Restorations: German Political Traditions and the Interpretation of Nazism, 1945–1946." *Central European History* 26, no. 1 (1993): 21–55.

Heusinger, Adolf von. *Befehl im Widerstreit, Schicksalsstunden der deutschen Armee, 1923–1945*. Tübingen: Leins, 1950.

Hoffmann, Peter. "Colonel Claus von Stauffenberg in the German Resistance to Hitler: Between East and West." *Historical Journal* 31, no. 3 (1988): 629–50.

———. *The History of the German Resistance, 1933–1945*. 1977 trans. ed. Cambridge MA: MIT Press, 1970.

———. "Warum misslang das Attentat vom 20. Juli 1944?" *Vierteljahrshefte für Zeitgeschichte* 32, no. 3 (1984): 441–62.

Hofmann, Hanns Hubert, ed. *Das deutsche Offizierkorps, 1860–1960; Deutsche Führungsschichten in der Neuzeit*, vol. 11. Boppard am Rhein: Boldt, 1980.

Holler, Regina. *20. Juli 1944, Vermächtnis oder Alibi?: wie Historiker, Politiker und Journalisten mit dem deutschen Widerstand gegen den Nationalsozialismus umgehen: eine Untersuchung der wissenschaftlichen Literatur, der offiziellen Reden und der Zeitungsberichterstattung in Nordrhein-Westfalen*

von 1945–1986; Kommunikation und Politik, vol. 26. Munich New Providence: K.G. Saur, 1994.
Hughes, Michael L. " 'Through No Fault of Our Own': West Germans Remember Their War Losses." *German History* 18, no. 2 (2000): 193–213.
Hürten, Heinz. "Das Offizierkorps des Reichsheeres." In Hoffman, ed., *Das deutsche Offizierkorps*.
Jacobsen, Hans Adolf, ed. *July 20, 1944: The German Opposition to Hitler as Viewed by Foreign Historians*. Bonn: Press and Information Office of the Federal Government of Germany, 1969.
Karner, Stefan. *Im Archipel GUPVI: Kriegsgefangenschaft und Internierung in der Sowjetunion, 1941–1956*. Vienna: Oldenbourg, 1995.
Kershaw, Ian. *The "Hitler Myth": Image and Reality in the Third Reich*. Oxford: Oxford University Press, 1989.
Kielmansegg, Johann Adolf von. "Gedanken eines Soldaten zum Widerstand." In *Aufstand des Gewissens: der militarische Widerstand gegen Hitler und das NS-Regime, 1933–1945: im Auftrag des Bundesministeriums der Verteidigung zur Wanderausstellung*, edited by Bundesministerium der Verteidigung and Militärgeschichtliches Forschungsamt, 205–18. Herford: E.S. Mittler, 1984.
Kitchen, Martin. *The German Officer Corps, 1890–1914*. Oxford: Clarendon Press, 1968.
Klemperer, Klemens von. *German Resistance against Hitler: The Search for Allies Abroad, 1938–1945*. Oxford: Clarendon Press, 1992.
Koller, Karl. *Der Letzte Monat: Tagebuchaufzeichnungen des ehem. Chefs des Generalstabes der Luftwaffe*. Munich: Bechtle, 1985.
Konasov, V.B. "K voprosu o chislennosti nemetskikh voennoplennykh v SSSR." *Voprosy istorii* 11 (1994): 187–90.
Körber, Hans, ed. *Soldat im Volk: Eine Chronik des Verbandes deutscher Soldaten; Schriftenreihe Verbände der Bundesrepublik Deutschland*, vol. 16. Wiesbaden: Wirtschaftsverlag, 1989.
Koselleck, Reinhart. "Der Einfluß der beiden Weltkriege auf das soziale Bewußtsein." In *Der Krieg des kleinen Mannes: Eine Militärgeschichte von unten*, edited by Wolfram Wette, 324–43. Munich: Piper, 1992.
Koshar, Rudy. *Social Life, Local Politics, and Nazism: Marburg, 1880–1935*. Chapel Hill: University of North Carolina Press, 1986.
Krüger, Dieter. *Das Amt Blank: Die schwierige Gründung des Bundesministeriums für Verteidigung*. Freiburg: Militärgeschichtliches Forschungsamt, 1993.

Kundrus, Birthe. "Nur die halbe Geschichte. Frauen im Umfeld der Wehrmacht zwischen 1939 und 1945 — Ein Forschungsbericht." In *Die Wehrmacht: Mythos und Realität*, edited by Rolf-Dieter Müller and Hans-Erich Volkmann, 719–35. Munich: Oldenbourg, 1999.

Kutz, Martin. *Realitätsflucht und Aggression im deutschen Militär*. Baden-Baden: Nomos Verlagsgesellschaft, 1990.

———. *Reform und Restauration der Offizierausbildung der Bundeswehr: Strukturen und Konzeptionen der Offizierausbildung im Widerstreit militärischer und politischer Interessen; Militär, Rustung, Sicherheit*, vol. 8. Baden-Baden: Nomos Verlagsgesellschaft, 1982.

Laqueur, Walter. *Europe since Hitler: The Rebirth of Europe*, rev. ed. New York: Penguin, 1982.

Large, David Clay. *Germans to the Front: West German Rearmament in the Adenauer Era*. Chapel Hill: University of North Carolina Press, 1996.

———. "Uses of the Past: the Anti-Nazi Resistance Legacy in the Federal Republic of Germany." In Large, ed., *Contending with Hitler*, 163–82.

Large, David Clay, ed. *Contending with Hitler: Varieties of German Resistance in the Third Reich*. Washington DC and Cambridge: German Historical Institute; Cambridge University Press, 1991.

Lipgens, Walter. *A History of European Integration*. Oxford: Clarendon Press, 1982.

Luck, Hans von. *Panzer Commander: The Memoirs of Colonel Hans von Luck*. New York: Dell, 1989.

Maschke, Erich, ed. *Zur Geschichte der deutschen Kriegsgefangenen des Zweiten Weltkrieges*, 15 vols. Munich: E. & W. Gieseking, 1962–74.

Meier-Welcker, Hans. "Der Weg zum Offizier im Reichsheer der Weimarer Republik." *Militärgeschichtlichen Mitteilungen* 1 (1976): 147–80.

Merson, Allan. *Communist Resistance in Nazi Germany*. London: Lawrence & Wishart, 1985.

Messerschmidt, Manfred. "German Staff Officers' Education since the Beginning of the 19th Century. Innovations and Traditions." *Militarhistorisk Tidskrift* 187 (1983): 9–19.

———. "The Wehrmacht and the Volksgemeinschaft." *Journal of Contemporary History* 18 (1983): 719–44.

———. "Die Wehrmacht im NS-Staat." In *Nationalsozialistische Diktatur, 1933–1945: Eine Bilanz*, edited by Karl Dietrich Bracher, Manfred Funke and Hans-Adolf Jacobsen, 465–79. Düsseldorf: Droste Verlag, 1983.

———. *Die Wehrmacht im NS-Staat: Zeit der Indoktrination.* Hamburg: R. von Decker, 1969.

Meyer, Georg. "Auswirkungen des 20. Juli 1944 auf das innere Gefüge der Wehrmacht bis Kriegsende und auf das soldatische Selbstverständnis im Vorfeld des westdeutschen Verteidigungsbeitrages bis 1950/51." In *Aufstand des Gewissens: der militärische Widerstand gegen Hitler und das NS-Regime, 1933–1945: im Auftrag des Bundesministeriums der Verteidigung zur Wanderausstellung,* edited by Militärgeschichtliches Forschungsamt, 465–500. Herford: E.S. Mittler, 1984.

———. "Soldaten ohne Armee: Berufssoldaten im Kampf um Standesehre und Versorgung." In *Von Stalingrad zur Währungsreform: zur Sozialgeschichte des Umbruchs in Deutschland,* edited by Martin Broszat, Klaus-Dietmar Henke and Hans Woller, 683–750. München: R. Oldenbourg, 1989.

———. "Zu Fragen der personellen Auswahl bei der Vorbereitung eines westdeutschen Verteidigungsbeitrages (1950–1956)." In Hofmann, ed., *Das deutsche Offizierkorps,* 351–65. Boppard am Rhein: Boldt, 1980.

———. "Zur inneren Entwicklung der Bundeswehr bis 1960/61." In *Die NATO-Option,* edited by Hans Ehlert, 851–1162. Munich: Oldenbourg, 1993.

———. "Zur Situation der deutschen militärischen Führungsschicht im Vorfeld des westdeutschen Verteidigungsbeitrages, 1945–1950/51." In Forester, ed., *Von der Kapitulation,* 577–736. Munich: Oldenbourg, 1982.

Militärgeschichtliches Forschungsamt, ed. *Aspekte der deutschen Wiederbewaffnung bis 1955.* Vol. 7 of *Militärgeschichte seit 1945.* Boppard am Rhein: Boldt, 1975.

———. *Aufstand des Gewissens: der militärische Widerstand gegen Hitler und das NS-Regime, 1933–1945: im Auftrag des Bundesministeriums der Verteidigung zur Wanderausstellung.* Herford: E.S. Mittler, 1984.

Mommsen, Hans. "Der Kreisauer Kreis und die künftige Neuordnung Deutschlands und Europas." *Vierteljahrshefte für Zeitgeschichte* 42, no. 3 (1994): 361–77.

———. "Social Views and Constitutional Plans of the Resistance." In Graml, et al.; eds., *German Resistance,* 55–148. Berkeley: University of California Press, 1970.

———. "Der Widerstand gegen Hitler und die deutsche Gesellschaft." *Historische Zeitschrift* 241, no. 1 (1985).

Mosen, Wido. *Bundeswehr, Elite der Nation? Determinanten und Funktionen elitarer. Selbsteinschatzungen von Bundeswehrsoldaten; Soziologische Essays*, vol. 67. Neuwied: Luchterhand, 1970.

Müller, Klaus-Jürgen. *The Army, Politics, and Society in Germany, 1933–45: Studies in the Army's Relation to Nazism, War, Armed Forces, and Society.* New York: St. Martin's Press, 1987.

———. *Der Deutsche Widerstand 1933–1945.* Paderborn: F. Schöningh, 1986. Uni-Taschenbucher, no. 1398.

———. "Die deutsche Militäropposition gegen Hitler. Zum Problem ihrer Interpretation und Analyze." In *Armee, Politik und Gesellschaft in Deutschland 1933–1945*, edited by Klaus-Jürgen Müller, 101–23. Paderborn: Schöningh, 1979.

———. "Die national-konservative Opposition vor dem Zweiten Weltkrieg: Zum Problem ihrer begrifflichen Erfassung." In *Militärgeschichte: Problem—Thesen—Wege*, edited by Manfred Messerschmidt, 214–42. Stuttgart: Deutsche Verlags-Anstalt, 1982.

Nelson, Walter Henry. *Germany Rearmed.* New York: Simon and Schuster, 1972.

Neuss, Raimund. "Wem gehört der deutsche Widerstand?—Der Streit zum 50. Jahrestag des 20. Juli 1944." *German Life and Letters* 49, no. 1 (1996): 101–19.

Nicosia, Francis R., and Lawrence D. Stokes, eds. *Germans against Nazism: Nonconformity, Opposition, and Resistance in the Third Reich: Essays in Honour of Peter Hoffmann.* New York: Berg & St. Martin's Press, 1990.

Noelle-Neumann, Elisabeth, and Erich Peter Neumann. *Jahrbuch der öffentlichen Meinung, 1947–1955.* Allensbach am Bodensee: Verlag für Demoskopie, 1956.

Ostertag, Heiger. *Ausbildung und Erziehung des Offizierkorps im deutschen Kaiserreich 1871 bis 1918: Eliteideal, Anspruch und Wirklichkeit.* Frankfurt/Main: Verlag Peter D. Lang, 1990.

Perrault, Gilles. *The Red Orchestra*, 1969 trans. ed. New York: Schocken (Random House), 1967.

Pollock, James Kerr, and James Hans Meisel. *Germany under Occupation: Illustrative Materials and Documents*, Ann Arbor: G. Wahr, 1947.

Rausch, Wolf Werner, and Christian Walther, eds. *Evangelische Kirche in Deutschland und die Wiederaufrustungsdiskussion in der Bundesrepublik: 1950–1955.* Gutersloh: Gutersloher Verlagshaus Mohn, 1978. Gutersloher Taschenbücher Siebenstern, no. 292.

Reich, Ines. "Die Tradierung des deutschen Widerstandes in der Bundesrepublik und der DDR." *Zeitschrift für Geschichtswissenschaft* 42, no. 7 (1994): 635–44.

Reich, Ines, and Kurt Finker. "Der 20. Juli 1944 in der Geschichtswissenschaft der SBZ/DDR seit 1945." *Zeitschrift für Geschichtswissenschaft* 39, no. 6 (1991): 533–53.

Ritter, Gerhard. *Carl Goerdeler und die deutsche Widerstandsbewegung.* Stuttgart: Deutsche Verlags-Anstalt, 1954.

Robel, Gert. *Die deutschen Kriegsgefangenen in der Sowjetunion: Antifa.* Vol. 8 of Maschke, ed., *Zur Geschichte.*

Roon, Ger van. *Neuordnung im Widerstand. Der Kreisauer Kreis innerhalb der deutschen Widerstandsbewegung.* Munich: R. Oldenbourg, 1967.

Rosenhaft, Eve. "The Uses of Remembrance: The Legacy of the Communist Resistance in the German Democratic Republic." In Nicosia and Stokes, eds., *Germans against Nazism,* 369–88.

Rothfels, Hans. "Das politische Vermächtnis des deutschen Widerstands." *Vierteljahrshefte für Zeitgeschichte* 2, no. 4 (1954): 329–45.

———. *Deutsche Opposition gegen Hitler. Eine Würdigung.* Munich: Institut für Zeitgeschichte, 1977.

Ruhm von Oppen, Beate. *Documents on Germany under Occupation, 1945–1954.* London and New York: Oxford University Press, 1955.

Schenck zu Schweinsberg, Krafft Freiherr. "Die Soldatenverbände in der Bundesrepublik." In *Studien zur politischen und gesellschaftlichen Situation der Bundeswehr,* edited by Georg Picht, 96. Witten and Berlin: Evangelische Studiengemeinschaft, 1965.

Scheurig, Bodo. *Verräter oder Patrioten: das Nationalkomitee "Freies Deutschland" und der Bund Deutscher Offiziere in der Sowjetunion, 1943–1945,* rev. ed. (orig. 1960). Berlin: Propylaen, 1993.

Schlabrendorff, Fabian von. *Offiziere gegen Hitler, nach einem Erlebnisbericht von Fabian v. Schlabrendorff.* Zurich: Europa Verlag, 1946.

Schmädeke, Jürgen, and Peter Steinbach, eds. *Der Widerstand gegen Nationalsozialismus. Die deutsche Gesellschaft und der Widerstand gegen Hitler.* Munich: Piper, 1985.

Schubert, Klaus von. *Wiederbewaffnung und Westintegration; die innere Auseinandersetzung um die militarische und aussenpolitische Orientierung der Bundesrepublik 1950–1952; Schriftenreihe der Vierteljahrshefte für Zeitgeschichte,* no. 20. Stuttgart: Deutsche Verlags-Anstalt, 1970.

Schulte, Theo J. *The German Army and Nazi Policies in Occupied Russia.* Oxford: Berg, 1989.

Smith, Arthur L., Jr. *Die "vermißte Million": Zum Schicksal deutscher Kriegsgefangener nach dem Zweiten Weltkrieg.* Edited by Karl Dietrich Bracher and Hans-Peter Schwarz; Schriftenreihe der Vierteljahrshefte für Zeitgeschichte, no. 65. Munich: Oldenbourg, 1992.

———. *Heimkehr aus dem Zweiten Weltkrieg: Die Entlassung der deutschen Kriegsgefangenen.* Edited by Karl Dietrich Bracher and Hans-Peter Schwarz; Schriftenreihe der Vierteljahrshefte für Zeitgeschichte, no. 51. Stuttgart: Deutsche Verlags-Anstalt, 1985.

———. *The War for the German Mind: Reeducating Hitler's Soldiers.* Providence RI: Berghahn, 1996.

Spires, David N. *Image and Reality: The Making of the German Officer, 1921–1933;* Contributions in Military History, no. 38. Westport CT: Greenwood, 1984.

Steinbach, Peter. "Teufel Hitler-Beelzebub Stalin? Zur Kontroverse um die Darstellung des Nationalkomitees Freies Deutschland in der ständigen Ausstellung 'Widerstand gegen den Nationalsozialismus' in der Gedenkstätte Deutscher Widerstand." *Zeitschrift für Geschichtswissenschaft* 42, no. 7 (1994): 651–62.

———. "'Widerstand hinter Stacheldraht': Zur Diskussion über das Nationalkomitee Freies Deutschland als Widerstandsorganization seit 1943." In Ueberschär, ed., *Der 20. Juli 1944*, 265–76.

———. "Widerstand im Dritten Reich—die Keimzelle der Nachkriegsdemokratie? Die Auseinandersetzung mit dem Widerstand in der historischen politischen Bildungsarbeit, in den Medien und in der öffentlichen Meinung nach 1945." In Ueberschär, ed., *Der 20. Juli 1944*, 79–100. Cologne: Bund-Verlag, 1994.

Steiniger, Rolf. "Some Reflections on the Maschke Commission." In Bischof and Ambrose, eds., *Eisenhower and the German POWs*, 170–80.

Stern, Frank. "Wolfschanze versus Auschwitz: Widerstand als deutsches Alibi?" *Zeitschrift für Geschichtswissenschaft* 42, no. 7 (1994): 645–50.

Streit, Christian. *Keine Kameraden: Die Wehrmacht und die sowjetischen Kriegsgefangenen.* Bonn: JHW Dietz, 1991.

Tarrant, V.E. *The Red Orchestra: The Soviet Spy Network inside Nazi Europe.* NY: John Wiley & Sons, 1995.

Tauber, Kurt. *Beyond Eagle and Swastika: German Nationalism since 1945*, 2 vols. Middletown CT: Wesleyan University Press, 1967.
Thompson, Wayne C., and Marc. D. Peltier. "The Education of Military Officers in the Federal Republic of Germany." *Armed Forces and Society* 16, no. 4 (1990): 587–606.
Tuchel, Johannes. "Das Ende der Legenden: Die Rote Kapelle im Widerstand gegen den Nationalsozialismus." In Ueberschär, ed., *Der 20. Juli 1944*, 277–90. Cologne: Bund-Verlag, 1994.
Ueberschär, Gerd R, ed. *Der 20. Juli 1944: Bewertung und Rezeption des deutschen Wilderstandes gegen das NS-Regime*. Cologne: Bund-Verlag, 1994.
Vogel, Johanna. *Kirche und Wiederbewaffnung: die Haltung der Evangelische Kirche in Deutschland in der Auseinandersetzungen um die Wiederbewaffnung der Bundesrepublik 1949–1956; Arbeiten zur kirchlichen Zeitgeschichte: Reihe B, Darstellungen*. vol. 4. Göttingen: Vandenhoeck & Ruprecht, 1978.
Volkmann, Hans-Erich. "Die innenpolitische Dimension adenauerscher Sicherheitspolitik in der EVG-Phase." In *Die EVG-Phase*, edited by Lutz Köllner, 235–604. Munich: Oldenbourg, 1982.
Weinstein, Adelbert. *Armee ohne Pathos, die deutsche Wiederbewaffnung im Urteil ehemaliger Soldaten*. Bonn: Köllen Verlag, 1951.
Whalen, Robert Weldon. *Assassinating Hitler: Ethics and Resistance in Nazi Germany*. Selinsgrove PA: Susquehanna University Press, 1993.
Wiggershaus, Norbert. "Zur Bedeutung und Nachwirkung des militärischen Widerstandes in der Bundesrepublik Deutschland und in der Bundeswehr." In *Aufstand des Gewissens: der militärische Widerstand gegen Hitler und das NS-Regime, 1933–1945: im Auftrag des Bundesministeriums der Verteidigung zur Wanderausstellung*, edited by Militärgeschichtliches Forschungsamt, 501–28. Herford: E.S. Mittler, 1984.
Zoll, Ralf, Ekkehard Lippert, and Tjarck Rössler, eds. *Bundeswehr und Gesellschaft: Ein Wörterbuch; Studienbücher zur Sozialwissenschaft*, vol. 34. Opladen: Westdeutscher Verlag, 1977.

Index

08/15, 26–27, 60
Der 20. Juli, 161
20 July coup attempt: 153–80; and Bundeswehr, 153, 179; and conspirators' anticommunism, 161, 172; and conspirators' European ideas, 137–38, 171–73; events of, 155; films on, 160–61; Frießner on, 46–47, 174–76; officers' reaction to, 153–54, 164–80, 183; reception in FRG, 156–64, 223 n.15 n.17; reception in GDR, 156–57; Rommel's involvement in, 36, 155; and soldiers' oath, 130, 168–69, 178–79; as treason, 132, 167–68, 174, 176–77, 183; VDS's official stance on, 175; and Wehrmacht, 70, 155, 167, 214 n.92

Adenauer, Konrad: advisers to, 112, 166–67, 189 n.7, 222 n.12; interview with *Cleveland Plain Dealer*, 22, 104; corporate approach to politics of, 19, 111; creates Blank Office, 106; and rearmament, 4, 22, 48, 104, 106, 108, 110, 147, 157, 183; and 20 July coup attempt, 153, 157–59, 175–76; and veterans' organizations, 50, 99, 101, 111, 148
Albrecht, Konrad, 114
Allied Control Council: 13–15, 20, 28, 100; Directive 38 of, 20; Law 8 of, 13, 28; Law 16 of, 28–29; Law 34 of, 13, 14, 15, 16, 24; and Proclamation 2 of, 13
Allied High Commission: 15, 104, 106; Law 16 of, 15
Allied occupation regimes: lobbied by Hansen, 29, 99–100; officers' attitudes toward, 59, 145; and pensions, 191 n.12; powers of, 2, 183; and rearmament, 104; and resistance groups, 127; as shield for West German government, 16, 92; stabilizing effect of, 1, 9–10. *See also* Allied Control Council; Allied High Commission; demilitarization; denazification
anticommunism: and European unification, 125–27, 135–36, 138–51; of officers, 8–10, 139–43, 146–51, 181, 183, 185; of prisoners of war, 91, 135; of radical right, 132; and 20 July, 161, 172, 228 n.73; and World War II, 133. *See also* KPD
Arnim, Jürgen von, 90

Basic Law, 17–19, 98, 158
Baudissin, Wolf von, 31, 105, 129, 142, 143, 189 n.7
Beck, Ludwig, 155, 168–70, 173, 179
Behr, Heinrich 167–68
Bergmann, Walter von, 203 n.17
Berlin: 75, 148; blockade, 146; construction of Berlin Wall, 147; postwar division of, 41, 132; and 20 July, 155, 157, 163; unrest in 1919–20, 67–68; unrest in 1953, 147, 159
BEWAH (Betreuung ehemalige Wehrmachtsangehöriger und derenHinterbliebene), 194 n.68
Bielefeld Soldier's Circle, 119
Bismarck, Otto von, 99, 138
Blank, Theodor: 36, 107, 129, 159, 160; named to Chancellor's Office, 106; swears in Bundeswehr recruits, 119; and VDS, 44, 51–52, 113–14, 121. *See also* Blank Office
Blank Office: creation of, 106; favors General Staff officers, 36; legality of, 28; reform ideas of, 115, 120–21, 182, 189 n.7, 227 n.60; relations with officers and veterans' organizations, 44, 51,

Blank Office (*continued*)
  56, 58–60, 112, 115, 117–18, 120–21,
  129, 142, 183, 226 n.50. *See also* Blank,
  Theodor
Blomberg, Werner von, 61
Blücher, Gebhart Leberecht von, 169
Blum, Léon, 133
Blumentritt, Günther, 228 n.74, 229 n.89
Brandstädter, Kurt, 118
Brennecke, Kurt, 168
Bruhn, Hans, 22
Bundestag: creates PGA, 159; delegates honor soldiers, 19–20, 50, 168–69; officers critical of, 96, 102; officers lobby, 31, 149, 211 n.53; reaction to Frießner, 47; soldiers as delegates to, 21, 27, 118
Bundeswehr: creation of, 119; education and training in, 67, 204 n.31; former officers join, 22–23, 36, 59, 94, 113–14, 186–87, 213 n.76, 214 n.92; impact of 20 July coup attempt on, 153, 168–69, 179–80; impact on veterans' organizations, 116–17, 230 n.6; opposition to, 26, 107, 115, 148, 166–67, 211 n.43, 213 n.71; plans for, 4, 40, 59, 100, 104–5, 115–23, 139, 189 n.7. *See also* rearmament
Bundeswehr League (Bundeswehrverband), 121, 187
Bussche, Axel von dem, 28–29, 44
BvW (Bund versorgungsberechtigter ehemaliger Wehrmachtsangehörige und ihrer Hinterbliebene—League of Pension-Entitled Wehrmacht Personnel and Their Next-of-Kin): and Bundeswehr, 22; as German Soldier's League (DDSB), 45; goals of, 30–31, 33–36, 50, 102, 110, 173, 175; influence on later organizations, 33–36; merges with VDS, 29, 43, 45, 48–49, 56
Byrnes, James, 127

Canaris, Wilhelm, 176
Cappele, Jobst von, 56–57

Christian Democratic Union (Christlich-Demokratische Union—CDU), 99, 101–3, 106, 116–17, 157, 162 table 1, 222 n.12, 224 n.29
Christian Officers' Union, 135
Christian Social Union (Christlich-Soziale Union—CSU), 117
churches. *See* religion
Churchill, Winston, 127
civil service, 5, 18, 20–21, 103, 191 n.26
Claes, Heinrich, 109
Clasen, Carl Wilhelm, 26
Cold War: 3, 186; impact of 20 July coup attempt on, 156, 172, 228 n.73; spurs rearmament, 22, 104, 153; strengthens officers' negotiations, 4, 31, 100–101, 134, 183
Common Coal and Steel Market, 128
Comrades of Light Anti-Aircraft Battery 71 (Kameradschaft Leichte Flakabteilung 71), 8
Conrady, H. D. von, 116
Cordes, August, 228 n.83
Council of Europe, 128
Crüwell, Ludwig, 37, 52, 115, 198 n.44

DAK (Verband ehemaliger Angehöriger Deutsches Afrika Korps—League of Former Members of the Africa Corps): 29, 33, 53–55, 59–61; and *Die Oase* (newsletter), 36–37, 38–39, 60, 146; organizational ideology of, 36–40, 50, 52, 60–61, 146; and rearmament, 115–16; and VDS, 45, 50, 52
defamation: 5, 12, 83; campaign against militarism as, 14–16, 57–58, 109; by German public, 24–27, 30–31, 40, 86, 149, 166, 179, 181; veterans' organizations fight against, 35, 49
demilitarization, 2, 4–5, 12–14, 73, 101–2
denazification, 2, 10, 12–14, 16, 79, 81
Dethleffsen, Erich: links to Blank Office, 44–45, 52, 111–12, 131; on rearmament 107–8, 110, 114–15, 136, 141; and VDS, 43–44, 216 n.18, 226 n.50. *See also*

Wirtschafts-politische Gesellschaft von 1947
Dickfeld, Adolf, 159–60
Dien Bien Phu, 192 n.37
Diester, Hans, 87, 88
Dittmar, Kurt, 108
Donat, Hans von: 55, 88, 132–33, 216 n.18; and BvW/VDS, 28, 31, 34, 173; on economic situation of veterans, 16–17; reaction to Frießner, 48–49; and political parties, 97, 101, 102, 209 n.12
Dönhoff, Marion, 160, 177–78
Dönitz, Karl, 114

Eberbach, Heinrich, 58, 129–30, 138–40, 178
Ebert, Friedrich, 64–65. *See also* Ebert-Groener pact
Ebert-Groener pact, 68
Economic Miracle. *See* Federal Republic of Germany: prosperity
Emergency Groups, 28–29, 30, 48, 54
employment: 2–4, 133; for veterans, 4–5, 12, 16, 20–24, 87, 94, 114–15, 184, 206 n.72; veterans' organizations as sources for, 28, 30, 53, 54, 61, 200 n.78. *See also* unions: boycott against officers
Erler, Fritz, 129
Es Geschah am 20. Juli, 161
Europe: 8, 39, 96, 130, 133, 142, 209 n.11; defense of, 22, 38, 48, 56, 100, 105, 109, 125–28, 140–43, 209 n.21, 218 n.45, 219 n.53; unification of (*see* European unification)
European Defense Community (EDC), 105, 116, 118, 143
European Economic Community (EEC), 128
European unification: as anticommunist bloc, 98, 126, 136, 138–51, 183; background, 127–28, 186; Germany's role in, 59, 92, 125–28, 132, 136, 181; impact of 20 July coup attempt on, 137–38, 160, 172–73
Evangelical Academies: background, 128, 206 n.72, 216 n.18; and European unification, 135–51; and moral foundation for Germany, 97, 131–35; and POW problem, 87, 89; and rearmament, 122–23, 128–31, 139–42, 145–46, 149–51, 186; and 20 July coup attempt, 163, 169

Federal Border Guard (Bundesgrenzschutz—BGS), 22, 118, 213 n.76
Federal Republic of Germany (and pre-1949 western zones of occupation): Basic Law of the, 17–19, 98, 158; corporate style of government, 19, 111; Defense Ministry (*see* Blank Office); Federal Constitutional Court, 163, 196 n.22; Federal Office for Political Education, 160; Federal Press Office, 47, 160; foundation of, 15, 18, 33, 95; on Frießner, 47–48; Interior Ministry, 118; postwar situation of, 1–4, 23–24, 181; POWs return to, 80, 85; prosperity, 3, 86, 114; rearmament of (*see* rearmament); relations with veterans' organizations, 20, 23, 28–29, 32, 33–35, 49, 52, 59, 62, 63, 103, 116, 122–23, 125, 129, 147–48, 154, 183–84, 186; and 20 July coup attempt, 153–54, 156–64, 172, 177, 179, 223 n.15 n.17; unification of, with GDR and lost provinces, 41, 52, 142, 183, 184, 186
Fette, Christian, 45
Finet, Albert, 218 n.45 n.49
First Panzer Division, 39
Foertsch, Hermann, 209 n.21
Der Fortschritt, 95
Fourth Panzer Division, 58, 142–43
France: 37, 40–41, 127, 133, 136, 137, 139, 172; opposition to German rearmament, 105–6; and POWs, 80–81, 87; zone of occupation, 2, 13, 17
Frank, Engelbert, 29–30, 194 n.68
Free Democratic Party (Freie Demokratische Partei—FDP): on Frießner, 47; relations with veterans' organizations, 99, 102, 117, 168–69; on 20 July coup

250 Index

Free Democratic Party (continued)
  attempt, 162 table 1; veterans as delegates of, 21, 118–19, 210 n.29
French Foreign Legion, 22
Frießner, Johannes: 25, 87, 97, 186, 193 n.48, 194 n.57; on captivity, 85–88; and European defense, 134–35, 140–41, 147, 219 n.57; press conference, 45–49, 50–51, 60, 174–76, 179, 229 n.85; on rearmament, 109, 112, 119, 208 n.4, 219 n.54; on 20 July coup attempt, 174–76; and VDS, 43–45
Fromm, Fritz, 155
Fuchs, Werner, 168

Gale, Richard, 38
Gaulle, Charles de, 127
Geneva Convention, 74
German Community (Deutsche Gemeinschaft), 97, 99, 102
German Democratic Republic (GDR) (and pre-1949 Soviet zone of occupation): threat to West Germany, 4, 12, 22–23, 50, 104, 148–49; treatment of veterans, 18, 20, 148, 221 n.81; and 20 July coup attempt, 153, 156–57, 163, 224 n.27; veterans' hatred of, 41, 80–81, 132, 147, 196 n.30
German Federation of Trade Unions (Deutsche Gewerkschaftsbund—DGB), 9, 21
German Union (Deutsche Union), 96, 98, 102
Gestapo, 73, 155, 157, 167, 177, 223 n.20
Gneisenau, August von, 52, 169, 227 n.60
Goebbels, Joseph, 98, 126, 134, 135
Goerdeler, Carl, 137, 156, 171–73
Göring, Hermann, 164
Görlitz, Walter, 136–37
GPURKKA (Russian Special Committee on Political Administration of the Red Army), 76
Grafischen Post, 26
Great Britain: 127, 133, 136, 146, 150, 215 n.1, 216 n.26; Foreign Office, POW Division, of 82; zone of occupation of, 13, 28, 99, 136, 145
Great Depression, 133
Groener, Wilhelm, 65. *See also* Ebert-Groener pact
Großdeutschland: 29, 33, 35–36, 39–41, 45, 50, 52–53, 168, 199 n.72; and *Die Neue Feuerwehr* (newsletter), 39–41, 168
Guderian, Heinz, 108–9, 129, 167, 198 n.44, 216 n.18, 219 n.57
Gümbel, Ludwig, 167–68, 198 n.44, 226 n.50
Günther, Gerhard, 44

Hagen, Hans, 163–65, 174, 178
Hansen, Gottfried: as early organizer, 14, 15, 17, 21, 22, 23, 28, 30–31, 33–35, 99, 128, 136, 145–46; and rearmament, 105, 110–12, 118, 119, 213 n.77; relations with political parties, 99–102, 131; on 20 July coup attempt, 167–68, 175–76, 179, 225 n.33; and VDS, 43–45, 49–52, 54, 61, 103, 198 n.44, 201 n.87, 216 n.18
Hassell, Ulrich von, 156
Hauck, Friedrich Wilhelm, 122–23, 142
Hausser, Paul, 198 n.44, 228 n.74
Heinrici, Gotthard, 129
Helfer, Karl Heinrich, 171, 173
Herr, Traugott, 198 n.44, 228 n.83
Heusinger, Adolf, 31, 51, 112, 167, 176, 189 n.7
Heuss, Theodor, 101, 158–60, 169
Heydte, Friedrich-August von der, 228 n.74
Heye, Heinrich, 210 n.29
Hilfsverein für ehemalige berufsmässige Angehörige der Deutschen Wehrmacht und ihrer Hinterbliebenen, 29–30
Himmler, Heinrich, 164
Hindenburg, Paul von, 5, 69
Hitler, Adolf: and control of Germany, 6, 68, 98–99; officers' association with, 17, 68–71, 105, 181; soldiers' oath to, 25,

69–70, 72, 77, 83, 130, 131, 154, 163, 165, 168, 170, 175, 178, 205 n.47, 230 n.98; and 20 July coup attempt, 36, 103, 153, 155–57, 159, 161, 163–64, 167, 169, 172–78; and World War II, 5, 40, 47, 88, 132–35, 138, 147, 181, 185, 227 n.60. *See also* National Socialism
Hitler Youth, 1, 76, 130
Hohenzollern monarchy, 4, 64–65. *See also* Wilhelm II
Hossbach, Friedrich, 144

Innere Führung, 120–21, 168, 214 n.82

Jackson, Robert H., 15
Jodl, Alfred, 164
John, Otto, 163, 176, 177 n.92

Kapp, Wolfgang, 68. *See also* Kapp putsch
Kapp putsch, 6, 67–68, 203 n.17
Karst, Heinz, 58, 142
Keitel, Wilhelm, 167, 176, 179
Kieler Nachrichten, 100
Kielmansegg, Johann Adolf, 31, 44–45, 112, 168, 175–76, 189 n.7
Koller, Karl, 143
Korean War, 4, 43, 94, 100, 101, 104, 107, 109, 130, 153
Korte, Hans, 109, 148, 166
KPD (Communist Party of Germany): 66, 67, 133; declared unconstitutional, 196 n.22; relations with veterans, 25, 39–40, 57–58; resistance to Nazism, 156–57; Rote Fahne, 66, 67; uprisings in Berlin and Ruhr in 1919–20, 67. *See also* anticommunism
Kreisau Circle, 137, 156–58, 160, 170–72, 225 n.32, 228 n.73
Krelle, W., 141
Kretschmer, Alfred, 200 n.78
Kühne, Gerhard, 30
KVP (Kasernierte Volkspolizei), 22–23, 104, 148, 149, 153, 210 n.36
Kyffhäuserbund, 33, 51, 54

Langer, Helmar, 134–36, 147

Lauinger, Josef, 25
Law for Liberation from National Socialism and Militarism, 14
Law Relating to Basic Law Article 131, 18–19, 54
Leadership Circle of German Soldiers (Führungsring deutscher Soldaten), 57
League of German Officers (Bund deutscher Offiziere—BdO), 78–79, 157, 176
League of German Soldiers (Bund deutscher Soldaten—BDS), 45, 226 n.50
League of German War-Disabled and Survivors (Bund Deutscher Kriegsbeschädigter und Kriegerhinterbliebener—BdKK), 7
Leber, Julius, 172
Lebius, Max, 17
Lehr, Robert, 52
Lemmer, Ernst, 159
Lempp, Hans, 89
Lenz, Otto, 222 n.12
Lerch, Archer, 81–82, 84
Linde, Kurt, 31, 51, 116
Luck, Hans von, 105–6, 114
Luftwaffe, 143
Lukaschek, Hans, 160, 222 n.12, 224 n.29
Lüttwitz, Smilo von, 94, 129, 216 n.18
Lüttwitz, Walther von, 68

Maislinger, Hans, 148–49
Malmédy, 219 n.57
Manstein, Erich von, 129, 131
Manteuffel, Hasso von: as Bundestag delegate, 21, 118–19, 210 n.29; and rearmament, 108–9, 112, 118–19; on 20 July coup attempt, 164, 174; as veterans' leader, 22, 43, 46, 198 n.44, 208 n.5
Mantey, Friedrich von, 133
Marshall Plan, 128
Mayer, Ernst, 47
Mazière, Ulrich de, 106
Mende, Erich, 168–69
Mewis, Raul, 194 n.68
militarism, 8, 12–15, 20, 24, 50, 102, 130

252 *Index*

Mölders, Werner, 169
Moltke, Helmut James von, 137–38, 170, 172–73
Montgomery, Bernard Law, 108
Müller, Eberhard, 130, 138, 140, 141–42, 143
Müller-Brandenburg, Hermann, 109

National League of German Officers (Nationalverband deutscher Offiziere), 5
National Socialism: and anticommunism, 133–34; concentration camps, 90; coordination (Gleichschaltung), 62, 169; Fortress Europe (Festung Europa), 182; Lebensraum, 131, 182; legacies of, 3–4, 12, 15, 48, 57, 81, 86, 91, 102–3, 122, 128, 130–32, 144, 181, 183, 226 n.50; Nazi party, 12, 46, 69, 122; resistance to, 154, 156–58, 161–62, 177–79; similarity of veterans' ideas to, 61, 70–71, 76, 78, 79, 81–84, 94, 96, 98, 133–36, 149–50, 154, 166, 181–82, 185–87, 197 n.39 (44); soldiers under, 5, 9, 16, 17, 18, 24–25, 69–72, 100, 169, 177–79, 185, 217 n.28; Volksgemeinschaft, 61, 182. *See also* denazification; Hitler, Adolf; Night of the Long Knives
National Unification (Nationale Vereinigung) (Weimar officer group), 6
nationalism: as counter to communism, 58, 136, 138, 142; officers' espousal of, 5, 8, 31, 58–59, 63–66, 84–85, 91–92, 93–95, 96, 98, 105, 113, 125–27; as postwar problem, 131–33
NATO (North Atlantic Treaty Organization), 105, 109, 128
Night of the Long Knives, 69, 217 n.28
NKFD (Nationalkomitee Freies Deutschland—National Committee for a Free Germany), 77–79, 157, 179
Noske, Gustav, 65, 68
Nuremberg trials. *See* war crimes trials
NVA (Nationale Volksarmee—National People's Army), 148

oath. *See* Hitler, Adolf: soldiers' oath to

Operational History (German) Section, 136, 219 n.54
Organization for European Economic Cooperation, 128
Ostau, Joachim von, 95, 96, 208 n.6, 209 n.12
Oster, Hans, 176

Parliamentary Council, 3, 18
Paulus, Friedrich von, 137
pensions: as regulated by Law Relating to Basic Law Article 131, 18–19, 54; regulation of, prior to 1945 (WFVG/WEFVG), 191 n.25; revocation of, 13, 15–17, 23–25, 91, 181, 191 n.21; veterans' organizations struggle to reinstate, 17–20, 23–24, 30, 32, 33, 49, 53–54, 61–62, 64, 94, 100, 102–4, 109, 114, 117–18, 173, 183–84, 185–86
Peucker, Eduard von, 67
PGA (Personalgutachterausschuß—Personnel Screening Committee) 23, 51–52, 159, 208 n.4, 210 n.39, 213 n.72
POWs (prisoners of war): 4, 31, 72–92, 135, 182, 206 n.72; in British camps, 81–84; casualties among, 195 n.7, 200 n.85, 205 n.43; effects of captivity, 85–92; in French camps, 22, 80–81; Maschke commission on, 204 n.32; reeducation of, 76–79, 81–85, 205 n.54; Soviet Antifas (reeducation), 76–79, 82; in Soviet camps, 55, 73–80, 135, 229 n.91; in United States camps, 81–82, 84–85; veterans' organizations seek freedom for, 30, 40–42, 49

Raeder, Erich, 114
rearmament: 104–23; aids veterans organizers, 33, 43, 100, 104–5, 183; opposition to, 26, 107, 115, 148, 166–67, 211 n.43, 213 n.71; and 20 July coup attempt, 153; veterans and, 31, 42, 44, 48, 56–57, 59, 94, 105–6, 107–23, 129–31, 139, 148, 182, 189 n.7, 212 n.62. *See also* Bundeswehr

Reben, Herbert, 25
Red Cross, 8, 35, 54
Red Orchestra, 157, 222 n.11
refugees, 2, 12, 25
Reichswehr, 64, 65, 67, 68, 69, 119, 205 n.47
Reichwein, Adolf, 172
Reinhard, Wilhelm, 198 n.44, 201 n.87
Reinhardt, Walter, 203 n.17
religion: 3, 128–30; and politics, 96, 99; and POWs, 81, 84, 135; and rearmament, 141–44; and opposition to rearmament, 107, 211 n.43; and resistance to Hitler, 159, 227 n.68
Remer, Otto, 165, 162, 163, 165, 196 n.22
Robertson, Brian, 100, 149
Rommel, Erwin, 36–38, 47, 52, 54, 115, 155, 169
Der Ruf, 84–86, 90–91, 206 n.68
Rundstedt, Gerd von, 164

SA (Sturmabteilung—National Socialist Storm Troopers), 4, 69, 72
Salchow, Richard, 38–39
Scharnhorst, Gerhard von, 52, 64, 169, 227 n.60
Schleicher, Kurt von, 68
Schmid, Carlo, 19–20
Schmidt (interior minister of North Rhine-Westphalia), 21
Schoettle, Erwin, 47
Schörner, Ferdinand, 169, 227 n.60
Schramm, Wilhelm Ritter von, 137–38, 160, 225 n.33
Schreiber, Jürgen, 33
Schubert, Günther, 30
Schumacher, Kurt, 21, 26, 45
Schwerin, Gerhard von, 106
Seeckt, Hans von, 64, 65, 66, 67, 68, 70, 72, 90, 92, 99, 183
Selle, Herbert, 178
Sievert, Anita, 23–24
Society for Defense Information (Gesellschaft für Wehrkunde—GfW), 56, 113, 168, 201 n.87, 229 n.86

Society of Carriers of the German Knight's Cross (Gemeinschaft Deutscher Ritterkreuzträger), 160
Sodenstern, Georg von, 28, 31, 135, 147, 178
Soviet Union: POWs in, 73–80, 85, 87–91, 135, 229 n.91; Red Army of, 2, 76, 77; and Reichswehr, 68; threat to West Germany, 4, 9–10, 46, 100, 104, 106, 109, 125–26, 139–40, 143, 146–47, 153; and 20 July coup attempt, 157, 163, 172, 176–77; veterans' hatred of, 39, 41, 52, 85, 87–91, 146, 150; and World War II, 135–36; zone of occupation (*see* German Democratic Republic)
SPD (Sozialdemokratische Partei Deutschlands—German Social Democratic Party): on Frießner, 47; and rearmament, 104, 107, 123, 129; relations with veterans' organizations, 19, 21, 25, 26, 30, 50, 55, 97, 99, 101–3, 132, 185–86; and 20 July coup attempt, 156, 162 table 1, 172, 173; *Vorwärts*, 26; in Weimar, 64–65. *See also* Schumacher, Kurt
Speidel, Hans, 112, 115, 166, 224 n.27, 228 n.74
Spindler, Gert, 15, 95–96, 167–68
SRP (Sozialistische Reichspartei—Socialist Reich Party), 132, 161–62, 162 table 1, 196 n.22
SS (Schutzstaffel—National Socialist Elite Guard), 4, 69, 72, 141
Stahlhelm, 25, 33, 35–36, 43, 45
Stalingrad, 225 n.34
Stalingrad, 76, 77, 137
Stauffenberg, Claus Schenk von: actions on 20 July 1944, 155–56, 162, 174, 177, 179, 183, 185; as officer, 154, 169–70, 173; political ideas of, 78, 171–73, 228 n.73; postwar canonization of, 153–54, 158, 163, 168
Stauffenberg, Hans Christoph von, 172, 228 n.73
Steltzer, Theodor, 222 n.12

Student, Kurt, 174, 198 n.44
Stülpnagel, Siegfried von, 129

Tatgemeinschaft freier Deutscher (Free Germans' Action Community), 96
Tauroggen, 137–38
Teich (communist speaker), 57–58
Teichert (Schleswig-Holstein Office for People's Education), 20
Des Teufels General, 225 n.34
Third Reich. *See* National Socialism
Tholens, Hermann, 133
Tillmanns, Robert, 139–40
tradition societies, 8, 29, 33, 56
Tradition Society of the 65th Infantry Division (Traditionsgemeinschaft 65er Infanteriedivision), 8
Trott zu Solz, Adam von, 137–38, 173

unions: Blank's links to, 106; boycott against officers, 4, 12, 21, 30, 103, 149; opposition to rearmament, 107, 211 n.43; and veterans' organizations, 9, 21, 26, 198 n.45
United States of America: and European unification, 127–28, 140, 144, 150; POW camps in, 80–82, 84–85; and rearmament, 94, 104–6, 136, 140, 145, 153, 218 n.45; veterans' attitude toward, 37, 114, 117, 145–47, 183; and World War II, 47, 135, 215 n.1; zone of occupation, 2, 9, 23, 25, 133

Vandenberg, Arthur, 23
VdH (Verband der Heimkehrer—Association of Former Prisoners of War): 7, 41–42; and *Der Heimkehrer* (newsletter), 42
VDK (Verband der Kriegsbeschädigten, Kriegshinterbliebenen und Sozialrentner Deutschlands—German Association of War-Disabled, War Survivors, and Social Pensioners), 7
VDS (Verband Deutscher Soldaten—League of German Soldiers): aims of, 33, 49–54; and Bundeswehr, 121, 186–87; composition of, 121, 187, 199 n.61, 230 n.6; creation of, 29, 34, 43–50, 199 n.72; and European defense, 135–35, 142–43, 148; and *Der Fortschritt*, 95; Frießner as president of, 45–49, 60–61; membership of board, 198 n.44; and rearmament, 56–58, 97, 113–14, 116–18; relations with government, 44–45, 47–48, 50–52, 59, 62, 111, 113–14, 118, 213 n.72; relations with political parties, 93, 116–18; as soldiers' occupational representative, 51–52; stance on 20 July coup attempt, 174–75, 225 n.33, 229 n.85; stance on war criminals, 111, 198 n.60
Veiel, Rudolf, 28, 34, 102, 103, 149
Versailles Treaty, 65–66, 147
veterans' organizations: 11–62; ban on, 15, 24; composition of, 6–10, 33–34, 186–87, 189 n.7, 192 n.28; early types of, 27–32; as lobbyists, 93, 102–3, 108, 117, 121–22, 182; loyalty to FRG, 61–62, 182–84; organizational ideologies, 34–42; and rearmament, 105, 110, 119, 122–23; social aspects of, 8, 53–61; and 20 July coup attempt, 173–76; women's involvement in, 7, 8, 15, 30–31, 37, 42, 55, 60, 101, 197 n.36, 199 n.61. *See also* BvW; DAK; Großdeutschland; tradition societies; VDS
Vietinghoff, Heinrich von, 123, 129
Viking-Ruf, Der, 141
VVN (Vereinigung der Verfolgten des Naziregimes—Union of Those Persecuted by the Nazi Regime), 156–57, 163

Waffen-SS, 45, 141, 150, 192 n.28, 219 n.57, 226 n.48
Waldburg zu Zeil und Trauchburg, Erich von, 218 n.49
war crimes trials: 4, 181; Manteuffel trial, 41; Nuremberg trials, 14–15, 46, 100, 164. *See also* Malmédy; war criminals
war criminals: 18, 40–41, 75–76, 181, 212 n.61; veterans' organizations acting on

behalf of, 30, 35, 42, 49, 108–9, 112, 119, 131, 184, 198 n.60. *See also* war crimes trials
Wechmar, Kurt, 45–46
Wehrmacht: crimes of, 14–15, 17, 20–21, 86, 90, 103, 110, 130; defamation of (*see* defamation); dissolution of, 13, 181; General Staff of, 13, 14, 28, 36, 65, 66, 89, 90, 143, 155, 214 n.92; High Command of, 14, 228 n.74; role of, in Third Reich, 4–5, 61, 64, 70–72, 154, 178, 181–82, 192 n.28; and tradition, 8, 37, 89–90, 97, 141, 153, 214 n.92; and 20 July coup attempt, 154–57, 164, 166–67, 178; and World War II, 7, 72, 76, 103, 110, 112, 132, 134, 136, 205 n.43, 215 n.1, 217 n.28, 227 n.60
Wehrmachthelferinnen, 7
Weimar Republic: democracy and, 1, 3, 9, 96, 98, 121–22, 172, 181, 211 n.48; officers and, 4, 5–6, 63–70, 72, 95, 98, 183, 217 n.28
Weinstein, Adelbert, 112
Die Welt, 100
Wilhelm II, 4, 64, 95, 134
Wirmer, Ernst, 222 n.12
Wirtschafts-politische Gesellschaft von 1947, 197 n.43
Witzleben, Erwin von, 155, 158, 170

Wlottkowski (refugee who argued against officers' pensions), 25
Wolfschanze, 155
women: attitude toward 20 July coup attempt, 161, 162 table 1; and revocation of widows' pensions, 13, 15, 17, 101. *See also* veterans' organizations: women's involvement in
World War I, 63, 95, 113, 116, 119, 127, 134, 147
World War II: Allied bombing raids during, 2, 16; Frießner on, 46–47; German surrender in, 2, 24, 41, 78, 126; officers' role in, 5, 14, 25–27, 71, 110, 169, 179, 181; postwar effects, 36–41, 52, 63–64, 133–36, 138, 183
Wunsch, Gerd-Peter, 144
Wurm, D. Theophil, 138
Wüst, Joachim, 5

Yorck von Wartenburg, Ludwig, 52, 137, 169
Yorck von Wartenburg, Peter, 170, 223 n.15

Zahn, Peter von, 47
Zeitzler, Kurt, 175
Zero Hour, 3, 162
Zydowitz (speaker on rearmament issues), 56–57, 58